D0845660

Between Two Shores

David Philip
Cape Town & Johannesburg

Between Two Shores

FLORA AND FAUNA OF THE CAPE OF GOOD HOPE

TEXT BY
MICHAEL FRASER
ILLUSTRATIONS BY
LIZ McMAHON

Grateful acknowledgements are due to First National Bank, whose generous financial assistance has helped to reduce the published price of this book.

To the memory of the Rev. Ian W. Fraser

Indemnity

Many areas of the Cape of Good Hope Nature Reserve, particularly the cliffs, are hazardous and some of the beaches have strong currents. Poisonous snakes and other potentially dangerous animals (particularly baboons) also occur here. The author, artist and publisher of *Between Two Shores* take no responsibility for any loss or injury sustained at the reserve.

Please take care

Do not stray off the paths; do not go near the edges of cliffs; do not go swimming, diving or angling on your own.

Please do not feed the baboons!

Do not break the reserve rules! They exist for your benefit and the welfare of the wildlife.

First published 1994 by David Philip Publishers (Pty) Ltd, 208 Werdmuller Centre, Claremont, 7700 South Africa

© 1994 Michael Fraser (text) and Liz McMahon (illustrations). All photographs copyright Michael Fraser, apart from pages 22 & 29 (Cape Archives) and pages 28 & 35 (Cape of Good Hope Nature Reserve Archives)

ISBN 0-86486-224-5

All rights reserved

Maps by Accessible Graphics (Ryan & Moloney), Rondebosch

Cover design by Abdul Amien

Reproduction and setting by Hirt & Carter

Printed by Singapore National Printers, Singapore

Errata

Page 75: *Hesperantha falcata* should read *Geissorhiza juncea*.
Page 124: *Evota harveyana* should be *Evota bicolor* and vice versa.

Contents

Foreword

For almost thirty years I have been intimately involved in the international art world and that of the bibliophile specialising in the fields of ornithology and botany. During this time I have rarely experienced such dedication and skill as are apparent in Liz McMahon's superb paintings and Mike Fraser's knowledgeable, witty and readable text in *Between Two Shores*.

These two enthusiasts have, through their particular knowledge of and affinity for natural history, created a book which will visually appeal to and fulfil the scholarly needs of all who read it. Their many years of study, hands-on experience, and love of the flora and fauna of the Cape of Good Hope Nature Reserve have succeeded in changing a dream into a reality with the publication of this book. They should be proud, and I am well satisfied.

To be fortunate enough to acquire the collection of Liz McMahon's delicate and sensitive watercolours is one thing, but to have the pleasure of being so closely involved in Liz and Mike's endeavours is something very special. I feel honoured to have been part of this book, in however small a way. I can confidently say that this monograph on the flora and fauna of the Cape will be a source of pleasure and knowledge for years to come.

The need for involvement by the corporate world in projects of this nature should not be underestimated. A great deal of money is spent around the world on social development programmes, and rightly so. Nevertheless, support for publications such as *Between Two Shores*, which is at once creative and instructive, is often forgotten or considered to be irrelevant. This is regrettable, as we should never lose sight of the need to educate ourselves on subjects of such importance close to home.

In this wonderful country we find worlds within worlds, and ecosystems unlike any other. It is only through education, bringing with it an awareness of the necessity for conservation, that future generations will have the pleasure of experiencing these worlds and ecosystems as well as their plants and animals which we, in our lifetime, are fortunate enough to witness.

In their first book, *A Fynbos Year*, Liz and Mike described and illustrated the small and fragile Cape Floral Kingdom, in which some of the world's rarest and most beautiful plants thrive. I use the word 'thrive' with some trepidation, as human activities have taken their toll of fynbos plants and animals and will continue to do so unless this unique ecosystem is successfully managed by those in authority, with the guidance of conservationists. Most important, everyone should be made aware that for much of the wildlife found in this part of the world there is a very thin line between survival and extinction. Harsh words but true!

In his famous monograph *Coloured Engravings of Heaths. The Drawings Taken from Living Plants Only* (1802) which depicted the indigenous flora of the Cape, the artist H. C. Andrews drew his exquisite illustrations of ericas from specimens growing in the greenhouses of the Marquis of Blandford. How interesting it is for me that these Cape plants were admired to the extent that they were successfully cultivated more than a century ago in England.

We are now afforded the opportunity to compare these historical records and descriptions with contemporary ones. I am only too aware of the importance of continuing the work of recording for posterity something as special as our fauna and flora, and of the responsibility borne by Liz and Mike and others in contributing to this task.

As the world changes, we must be thankful that so much has been done to document our natural resources and surroundings. We must encourage such work, as paintings and descriptions of the kind presented in *Between Two Shores* will, in future, allow us to experience today's plants and animals in their natural milieu. One wonders what the future holds for much of the Cape's natural glory.

Let the words and visual beauty in these pages remind us of our paramount responsibility to conserve what is left.

STEVE BALES
Custodian of Art
First National Bank of Southern Africa Limited
Johannesburg, July 1994

Preface

❀

Early in 1994 we celebrated ten years of association with the Cape of Good Hope Nature Reserve. A decade ago we left Scotland and arrived, ignorant and blissful, at the Cape. Having landed in the rain and been greeted by fellow immigrants in the form of pestilential House Sparrows and European Starlings in the suburbs, and finally been deposited at the reserve to the welcoming calls of Sandwich Terns at sea, Greenshanks on the beach and hillsides covered with lots of scrubby plants which all looked like heather (even to the extent of having Stonechats perched on top of them), we were ready to sue our travel agent for incompetence. Surely this was not Africa?

Thankfully, our misgivings were short-lived and we quickly discovered that the Cape and Scotland were only superficially similar. With a mounting succession of sighs of relief at each discovery of something different, we soon became immersed in the fascinating world of fynbos and all the peculiar natural splendours that this corner of the continent has to offer.

For two years we were ensconced in the S. H. Skaife Centre for Environmental Education ('Skaife' to its friends) near Olifantsbos on the west coast of the Cape of Good Hope Nature Reserve. Miles from anywhere, Skaife is ideally positioned to monopolise shelter and vista, and provided us with a superlative setting in which to indulge our passion for natural history. These were the good old days, when the building's facilities extended to little more than hot-and-cold running baboons. It is a most delightful spot, with its sea-and-sunset view, beach virtually on the bottom step, and resident rock thrush warbling from the gable end.

Within a short time of arriving at the Cape of Good Hope we decided that the reserve would be an ideal subject for an illustrated book. It takes time to get to know a place well enough to embark with even a modicum of confidence on a description which would do it any justice. Two years was definitely not enough to get more than a superficial insight into fynbos, the coast and their plants and animals, and how they tick. Ten years is an improvement but, we appreciate, also not nearly long enough! Plans to put together something specifically on the reserve were, however, reluctantly shelved when we moved to Stellenbosch to extend our fynbos study area. But the idea of a book of some sort persisted, and with a wider catchment of sites and wildlife to draw upon, we set about putting together *A Fynbos Year*. This was published in 1988.

Having completed the academic side of our fynbos research, we refocused attention on the Cape of Good Hope. We migrated back to the Peninsula and set about resurrecting the project, although various constraints have decreed that the production has taken longer than anticipated. We do not feel this has altogether been a drawback; the opposite to some degree, as the passing years have allowed us to get to understand the place a little better and to depict a wider spectrum of plants, many of which emerge only after fire.

For the time we have spent working on this book we have approached the reserve much like any other visitor. An exception to our status as ordinary citizens has been the permission granted by the authorities to collect certain plant and animal specimens and occasionally to drift off the trails and into the few areas closed to the public. If we do give the impression that there is free rein to ramble over the reserve as you wish, this is not the intention. But do not despair; the reserve is one of very few in which visitors are encouraged to leave their cars and explore. Many areas are accessible by roads and footpaths and, with the exception of the reserve headquarters at Klaasjagersberg, the lighthouse buildings, the Brightwater enclave and the sanctuary at Die Mond, are open to everyone. But we have been privileged, greatly so, to have been permitted to wander around at will. Lest you feel you are unfairly discriminated against, it is true to say that all the subjects portrayed in *Between Two Shores* can be found 'legally', that is by the roadside, on the beach or along one of the excellent trails that are being laid out with the very aim of bringing the real pleasures of the reserve within reach of more people. Indeed, not only is following the trails easier than crashing through the veld but, by their nature, the footpaths are designed to lead the visitor through areas of particular natural beauty and interest. One loses little or nothing by sticking to the paths, and the vegetation gains immeasurably through not being trampled, and the birds and other animals by not being disturbed.

Between Two Shores is not a field guide, but an illustrated description of the reserve designed to make your visit there more meaningful and enjoyable. Although we aim to keep this account well and truly down to earth, we could hardly deny that many of the reserve's sights and sounds are inspiring. We do, however, assure readers of a sensitive disposition that nothing will stand in 'mute testimony' to anything else, and that no view will be splendid, plant dazzling or animal remarkable because 'mother nature has conspired' to make it so.

The artist's impressions

Fired with enthusiasm after the publication of *A Fynbos Year* in October 1988, work started immediately on *Between Two Shores*. The first painting completed was the rather rare orchid *Acrolophia bolusii*. There followed in quick succession the graceful *Ixia dubia*, a collection of orchids and *Pelargonium triste* from Klaasjagersberg, and the diminutive *Pelargonium longifolium*.

Work on the illustrations then came to an abrupt halt with the arrival of *The Fynbos Collection*. This was a merchandising venture which we based upon the theme of *A Fynbos Year* and was destined to take up far more time than anyone, not least ourselves, had anticipated. By early 1994 we finally were back on track. Now, at last, we were able to concentrate on catching up with all those plants and animals which had been waiting throughout the preceding years.

Many of the paintings start life as drawings in my sketchbook and, whenever possible, I work from life, whether painting a flower or a frog, simply because this is more enjoyable and immediate. Working from photographs can be useful, especially when checking details, but I have found that they certainly are no substitute for the real thing.

A series of sketches of a living, moving animal helps to build up a picture of that particular individual's character. Ideally, having worked through these drawings I gain enough confidence to tackle a final painting. What you see within the pages of this book, therefore, are not these field or preliminary drawings but illustrations based on these and an accumulation of field experience.

I have been fortunate over the last few years to have a circle of friends who do not meet the request for dead bodies with raised eyebrows. The unfortunate road casualty or beached bird in good condition can provide invaluable reference material. As a result, our freezer is filled with everything from Puff Adders to Dassies and all sorts of birds and other beasts in between. Once thawed out, these animals can be manipulated more effectively and measured more accurately than the stuffed specimen or museum study skin. Plants, in contrast, are more cooperative subjects and at least

stay still. Fynbos by its nature has many species of plants crowded into small areas. The sheer richness of the flora and the overabundance of beautiful flowers in bloom at one time made the choice of species to illustrate a difficult one. Particularly in spring, I found my pages becoming increasingly busy as the season progressed, and the temptation to cram as many plants as possible into each picture had to be resisted!

The illustrations are, in the main, life-size; that is, the size of the plant or animal which you see on the page is the size of it in life and of the original painting. Of the birds and mammals, only the sunbirds, Cape Sugarbird and Vlei Rat are, however, small enough to paint and reproduce this way.

Working specifically to a set page size can be restricting. In an effort to break out of this framework and to cater for a greater diversity of shapes and sizes of plants and animals, a number of the paintings extend over two pages. Some subjects refused to fit comfortably even into this format; these were given a little more breathing space by increasing the size of the original paintings by 25 per cent. This applies to the Candelabra Flower, Yellowtail, Bontebok, Ostrich and Baboons.

I have used a variety of papers in the book, from Fabriano NOT and Arches HP for watercolours to Canson and Fabriano pastel papers, in their varying colours, when working in gouache. I usually alternate between these two media, and together they account for the majority of paintings. Every now and then I experimented with acrylics, the results being the Blacksmith Plover, the angling fish, the Candelabra, April Fool and Kukumakranka flowers, as well as the rare plants in the final chapter.

While we worked on this book our home was constantly full of small livestock – insects of one sort or another, a Vlei Rat, frogs, scorpions and more. A veritable mini-zoo, or at least a zoo of mini-animals. An acute shortage of space often dictated that we sat down to supper with an Evil-eye Puffer Fish or shared the breakfast table with a tank full of waving goose barnacles.

With the exception of the edible fish (which were delicious), all our animals were released at their site of capture after we had finished with them, although some did make their own bids for freedom. The disappearance of the Leopard Toad led to full-scale upheaval while a search was embarked upon. Some hours later, and having found only evidence of months of neglected housework, we sat down exhausted with a cup of tea, only to spot him in a pot of African Violets!

Between Two Shores has been fun. We hope you will share this enjoyment as you leaf through the pages. Most of all, we hope it encourages you to visit the Cape of Good Hope Nature Reserve and support its staff and the efforts of all those who work to conserve it and the precious few remaining unspoilt areas beyond the boundary fence.

Acknowledgements

❀

Our association with the Cape of Good Hope Nature Reserve began with research undertaken by M.F. while a member of the Percy FitzPatrick Institute of African Ornithology (PFIAO) at the University of Cape Town (UCT). Dr Robert Prŷs-Jones (PFIAO; now the British Museum, Tring) was instrumental in setting up the project and securing our involvement in it. While based at Olifantsbos, we enjoyed the support and cooperation of Chief Warden Gerald Wright (now Helderberg Nature Reserve, Somerset West) and his staff (Rangers Derek Clark, Otto von Kaschke and Kevin Foster).

Fieldwork at the reserve for *Between Two Shores* was carried out with the permission of the Western Cape Regional Services Council (WCRSC), which also granted access to sanctuary areas and a permit to collect specimens. Chief Conservation Officer Howard Langley and Senior Conservation Officer Adam Mecinski approved the project. They and Law Enforcement Officer Carl Nortier, Interpretive Officer Jim Hallinan, Veld Manager Roy Ernstzen and former Conservation Officers Fanie Fouché, Alec Woods and Philip Stewart supplied information and observations. The cooperation and help of other past and present reserve staff, particularly Kathy La Grange, Jeffrey Lemine, Micky Heydenrych, William Moni and Johnny Brooks, were also invaluable.

Plants and animals were provided or identified by Howard Langley, Carl Nortier, Roy Ernstzen, Fanie Fouché, Kim Collett, Craig Spencer, Justin Buchmann, Harold Carpenter and Chad Cheney (Cape of Good Hope Nature Reserve); Bill Liltved (Kommetjie); Drs Peter Ryan and Coleen Moloney (PFIAO); Prof. Jenny Jarvis, Dr Mike Picker and students of their UCT third-year zoology field camps; Gill Wheeler, Dalton Gibbs, Tracy Botha and John Hartwick (Rondevlei Nature Reserve); George Underhill (Mowbray); Margaret Oatley (Glencairn); Fiona Powrie (National Botanical Institute, Kirstenbosch); Dylan Evans (Glencairn); and Aida Macdonald (Fish Hoek).

Mrs Antoinette Jacobson (Higgovale) translated and interpreted the Afrikaans place-names; and Dr Lisa Guastella (Oceanographic Research Institute, Durban) supplied information on angling catches, Rob Truter (Chief Surveyor's Office, Mowbray) on place-names. Details of ringed birds were provided by Dr Terry Oatley and the South African Bird Ringing Unit (SAFRING) at UCT.

Source material for the text was suggested or provided by Dr Peter Ryan, Rob Leslie (Sea Fisheries Research Institute), Gill Wheeler, Colin Martin (Dept of Surveying and Geodetic Engineering, UCT), Prof. Les Underhill (Avian Demography Unit, UCT), Dr John Rogers (Marine Geoscience Unit, Dept of Geology, UCT), Prof. Andy Smith (Dept of Archaeology, UCT), Dr Mike Cherry (South African Museum), and Diana and John Deeks (Glencairn). Dr Hamish Robertson (South African Museum) gave access to papers of the late Dr S. H. Skaife. We acknowledge a particular debt to Hugh Taylor's thesis and scientific papers emanating therefrom on the reserve's vegetation, and to Jim Hallinan's thesis on history and interpretative development.

Dr Coleen Moloney, Dr Peter Ryan and Jim Hallinan reviewed parts of the text. Any inaccuracies remaining therein are our own; the opinions expressed are our own and do not necessarily reflect those of the reviewers or their institutions.

Additional help and information came from Russell Martin and Ingrid Küpper (David Philip Publishers), Prof. Richard Cowling (Institute for Plant Conservation, UCT), Dr Shirley Pierce Cowling (Dept of Botany, UCT), Brian Eastman (WCRSC), Barry Rose (Irvin and Johnson), Herman Oosthuisen (Sea Fisheries Research Institute) and Susan Coetzer (Cape Archives). John Graham (Lakeside) and Andrea Plös (PFIAO) came to our rescue during a computer crisis.

The full-page illustrations have been acquired by Steve Bales on behalf of First National Bank's corporate art collection through Everard and Mark Read of the Everard Read Gallery, Johannesburg.

We extend our grateful thanks to all these people and institutions. A special thank you to Peter, Coleen and Gill.

MICHAEL FRASER & LIZ McMAHON

The sandstone sandwiches of Cape Maclear and the Cape of Good Hope viewed from Cape Point's guano-covered cliffs.

CHAPTER ONE

Sandstone and Southeaster

The Physical Setting of the Cape of Good Hope,
Its Landscape, Geology, Climate and Marine Environment

The Cape of Good Hope Nature Reserve occupies the tip of the Cape Peninsula at the southwestern corner of Africa. It is a windswept moorland, a sodden plain, a confusion of ragged rocks, a craggy snaggle-tooth of land jabbing the ocean. Its soils are thin and unyielding, its lakelets dark and uninviting, its seas cold and forbidding. It is far removed geographically and ecologically from traditional perceptions of the African landscape, especially African nature reserves with their thorn trees, wide savannas and animals crowded round a waterhole. The Cape of Good Hope is, nevertheless, every bit as African as these. It is also one of the most ecologically important reserves and remarkable tracts of wilderness in South Africa.

The principal theme of this book is the description and illustration of the wildlife, or some of it at least, found at the Cape of Good Hope. This certainly is a daunting task, as the 7,750 hectare reserve is home to over 1,000 species of plants, over 50 species of mammal and more than 40 reptile and amphibian species. Some 250 species of birds have also been recorded here. The diversity of insects is unquantified but likely to be prodigious and the wealth of marine life, from winkles to whales, is astonishing. Before we can broach the subject of natural history, however, or even begin to detail the species of plants and animals which occur here, we are obliged to provide a physical and cultural setting in which to place them. This also affords us the opportunity to describe what is, after all, a scenically beautiful and historically significant little promontory.

A Cook's tour

Perhaps the best way to describe the reserve's landscape is for us to accompany you on a tour through it. In so doing we confine ourselves largely to the tarred roads and limit descriptions of wildlife to a minimum, leaving the birds and beasts till later.

Lying 40 kilometres south of Cape Town, as the Pied Crow flies, the reserve is reached by the scenic drive over Chapman's Peak or along the False Bay coast through Simon's Town. Both routes will deliver you to the entrance above Smitswinkel Bay. From here the reserve's main road

runs the length of the remainder of the Peninsula, with off-shoots like the broken veins of a badly designed leaf weaving their way to places of interest and strategic importance. These roads encounter representatives of most of the land-form types – mountain, valley, plain and coastline – and thus provide a convenient route along which these can be described.

As the road gently rises and curves into the reserve, you emerge from the valley forming the floor of the fault line which slashes across the Peninsula from Smitswinkel to Schusters Bay. Behind you, and almost 600 metres above, the Swartkop and Klaasjagers mountains represent the edge of the massif from which the tip of the Peninsula has slipped and dropped, not quite completely, into the sea.

Once through the entrance gate, the panorama of False Bay unfolds to the east, the Hottentots Holland mountains across the water culminating in Cape Hangklip. On clear days, particularly in winter's early morning chill before the sea haze rises or Cape Town has dispatched its daily dose of aerial filth in a southerly direction, the mountains and coastal plains of the Overberg can be discerned over 80 kilometres away, petering out into the sea at Danger Point.

The road then curves around the girth of Rooihoogte ('Red Hill'), so called because of the rusty, iron-tainted outcrops of ferricrete on its eastern flank. Once around the corner, the reserve stretches below and beyond. The Smitswinkel Flats to the west (your right) are a great expanse of low-lying reedy plains, dotted with rocky islands and sweeping to the low coastal escarpment which forms the western bulwark of the reserve. The plains form a major catchment, gathering the water that drains from the high ground and holding it in myriad seeps and seasonal vleis before releasing it into the streams which converge in the Krom River valley in the northwest.

The peaks to your left represent the start of the knobbly and crumbling spine which runs the length of the reserve's False Bay coast. The vertebrae take the form of Judas Peak, Die Boer and Paulsberg (at 366 metres, the highest point of the reserve). These are curious round-shouldered half-mountains whose eastern flanks, undercut by waves, have

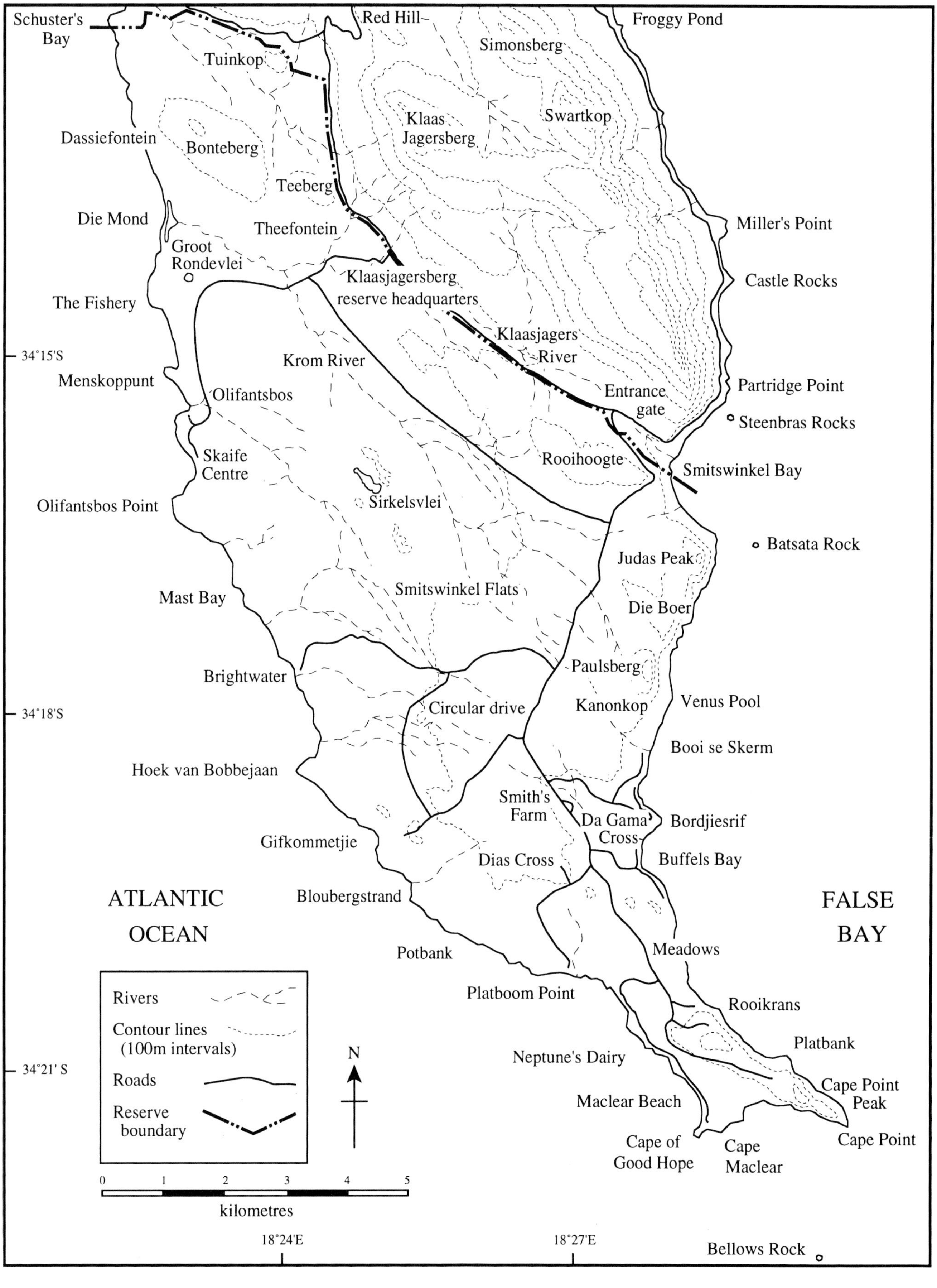

Schuster's Bay
Red Hill
Froggy Pond
Tuinkop
Simonsberg
Swartkop
Klaas Jagersberg
Dassiefontein
Bonteberg
Teeberg
Miller's Point
Die Mond
Theefontein
Castle Rocks
Groot Rondevlei
Klaasjagersberg reserve headquarters
The Fishery
34°15'S
Krom River
Klaasjagers River
Menskoppunt
Olifantsbos
Entrance gate
Partridge Point
Steenbras Rocks
Skaife Centre
Rooihoogte
Smitswinkel Bay
Olifantsbos Point
Sirkelsvlei
Batsata Rock
Judas Peak
Mast Bay
Smitswinkel Flats
Die Boer
Brightwater
Paulsberg
Venus Pool
34°18'S
Circular drive
Kanonkop
Booi se Skerm
Hoek van Bobbejaan
Smith's Farm
Da Gama Cross
Bordjiesrif
Gifkommetjie
Dias Cross
Buffels Bay

ATLANTIC OCEAN

FALSE BAY

Bloubergstrand
Meadows
Potbank
Platboom Point
Rooikrans
Platbank
34°21'S
Neptune's Dairy
Cape Point Peak
Maclear Beach
Cape Point
Cape of Good Hope
Cape Maclear

Rivers
Contour lines (100m intervals)
Roads
Reserve boundary

N

0 1 2 3 4 5
kilometres

18°24'E
18°27'E
Bellows Rock

collapsed, leaving bare cliffs to drop all but precipitously into the sea.

A few slipped discs in our spine then follow – the more gentle hill of Kanonkop (yes, there is a cannon on its summit), and a yet gentler drop into the old undulating limestone hillocks and sandy hummocks through which runs the sparkling streamlet of the Buffels River, recently exhumed from a mausoleum of impenetrable alien thicket. The tall, cross-topped pillar down near the shore is a memorial to Vasco da Gama, pioneering Portuguese navigator and explorer.

The road at this stage takes you past Smith's Farm and traverses the old dunes of sand whipped up from Buffels Bay by millennia of southeasters. A focal point for visitors to the area for the last two centuries or more, Smith's Farm continues in this role today as the Homestead Restaurant. The building occupies the site of and incorporates some of the original farmstead but shows little evidence of its origins. A whitewashed and thatched outbuilding retains the charm and character of the original architecture and serves as a small field museum and information centre. This is run by the Friends of the Cape of Good Hope Nature Reserve, a volunteer group.

As you press south through the Meadows, where farmers grazed their stock in days gone by, the Peninsula narrows and rises. Soon you appreciate that you really are 'between two shores' and can see the ocean briefly on both sides before the eastern aspect is blocked by Vasco da Gama Peak. The road contours round the western flank of this 266-metre hill, the steep drop to the right allowing you a view of the Cape of Good Hope massif. It is easy to be disappointed – the uninspiring mound which is the genuine Cape may not fulfil the expectations of those with romantic notions of something more evocative and memorable. But fear not, more satisfying views of this landmark are to be had from Cape Point, the final and most dramatic precipice of the southern Peninsula.

The climb to the summit of Cape Point Peak (which is 206 metres above sea level, although you have to surmount only the final 126) and the old lighthouse there requires a short and mildly energetic stroll from the car park. If you arrive breathless and trembling at the top, then you haven't spent long enough pausing to admire the view, enjoy the plants or watch the birds. All the way along the trail, the neatly stratified buttress of Cape Maclear draws the eye westward. The name commemorates Sir Thomas Maclear, Her Majesty's astronomer at the Cape who made scientific observations here last century. Between it and you lies Dias Beach onto which the sea and cormorants surge. Beyond broods the rampart of the Cape of Good Hope, the last bastion of Africa, propping up the continent and tempering Adamastor's fury.

Little more than the drum-shaped metal base of the old lighthouse remains, but plans are afoot to restore it to something more closely resembling the original structure. The

Opposite: The Cape of Good Hope Nature Reserve at the tip of the Cape Peninsula, South Africa.

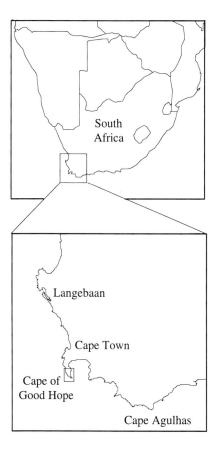

location is an inspiring one and allows 360° coverage of the sea, the Hottentots Holland mountains to the east and the broadening Peninsula behind you. The impression may be gained that looking straight out from here you should, somehow, be facing directly south. You are in fact gazing southeastward down the final furlong of the Point and out over the Atlantic. At the tip is the new lighthouse, an angle on it as well as a better one of the cliffs being had from the viewing sites back down the steps. If you get your bearings you will see to the west that Cape Maclear with the Cape of Good Hope beyond lies a fraction further south than Cape Point. The Cape of Good Hope thereby qualifies, by a whisker, as the southwesternmost tip of the African continent (at 34° 21' 25" South, 18° 28' 26" East, if you want to know precisely where it lies). If there is even a hint of a swell, white water can be seen breaking over Bellows Rock, about 3.5 kilometres to the south. This is a smooth granite outcrop which just breaks the surface at low tide; in stormy conditions it spawns the most enormous billows and spectacular spray (best appreciated through a telescope). It is famous as the rock which sunk the (at least *a*) *Lusitania* in 1911.

Time now to head back and explore the rest of the reserve through which we have overspeedily brought you. The first

Sparse vegetation and rocky outcrops characterise much of the reserve, but belie great natural richness and beauty.

turnoff is on your right and leads to Rooikrans, the aptly named Red Cliffs. Especially at sunrise, the brick-coloured sandstone precipices glow warmly. Look north along the coast to Buffels Bay and further on to the Paulsberg range and, beyond the boundary, the Swartkop. In the extreme distance lies the silver crescent of Strandfontein beach, with the Cape Flats disappearing into a horizon hatched by buildings and smudged by smoke. At the foot of Rooikrans are the ledges which are famous in the angling world; a well-worn cliff-edge track testifies to the generations of hopeful fishermen who have scrambled down to try their luck.

Next stop is the Cape of Good Hope itself, for which you must reconnect with the main road and, having scarcely done so, ease left down the slope and back along the west coast. Here you pass beaches of boulder and sand and rocky gulleys and enclaves with names which perhaps commem-

orate fishing expeditions and happy holiday outings – Neptune's Dairy where the waves and backwash whisk an airy froth like the best milkshake, and Pappiesbank where perhaps daddy was happiest to doze or where he caught his biggest fish. Just in from the coast there is evidence of old campfires and bivouacs; it is unclear as yet if these remains are a hundred or a thousand years old or come down to us from both eras.

At the road's end you can perch your car on the edge of the world. On a stormy day the sea washes up the beach and perilously close to the car park, but for most of the time you can relax and enjoy almost uninterrupted views of the glittering ocean. On the rocks ahead of you the cormorants roost, the few metres of water between them and you being security enough for their peace of mind. When you arrive a halo of gulls will form, Hitchcockian-like, around your car, evidence that visitors do feed them. Please don't be one of them. In doing so, you will inevitably encourage their bad habits and, even worse, attract a baboon.

If the baboon siege does not materialise and you are fit and able, climb up the steps to the top of the massif to view the cliffs and seascape. You will not regret the effort – an unrivalled scene presents itself, much more splendid, in our opinion, than that from Cape Point. Bear in mind that you are now perched at one of the most historical locations in the southern hemisphere, in which context we describe it more fully in Chapter Two. Having enjoyed the view from this spectacular and symbolic spot, retrace your route to the main road and the next junction.

This takes you west through marshy moorland past the Dias Cross and down to Platboom, the wind-cropped milk-wood bushes giving this spot its name ('Flat Tree'). A more distant aspect of the Cape of Good Hope is had from here, but the most striking feature is the stark, white dune which smothers the bottom of a narrow valley running parallel to the shore. When the wind blows from the southeast, it is easy to see how this dune has taken shape – stand for a minute or two and those sand grains which have not embed-ded themselves in your legs or accumulated in your socks will begin to form little drifts around your ankles. Magnify this a millionfold in time and space to see just how much material can be shifted by the wind from the beach and onto the dry land.

Dunes, rocks and sandy beaches in a picturesque setting combine to make Buffels Bay a popular recreational area. Back up the hill from Platboom, on to the main road and then first right will bring you to this spacious bay with its splendid views. Reserve management policy demands that recreation which is not strictly compatible with conserva-tion, but allows for an acceptable diversity of utilisation by visitors, should be focused on a small number of appropri-ate sites. This minimises the need for disturbance and devel-opment in the rest of the reserve. Thus we have parking

Sea spray whipped up below Paulsberg by a roaring 'black southeaster'.

areas, rolling lawns, a tidal swimming pool, *braai* places and ablution blocks at the bay. Although inevitably detracting from the natural qualities of the reserve, such facilities are essential to cater for a broad spectrum of demands from visitors. Carefully planned and controlled, the infrastructure need not necessarily introduce suburbia into the wilderness. Very busy over the summer holiday season, Buffels Bay is all but deserted for the rest of the year. This is a lovely spot, and it is easy to see why it is so popular with the picnickers and paddlers. Present-day visitors are not the first to appreciate the area – it has a long history of human occupation and utilisation, from vegetable farming to whaling. Today's users are, hopefully, more sensitive than their predecessors. As recently as the 1960s a fishing encampment was installed amongst the dunes. The domestic refuse emanating from this informal settlement has been largely removed, but a variety of material still surfaces from time to time. Chop bones and sea shells reflect the preferred diet of these latter-day strandlopers, an abundance of beer bottles their liquid leanings.

A second relatively intensively developed area not far away is at Bordjiesrif. Again, the swimming pool and picnic spots are very busy in the summer, particularly over Christmas and New Year. At other times there is little but the gulls to disturb the tranquillity of the boulder beaches and beckoning beds of kelp.

Further along the False Bay coast, the road runs along the foot of the hills and limestone outcrops to Booi se Skerm. We are told that years ago this was a veritable woodland of coastal shrubs and trees. A few remain, including an important relict patch of kloof forest, but most were chopped down to provide fuel for the local limekiln. Recently restored, this sits with a certain robust dignity under the outcrops which supplied its *raison d'être*. The small caves in the cliffs are known as Booi se Skerm, or 'Booi's Shelter'. This stretch of coast loses the sun quite early, being almost oppressively overshadowed by the mountains, but, whoever Booi was, he and previous occupants (who may date back thousands of years) of the caves chose a retreat which affords the finest views of False Bay and the mountains beyond and received the warming sun first thing in the morning.

We leave the coast now and take off across the Peninsula along Circular Drive. This narrow road was installed in an attempt to bring the people to the animals, the herds of buck, now recognised as inappropriate, which were introduced in response to a perceived demand from the public to stock the place with wildlife, the larger and more conspicuous the better. This formerly controversial issue we address in the final chapter; suffice it to say at the moment that if you have not yet seen a mammal larger than a mouse on your tour, that is a good, not bad, reflection of the state of the reserve. Do remember that this is first and foremost a botanical reserve, not a game park.

Circular Drive branches off the main road just north of Smith's Farm. It traverses what would appear to be an uninteresting stretch of veld, with little to disrupt the monotony of low, sparse vegetation for two-thirds of its length. For this reason it is unfortunately treated as some sort of race track by those drivers for whom an absence of elephants from a nature reserve is something to be regretted. This is a shame, as the drive, in common with the rest of the reserve's roads, should preferably be negotiated at a snail's pace to appreciate its finer points. The southern arm begins by traversing the gently undulating fossil dune which has its origins at Buffels Bay. A contrast between the dense, shrubby vegetation of the dune and the sparser Inland Fynbos is apparent before one drops gently down onto a wide and almost featureless plain, the Rietveld, or 'Reed Meadow'. The western arm of the road traverses some more inspiring landscape, with rocky outcrops, fine old protea bushes and panoramic views of the coast. For those who know where to look for it, the distant wreck of the *Thomas T. Tucker* at Olifantsbos Point is visible from here.

The offshoot to Gifkommetjie furnishes those who care to make this short diversion with fine views north and south along the west coast from a vantage point (nearby Kommetjieberg is, at 114 metres, the highest point on the west coast proper). There is some very rocky and bleak landscape here, but steeped in natural riches and beauty. The deep basin scooped out of the mountain side supports the finest tract of coastal thicket on the reserve and is of particular conservation importance in this context.

The final curve of Circular Drive leads back across the reedy plain and through the tussock marshes to the main road. The finer attractions of the habitat through which the road passes are elucidated in the following chapters. It certainly does support some of the nicest flowers and most interesting creatures of the whole reserve, although the finding and appreciation of the likes of *Schizodium obliquum* (an orchid just a few centimetres high) and the Cloud Cisticola (a small, brown warbler which, when not secreted in the tussock, lives up to its name by heading heavenward) do require some effort.

The final sector for you to explore is the northwest corner at Olifantsbos and environs. This is our favourite part of the reserve and is reached by driving down the long road which branches west off the main road at the foot of Rooihoogte, not far inside the main gate. This route, the Link Road (for it links the main road with the reserve headquarters at Klaasjagersberg), owes much to the Roman school of highway design. Its planners have taken two points and joined them by a straight line; a more meandering route would have served to increase enjoyment of the drive and slowed down the traffic. Parallel and to the north, the reserve boundary is flanked by a line of hills, Rooihoogte in the east being the highest, the peaks becoming less statuesque to the west until Kleinkoppie is reached. Between the two are old passes – Arnoldsnek and Snaartjiesnek, names which perhaps commemorate their discoverers. To the south is the shallow, marshy basin which converges in the Krom River valley. The ill-defined rise of Russouwskop would hardly merit the accolade of *kop* were the rest of the landscape not so featureless. Further north, the taller hills of Teeberg and Bonteberg serve as a natural boundary to the reserve. Below them the Klaasjagers River flows past the ruins of the farmstead at Theefontein and on to its meeting with the Krom River, before emptying into the sea at Die Mond.

The road then curves sharply south to Olifantsbos, down the long straight with the sea on your right and the rocky escarpment on your left. The coastal plain along which the road runs, straight and level, is a raised beach, a legacy of higher sea levels in prehistoric times. Near the end of the drive, a grove of oak trees is a reminder of the more recent past. Here a smallholding was lived and worked in as recently as the 1940s. With these last residents culminated a history of human occupation of Olifantsbos which stretches back tens of thousands of years.

Olifantsbos is journey's end for the car-bound traveller. Those who stay in their vehicles can still enjoy the views and watch the birds in the bay pottering amongst the highly malodorous kelp (which Mark Twain might describe as 'an insurrection in a gasometer'). The Skaife Centre lies a short distance south of here, and can be seen from the *Thomas T. Tucker* beach trail. To the north across the bay is Menskoppunt, 'Skull Point'. No one seems sure if this sinister name is really linked to some grisly discovery. About 15 kilometres north, and outside the reserve, the Slangkop lighthouse spikes up from its promontory near Kommetjie. This light works in tandem with the Cape Point beam to ward ships off the west coast's treacherous reefs and shoals.

This whistle-stop tour will take you a couple of hours or so, which hardly does justice to the finer-scale qualities of the landscape and its occupants. Hurtling around in your car and not taking time to linger in the reserve is about as satisfying as window-shopping, or scrutinising a restaurant menu but not savouring any of its delights. *Between Two Shores* is our attempt to winkle you out of your comfortable car, stretch your legs and take a look at what makes the reserve 'tick'.

At the bottom line, the functioning and composition of the reserve's plant and animal communities and, perhaps a little less directly, the history of humankind in this landscape, are products of the fundamental environmental factors which impinge upon them. These are the rocks and soil, in and amongst which they sit, and the weather which bears down upon them.

Monoliths and monkey stones

The geological history of the reserve is a mercifully uncomplicated one. Six-hundred million years ago, the southern Cape lay beneath the sea at the edge of Gondwanaland, the landmass which ultimately gave rise to the continents of the southern hemisphere. At this time, volcanic activity raised the seabed above the water; where the lava burst through the overlying shales, it cooled to form smooth, rounded granite domes. The infant Cape then sank beneath a shallow sea once more. For the next 200 million years great thicknesses of sediments were deposited upon it, swept down from the adjacent landmass, their component grains, pebbles and boulders tumbled and sorted by the torrents, winnowed and washed by tide and storm. These settled and solidified to create the coarse-grained, almost pure quartz sandstones which, much reduced and modified by subsequent erosion, form the basis of today's landscape. Known as the Peninsula Formation, these sediments are part of the Table Mountain Group.

The reserve thus comprises a great thickness of gently inclined quartzitic sandstone resting upon a granite foundation. The latter is an immensely hard, erosion-resistant rock and has prevented the Peninsula from being consumed by the waves long ago. Where the overlying sediments have been eroded away, granite outcrops are visible in places. The coastline from Simon's Town to Smitswinkel, for example, is dominated by granite which is visible as the huge, rounded, cormorant-bedecked silver-grey boulders off Miller's Point and Partridge Point. Once in the reserve the granite–sandstone interface runs out to sea and disappears. At the base of Cape Point Peak, however, some intruded granite is exposed. Its contours, almost pearly smooth at a distance, contrast with the no-nonsense strata of sandstone above, a multi-layered geological *mille-feuilles*. Granite outcrops are also manifested by patches of churning white water not far offshore. These almost, but not quite (or perhaps only at low tide), break the surface; as such, they have constituted a great hazard to seafarers over the centuries.

Back to dry land. As you will have gathered by now, we feel strongly that the biggest attractions of the reserve are its smallest occupants. This applies as much to its mineral as to its animal and vegetable features, and close scrutiny of the rocks can be very rewarding. The sandstones which comprise the great majority of exposed rock at the reserve are very hard and erosion-resistant. Look closely and you can see geological history encapsulated in the different-sized particles bound together in layers in a lump of sandstone. The sandstone at our seawatching site at the Cape of Good Hope, for example, is fine-grained and shows swirly ripple marks. These are the consequence of deposition in shallow water with swift currents. At the base of Cape Maclear and in the isolated outcrops on Dias Beach, older, finer-grained sediments of the Table Mountain Group are to be found, comprising small grains cemented by red or purple muddy sand. These rocks belong to the Graafwater Formation, and were laid down some 450 million years ago. Erosion of these relatively soft sediments at the base of the cliffs has led to deep overhangs and recesses at sea level.

The sandstones which typify the exposed rock further north in the reserve are, in contrast, generally coarser and comprise relatively large particles, the result of deposition, all those millions of years ago, in turbulent, nearshore

waters. Entombed in the rough, shapeless lumps are intricate and beautiful mosaics of quartz grains, milky pebbles in a crystal matrix. Because of its hardness, these quartz grains are often the sole survivors of erosion and transportation, processes which dissolve or disintegrate the softer and more soluble minerals. The shape of the grains indicates how far they have been transported from their source or how long they have been tumbled around in the water. The well-worn, smooth grains have been subjected to aquatic wear and tear for a long time; the coarse, sharply-edged ones have spent less time underwater. Below some of the rocks are perfect pools of these milky pebbles, untouched and unblemished, which have fallen like teardrops from their parent.

The often jagged and chaotic bouldery landscape and rock formations that characterise the reserve are the result of nature's sculpting over millions of years. Although hardly on the scale of the Grand Canyon, and not so much Michelangelo as Henry Moore with a hangover, some of the sculptures are impressive in their own way. These include the tumbled henges on Bonteberg and the mysterious standing stones in the Krom River valley. The escarpment above Olifantsbos exhibits some fine monolithic mazes and stark surrealistic carvings. Some could have stepped straight out of science fiction (a bug-eyed monster would not look out of place perched on them); some, with their battlements and machicolations, from medieval fortresses.

Rocks of all sizes are often pocked with hollows and depressions to form so-called monkey stones. This selective erosion of soft stone within hard can result in honeycomb-like formations decorating the rock faces or, when scoured from their tops, the most delightful natural birdbaths. Many attractively weathered stones have, in the past, undergone rapid transportation and subsequent deposition in Cape Town gardens. It has to be said that the monkey stones look much better in their natural surroundings than perched in the middle of a suburban garden supporting an angling gnome.

At two locations in the reserve, conspicuous outcrops of wholly brown, red, or yellowish-hued rocks occur. These are made of ferricrete, a sandstone whose constituent grains have been cemented together by iron to form hard pans or lenses. About half the bulk of Rooihoogte is composed of ferricrete, and adjacent to the Rooikrans road there is another conspicuous outcrop. Known as 'koffieklip', this material was once quarried and broken up to provide gravel for road building. The scars of these excavations are visible at both sites.

Fossil sediments

Geological features of more recent vintage than the sand-stones and granite are limestone outcrops and fossil dunes. Limestone essentially is the fossil remains of marine shells deposited on the sea bottom. Its appearance on land is a consequence of ancient sea levels being higher than that of the present day. With the retreat of the sea, the accumulated limestone sediments are exposed, thereafter to be cemented together by calcium salts to form calcrete, which in turn is weathered and eroded. On the False Bay coast a narrow band of limestone forms a broken escarpment along the hillside between Buffels Bay and Noupoortjie. The escarpment is dark grey in colour and rendered rough, sharp and brittle in texture by its component sand and shell grit. A source of high-quality lime for making cement, the calcrete cliffs here were quarried in the last century. The caves at Booi se Skerm are probably a combination of natural erosion, mainly by the sea, and quarrying.

Fossil dunes are just what the name implies. The major one all but bisects the reserve as it snakes across the Peninsula from Buffels Bay to Papkuilskloof; smaller, isolated ones occur at Olifantsbos and elsewhere. In the case of the trans-reserve dune, thousands of years of southeaster have blown sand from the exposed seabed of False Bay. When the source of sand was exhausted or extinguished by the rising sea, the dunes stabilised and hardened.

The to-ing and fro-ing of the sea has altered the extent and height of the reserve's coastal shelf or foreland. About 20,000 years ago the sea was some 140 metres lower than today, this level having been reached at least four times during the last million years as a result of expansion of the polar icecaps (the freezing ice draws up water from the world's oceans, lowering their level). Some six thousand years ago it was two metres higher than at present. When the sea level was at its lowest, False Bay would have been empty and transformed into a wide grassy plain, supporting herds of grazing animals. Higher sea levels, such as we see today, inundated False Bay and the reserve's coastal forelands, such that the only extensive area of this landform is the Krom River plain in the northwest. The road to Olifantsbos takes you along the foreland – on your left you will see the sandstone escarpment; between it and the sea lies the level sandy plain of the coastal shelf. This is essentially an old beach lying between 6 and 18 metres above the average sea level.

Of interest to the botanist is the fact that the soils of the raised beaches, limestone outcrops and ancient dunes have different chemical properties from the sandstones over which they have encroached. They have thus introduced coastal conditions to an inland setting and support plant communities more akin to those found nearer the sea than in the interior.

Soils ancient and modern

Soils in their most basic form are the breakdown product of rock. Where the parent material is hard and coarse, the soils have similar characteristics. Such is the case at the reserve, where the weathering of the Table Mountain Group sandstones gives rise to shallow, coarse, quartzitic sandy soils. These also tend to be well drained, acidic and very low in nutrients. On the rocky hills the soil is created on the spot from the almost immeasurably slow breakdown of the rock. In such positions the soil is very thin, shallow, and sugary in texture. On the lower slopes and flats accumulation of material from the hills above gives rise to soils with smoother and finer particles. Soil depth can extend to a metre, but in general the bedrock is rarely far beneath the surface.

Coastal soils are derived from marine sand, often containing large shelly fragments, or are a combination of this and inland material, blown or washed together over many years or from recent storms, fires or windy summers. These form mixtures which vary greatly in texture and acidity from place to place.

Soils also contain organic matter, the product of decomposed plants. Again, in the hills, there is little accumulation of such material. On the wetter lower slopes and poorly drained flats, more compost gathers. The soils here have a correspondingly greater organic content. This renders them very dark brown or black (most noticeable in the dried-out vleis in summer), in contrast to the white or pale grey soils of the mountains and rocky areas.

The reserve thus contains a small number of rock types, but a large variety of soils derived from them and other sources. The diversity of soil types is a major factor determining plant distribution and the species composition of communities, and contributes to the immense floral richness of the reserve and the fynbos region as a whole. Another important influence on the biological processes and on the character of the reserve's human and other visitors and inhabitants is the weather.

The Cape of Storms

'It's a lot of weather we've been having recently' was one of Oliver Hardy's least successful chat-up lines. But his reflections on things climatic would not be out of place at the Cape of Good Hope, which certainly does experience a lot of weather, much of it windy. Cape Point itself is the most exposed spot on the coast of South Africa, and the all but constant wind it receives is only moderately tempered over the narrow spit which forms the rest of the reserve. In summer the southeaster blows gale force for week after week; in winter horizontal rain from the northwest is the order of the day. 'The Cape of Storms' reflects the experiences of early navigators who braved these turbulent waters. Within and between these predominating patterns are spells of the most blissful calm and soporific warmth which, somehow, make all the tediously wet and monotonously windy ones worth enduring. Also in its favour is the gentle transition between summer and winter which gives rise to prolonged spring and autumn. These are quite the nicest seasons here.

The climate of the reserve is, in common with that of the rest of the southwestern Cape, classified as 'Mediterranean type', resembling as it does that experienced in that part of the world and other places on similar latitudes (Chile, California and southwestern Australia, for example). This climate can conveniently be summarised as having warm, dry summers and cool, wet winters. Although this is the overriding pattern, the reserve does display characteristics of its own. Prevalent among these are the variation in annual rainfall within short distances and the particular ferocity and persistence of the southeast wind in summer. Rainfall is relatively low (402 millimetres a year) at the exposed Point, but higher (565 millimetres) at Klassjagersberg. The former site experiences a maximum temperature of 26.2°C, dropping to a minimum of 7.8°C in winter. Its average temperature is 15.6°C. Perhaps the most interesting aspect is that Cape Point experiences the most equable of all climates in South Africa. That is to say, the differences between the lowest and highest temperatures on a daily and annual basis are the least recorded anywhere in the subcontinent. This is because the sea keeps the Point, and the reserve as a whole, cool in summer and warm, in a relative sense, in winter. In essence, the climate of the reserve is that of the sea around it.

Of all the weather conditions which the reserve experiences, the roaring southeaster leaves the most powerful and lasting impression on visitors and locals alike. Known as the 'Cape Doctor' because it sweeps clean the streets and blows all the dirt and dust out to sea, the southeaster is as much a part of Cape Town and environs as Table Mountain and the Cape of Good Hope itself. At the reserve, and over False Bay in particular, the summer southeaster is particularly ferocious because the wind is compressed vertically as it is forced over the mountains at the eastern entrance to False Bay and laterally as it is funnelled between these and the Peninsula mountains in the west. Cape Point's average wind speeds (35 kilometres per hour) are almost double those of Cape Town's airport, 40 kilometres to the northeast on the Cape Flats. At Olifantsbos the average wind speed is 24 kilometres per hour. The wind emanates from the southeast for 35 per cent of the year, outblowing any other direction, although between them, and largely in the winter months, west and north- and southwest account for 34 per cent of the wind direction.

Calm days are rendered even less frequent because of sea breezes – the movement of cool air from the ocean to replace air which has warmed and risen over the land as the day heats up. These breezes keep the temperature down to an extent that can render the reserve uncomfortably chilly on a summer's day. But perhaps we should be grateful, as it is true to say that if we did not have the wind to complain about, we would be moaning about the insufferable heat! The sea breezes may also shroud the coast in fog, and one or other of the reserve's shores can be swathed in thick, clinging cloud, while a hundred or two metres inland all is bright and sunny. The west coast in autumn is particularly prone to being fogbound. Moist, humid air rising from the relatively warm waters out to sea condenses when it passes over the colder nearshore waters of the Benguela Upwelling, and enshrouds a ribbon of coastline the length of the reserve.

In winter, successions of cold fronts sweep across the Peninsula from the west and northwest with almost monotonous regularity. Some days can be decidedly stormy. A memorable 'blow' occurred in May 1984 when, following a rapid drop in atmospheric pressure, the wind exceeded 100 kilometres per hour over the Cape west coast, and waves 16 metres high were recorded at Slangkop. At the reserve itself the seas were impressive, to put it mildly, as the wind howled from the northwest and the coast was pounded by massive surf. Seaweed was even dumped on the steps of Skaife stoep, a spot which the previous day had been 20 metres from the highest of high-tide lines! Storms of such ferocity – an intrusion of the 'Roaring Forties' into Cape waters – are rare but are salutary reminders of the power of wind and waves.

On a more general level, the distinct seasonal shift of wind direction from southeast in summer to northwest in winter is an important one, not least in the circulation of water in False Bay, and in the rain which arrives with a vengeance. On the bright side, 74 per cent of the rain is confined to the months of April to September, so we can look forward confidently to long, dry spells in the summer. Nevertheless, we have to confess that our favourite season at the reserve is winter. Not the tempestuous cloudbursts and furious winds (although these do have their attractions), but the deliciously warm and windless days which are such a relief from the tedium of summer gales and winter downpours. Such days occur when the depressions have passed and the northwest wind moderates and backs to southwesterly, later to southerly with clearing skies. Such conditions may persist for a week and happily coincide with the burgeoning of plant growth and the almost total absence of visitors. Few people, therefore, have seen the reserve clothed in its very finest apparel in June and July – great sweeps of dazzling leucadendrons draping the plains and hills with a veritable cloth of gold; the dark riverlets exuberantly bursting their banks and splashing, boisterous and unconfined, through the reedy marshes; the proteas alive with prattling sugarbirds and dashing, glinting sunbirds; and the promise of spring at hand with feverishly sprouting shoots and energetic foliage. There is a new-found vigour and freshness to the landscape, a determination to make good after the dry and dusty summer and, in the awakening bulbs and seeds, a bubbling of subterranean energy ready to erupt in a verdant volcano.

One ocean?

'Placed on a spot of the globe the most favourable perhaps for the grand spectacles, I had on my right the Atlantic and on my left the Indian, and before me the Southern Ocean, which breaking with fury at my feet seemed as if desirous of attacking the whole chain of mountains and swallowing up my feet.' So wrote François Le Vaillant, the itinerant and rather eccentric French naturalist who visited Cape Point in the late eighteenth century. For a man not exactly given to lavish praise on the places he visited (he described Simon's Town as 'this dreary desert'), this was a generous and evocative description. But was it accurate? Do the oceans meet at Cape Point?

Le Vaillant's 'Southern Ocean' is a nebulous concept. The ocean of that name might be interpreted as comprising the southern sectors of the Indian and Atlantic oceans somewhere beyond 50° South and into the realms of the ice floes and the midnight sun. The view from Cape Point is certainly not *that* good!

The other two oceans in question are the Indian and the Atlantic, with their reputedly warm and cold waters, respectively, which are claimed to converge immediately below the Point. Many observers tell us that they have actually seen them banging into each other there, and tour guides are fond of regaling their clients with accounts of this oceanic rendezvous. The meeting of the oceans is, unfortunately, something of a myth.

Oceans are not hard-edged with tangible borders like

landmasses; they are dynamic systems whose boundaries, if they have any, are constantly moving and mixing. The concept of two independent oceanic bodies of water is thus an artificial one, particularly in respect of their so-called meeting at Cape Point. From the geographers' point of view, this is certainly a fallacy, as the Indian officially becomes the Atlantic and vice versa at 20° East at Cape Agulhas.

Two currents

What does occur at Cape Point every now and then is the mixing of two water systems, or bits of them – the Agulhas Current on the one hand and the Benguela Upwelling on the other. Granted, these systems do have their origins in the Indian and Atlantic oceans, respectively, but their meeting and mingling takes place over a huge area and varies greatly according to the time of year and weather conditions. The Agulhas Current originates in the warm waters of the South Equatorial Current of the Indian Ocean. Driven by the earth's rotation and wind and weather systems, it meanders down the south coast of South Africa in a narrow arc. The current flows close inshore along the south coast before being deflected offshore by the Agulhas Bank, the shallow submarine shelf that extends 200 kilometres offshore slightly east of Cape Agulhas. At this point, sea-bed topography and wind combine to create a whirlpool effect which forces the Agulhas Current back on itself at this zone of retroflection, as it is termed. It then heads back into the Indian Ocean. Rings of warm Agulhas water, up to 500 kilometres across, do occasionally cruise past the Point far offshore. These continue to drift westward, having detached from the main current as it turns.

On the west coast of the Peninsula, water chemistry and temperature are determined by the Benguela Upwelling System. Simply put, water at the sea's surface is blown parallel to the coast by the southeasterly wind. The Coriolis force, which results from the rotation of the earth, dictates that this northbound water is then deflected to the left of its direction of travel, so that it actually moves northwestwards and out into the open ocean. This creates a local drop in sea level, a 'vacuum' which is then filled by water moving up from the sea below. This input consists of relatively cold water that has its origins in the central depths of the South Atlantic at about 40° South. It rises from a depth of some 300 metres at a rate of about 30 metres a day to form the surface waters along the Cape west coast.

The sea surface temperature of the Atlantic just west of the region of upwelling is about 21°C; within the Benguela as a whole it is 13–15°C. This changes by only 2–4°C throughout the year because summer warmth is cancelled by the southeaster which promotes upwelling, bringing the cold water to the sea surface. Indeed, the water off the west coast is perhaps a touch warmer in winter, as upwelling is weakest in May, June and July, when the southeast winds abate, than at the end of summer and in autumn. The west coast is thus blessed with lovely beaches but blighted by chilly water. No more so than at Olifantsbos, where an intense tongue of upwelling occurs, lowering the temperature of the sea there to 9°C. Meanwhile, on the False Bay coast only a few kilometres away, the water can be as much as 6°C warmer than on the west, as the wind blows surface water, heated by the sunshine, against the shore. The overall trend is, thus, for west coast water to be cooler than the east. This does form something of a biological barrier to marine organisms and processes, and the intertidal fauna on the west coast is markedly different from that on the east of the Peninsula.

Plankton and productivity

For those who find the sea temperatures at the Cape of Good Hope just a trifle brisk, consolation may (or may not) be had from the fact that the Benguela Upwelling System is one of the most productive marine areas in the world, paralleling and exceeding similar upwellings off Peru and California. This is because nutrients are swept upwards in the rising cold water to the well-lit sea surface. This is essentially like spreading fertiliser on a field, and any plants that can grow there will benefit from this enrichment. In the Benguela, therefore, there are exceptionally high levels of biological productivity. In the nearshore environment, extensive kelp beds provide shelter and food for many marine organisms.

Floating in the surface waters are phytoplankton, tiny single-celled plants, which can directly utilise the fresh input of nutrients and are, in turn, eaten by other organisms, including larger zooplankton and small fish. These are eaten by larger and then yet larger fish, with various small seabirds finding themselves a niche, and so on up the food pyramid until it is topped by the biggest seabirds, seals, whales and dolphins, and ourselves.

The abundance of plankton gives a good indication of upwelling in action. On the first few days of a strong summer southeaster fresh, cold water is imported and the sea is beautifully clear (and crisp). Under such conditions the shallow, sandy-bottomed coastal stretches at Platboom and Olifantsbos are a startling turquoise in colour and put to shame the garish tropical seascapes so dear to the hearts of those who compile travel brochures. This freshly upwelled water harbours a few phytoplankton which have been dormant in the deep, dark water but are swept to the surface. Here they respond to the sunlight by multiplying rapidly. This leads to accelerated growth and population increase of other microscopic creatures, notably zooplankton, which feed on the phytoplankton. After a few days the resulting organic soup clouds and colours the water, until the wind moderates, the upwelling subsides and the plankton die off, or are eaten, and their eggs and dormant stages sink down into the depths again.

The original lighthouse on Cape Point Peak, commissioned on 1 May 1860.

CHAPTER TWO

Khoikhoi, Caravels and Candlepower

A History of Exploration and Discovery,
Shipwrecks and Lighthouses,
and the Establishment of a Nature Reserve

The enormous bulks of ocean-going cargo ships which lumber round the Cape of Good Hope are enacting a scene which, in one form or another, has taken place innumerable times over the last five hundred years; or, if credence can be given to Middle Eastern mariners, one which occurred even two millennia ago. Either way, it must be remembered that although the arrival of European navigators in the late fifteenth century was the first unequivocal encounter of 'modern' Man with this corner of the globe, these outsiders were not the first humans to experience the windswept moorlands of the Cape Peninsula.

There is still much to unravel and probably plenty to discover about the area's unnatural history, but an impression can be gained of life at the Cape from the artefacts and calling cards left by early occupants and passers-by. At almost the simplest level, heaps of shells of the edible and explosive varieties reflect a long and diverse history of land use of the area now occupied by the Cape of Good Hope Nature Reserve. More complex is the mythical, superstitious, symbolic, romantic and strategic aura which the spot has generated over the centuries. Here is the home of a Greek god (albeit a minor one), haunt of a nautical apparition, a gateway to the east, a milestone in maritime exploration, a new horizon, a turning point, a navigational beacon, a marker in the conquest of the globe, colonial expansion and the scramble for territory and trade. Such are the awe and importance in which Man has seen fit to hold a large lump of salty sandstone topped with scruffy bushes and jutting into the ocean.

The three Stone Ages of Man

Prehistoric people made their first imprint on the landscape here about 600,000 years ago. This they did within a kilometre of the Cape of Good Hope where traces of occupation by Early Stone Age peoples have been found in a wind-scoured depression. There remains little by which to remember them, but the fragments of their basic stone tools are sufficient to plot the first dot on the graph of human history on the reserve. These aboriginals were itinerant hunter-gatherers, their movements linked to the availability of fresh water and of food. When supplies of these became depleted in particular seasons or years, the people moved on.

The next dot on our graph was added by Middle Stone Age peoples. Dating back some 40,000 to 200,000 years they, like their predecessors, left little evidence of their presence. Artefacts, including scrapers and other fragments of worked stone, ascribed to this period have been found at about six sites in the reserve. At this stage, settlement patterns in the southwestern Cape as a whole do not follow a smooth progression, but are interrupted by periods when the climate was colder and humans may have been absent from the area.

This brings us up to more modern times, or at least from about 21,000 years ago to the arrival of Europeans at the end of the fifteenth century. This period occupies the Late Stone Age, and over a hundred sites of this vintage have been found at the reserve. Evidence of human activity at them ranges from a few discarded seashells and stone flakes scattered by tool-makers, to caves or rocky overhangs which house the trappings of the successive generations who used them for shelter. The early occupants of such caves, the San (or Bushmen) hunter-gatherers, relied on the seashore for much of their food. Their colloquial name, strandloper (beachwalker), reflects their littoral lifestyle.

Evidence of human occupation litters a small cave at the base of the cliffs at Smitswinkel. Here a midden (a prehistoric domestic refuse-heap) contained remains of over 20 species of shellfish, hare, dolphin, fur seal and five species of antelope. The bones of cattle and sheep indicate that these livestock were present perhaps as long as 1,400 years ago. This cave shelter thus reveals an interesting mix of hunter-gatherer (San) collectables and pastoralist (Khoikhoi) kitchen scraps.

Outnumbering the cave shelters by a hundred or more are less formal prehistoric sites dotted around the reserve. Evidence of human activity ranges from a few scattered rock fragments or pottery shards to shell middens of varying size. Most of the sites occur along the coastline, reflecting the foraging preferences of prehistoric humans. The technology for making pots seems to have arrived at the Cape at the same time as the Khoi herders and their livestock. However, Cape pottery has unique attributes and is of such a style that suggests it may have developed independently. Pottery shards at the reserve are normally plain, but some bear simple designs and decorations. These were scratched into the wet clay with a twig or fish bone, or impressed with a crab pincer.

Such finds provide a glimpse into the lifestyles of early peoples at the reserve, and the contents of their middens reflect the environmental conditions which prevailed. They are made all the more important because there are no written accounts which unequivocally refer to the indigenous occupants of the tip of the Peninsula. One author's writings may, however, describe this area and its people. It is hardly an objective or flattering view, but it does give an insight into their lifestyles, and the unwillingness of the author to judge by standards other than European. The author was Augustin de Beaulieu who visited the Cape in 1620. He writes:

'Those people who live near the point of the Cape are, in my opinion, the most wretched savages that up to now have been discovered. They know nothing of sowing, they possess no contrivances for ploughing or cultivating the soil, they cannot fish and they would not venture two paces into the sea. They are of a very low stature, especially the women, thin and always dying of hunger. Their common food is a root, white and about the size of a small chestnut, with a stalk like a leek, only narrow and not dentated. It bears a white flower and its taste is not unpleasant. They go along the seashore seeking shellfish. Should they light upon a dead whale or other carcass they make a hearty meal of it, however putrified it be, after roasting it a little.'

De Beaulieu goes on to describe with undisguised disgust the people eating a decomposing seal and other, to him, unpalatable items. Recent work by Professor Andrew Smith of the University of Cape Town (UCT) has indicated that beached seals, whales and dolphins were an important component of strandloper diet, comprising as much as 10 per cent of their food intake. Stranded animals were butchered and buried in the sand and, like game or venison which is hung before eating, exhumed when suitably 'high'. De Beaulieu's 'white stalks' were clearly the storage organs of the bulbous plants which are such a feature of fynbos. It is recognised that the distribution of Middle Stone Age peoples, at least, was determined by the availability of *Watsonia* corms. Burning of the vegetation was employed to stimulate the plants to sprout and flower. *Watsonias* develop an additional corm when they bloom, thus increasing the potential harvest for the 'fire stick' farmers.

1487 and all that

The report by de Beaulieu has advanced us somewhat, as his visit was made a century after the first visit to this corner of the continent by a European. He was Bartolomeu Dias, who is recognised as one of the great Portuguese pioneers of the late fifteenth century. The stimulus to Dias and subsequent Portuguese expeditions was to find a sea route to India which would outflank the Muslim merchants who held a monopoly on trade with Eastern countries.

Dias was bidden by King John II to locate the southern bounds of Africa, but as no first-hand account of his voyage remains, we rely instead on the writing of a sixteenth-century chronicler, João de Barros, for details of the journey.

Cabo de Boa Esperança

Dias set sail in August 1487 with a fleet of three ships – his own *São Cristovão*, the *São Pantaleão* under João Infante, and a supply ship commanded by Dias's brother. The two first-named ships were caravels – small, light vessels, with a shallow draught and lateen sails (triangular sails on long yards at 45° to the mast) which allowed them to sail into the wind. These attributes made them ideal, at least in the context of fifteenth-century marine technology, for sailing in shallow coastal waters and investigating bays and estuaries. Nonetheless, they were very tiny vessels (as small as 50 tonnes), which must have added to the loneliness, danger and unpredictability of long journeys.

Dias's fleet reached Walvis Bay on 8 December, whence the *São Cristovão* and *São Pantaleão* pressed southwards, only to be delayed some five days by gales in a bay just south of the Orange River. Having made numerous tacks to extricate themselves, they were compelled by further strong winds to keep their sails at half-mast for the next thirteen days. During this period they were blown out of sight of land. When the wind moderated, the two ships headed east once more, expecting to renew contact with the west coast. Having in fact overshot Africa, and unwittingly rounded the Cape of Good Hope, they sailed east for some days before heading north. This had the desired result, and landfall was made on 3 February 1488 at the Gouritz River mouth on the Cape's south coast.

Exciting as the journey must have been, many of the sailors were now exhausted and the novelty of discovery had worn a bit thin. Grumbling below decks obliged Dias to consult his crew and put the various options to the vote. The result was a majority in favour of turning about and going home, with a concession to Dias of three more days sailing along the coast. The fleet got as far east as Cape Infanta, named after the captain of the *São Pantaleão*, who was the first to step ashore. This itself was an historic moment, but for our purposes the most important event was their rounding of the Cape of Good Hope on the return journey. In the words of de Barros: 'Setting out thence, they came in sight of that great and famous Cape concealed for so many centuries, which when it was seen made known not only itself but also another new world of countries.' Powerful prose, which also raises the question of how the Cape was so great and famous if no one had seen it before?

Or was de Barros indulging in some retrospective grandiloquence?

Some authorities maintain that Dias christened this windy promontory Cabo Tormentoso, the 'Stormy Cape' or 'Cape of Storms', because of the 'perils and storms they had endured in doubling it'. On the return to Portugal, it was renamed by King John 'Cabo de Boa Esperança', the Cape of Good Hope, 'because it gave promise of the discovery of India, so long desired and sought for many years'. Or so we are told by de Barros, though two contemporaries credit Dias himself with its present name. One was Duarte Pacheco Pereira, a fellow sea captain, the other Bartolomeu Columbus, brother of Christopher, who met Dias on his return. Although Dias may have had a somewhat jaded opinion of the Cape, what with the storms encountered and his disappointment at having to turn back, it would hardly have been politically expedient of him to inform King John that the route to the east lay beyond a 'Cape of Storms'. The 'Cape of Good Hope', on the other hand, would surely have endeared Dias to his master and bestowed on his expedition a more salutary air.

Vasco da Gama

Conventional history records that it was not until Vasco da Gama's expedition of 1497 that the Cape received a second visit from the Portuguese. There may have been other visitors between times which were not recorded because of the secrecy that surrounded journeys of such economic and strategic importance.

Da Gama set sail from Portugal on 8 July 1497 with a fleet of four vessels, including a supply ship. Dias himself accompanied the expedition as far as the Cape Verde Islands. The other three ships sighted the Cape of Good Hope on 18 November and rounded it on the 22nd. Da Gama thereafter continued his voyage, sailing up the east coast of Africa until he found an Arab pilot who guided him the 3,000 kilometres across the ocean to India, arriving at Calicut on 20 May 1498.

The significance for us in da Gama's voyage is that a new world was indeed revealed and the Cape of Good Hope had justified its name. Promise had blossomed into achievement. Commemorative crosses have been erected at the reserve to honour Dias and da Gama, at Bordjiesrif and near Platboom, respectively. Together, and appropriately, they also serve as navigation beacons for vessels in False Bay.

Once the trade route to the east around the Cape of Good Hope had been established, traffic not surprisingly came thick and fast (in a relative sixteenth-century way) as the quest for land and resources intensified between the various European powers. The first fleet to follow in da Gama's wake was under the overall charge of Pedro Alvares Cabral, and one of the thirteen ships was commanded by none other than Dias. The fleet headed far west into the Atlantic and, before it set course back to the Cape, the coast of Brazil was sighted. But some 26 days after leaving Brazil, the appearance of a waterspout was interpreted as a sign of fair weather and moderating winds. Full sails were set but, contrary to their predictions, the wind freshened and quickly attained gale force. The sails of nine of the ships were reduced to shreds, allowing the vessels to remain upright. The four whose sails remained intact were blown over and, pinned down by the force of the wind, could not right themselves, and sank. Dias was one of the unlucky ones. He now lies somewhere off the Cape, which finally claimed him as he claimed it.

Greek gods and Portuguese poets

The fate of Dias and, indeed, the mysterious and ghostly *Flying Dutchman*, that most famous of maritime phantoms, may be interpreted as the modern extension and manifestation of a classical myth. A myth that involves, as so many of them do, a selection of human foibles (jealousy, anger, vindictiveness, that sort of thing), plus a dollop of transmogrification to raise it above the merely mortal. The story goes something like this:

Adamastor was a demi-god, one of the Titans, the twelve children of Uranus (personifying heaven) and Gaea (earth). He and his siblings were not, it seems, altogether happy with their position in life as minor deities, and attempted to overthrow the top gods and take control of heaven. They were defeated by the combined forces of Hephaestus and Heracles and condemned by Zeus to be transformed into stone at the outer limits of the earth. Adamastor's fate was to be was banished to, and petrified at, the farthest corner of Africa. At least inasmuch as the originators of these tales could visualise such a place, for they knew nothing of the continent south of the Sahara.

The existence of such a region was much speculated upon, at least by the likes of Aristotle and Ptolemy. Presumably this had some basis in fact, emanating from travellers' tales. Prior to Dias's voyage, therefore, a nebulous notion prevailed of some sort of land far to the south, the extremity of 'Ethiopia'. Through their voyages, Dias and his successors were able to confer pedigree on this mongrel of mythology, rumour and postulation.

Dias may or may not have had the imagination and expediency to give the Cape of Good Hope its name, but it fell to a poet to draw together the threads of fact and fable which spread from or led to the Cape and weave them into an epic to satisfy the mystic and materialist. This poet was arguably Portugal's greatest, Luís Vaz de Camões. In journeying to and from India, where he lived for 17 years, he made the same long and difficult voyage round the Cape which had been blazed by Dias and da Gama. He could, therefore, write from experience as well as from his imaginings. *Os Lusíadas*, the Sons of Portugal, is an account of Portuguese activities in the East, the journey to and from that region, and the invocation of diverse religious traditions, facets of the human condition and dynamic storytelling in celebration of these activities. At its simplest level, the poem is an amalgam of myth, history and narrative, a travelogue charged with symbolism and drama.

The Cape of Good Hope and the Portuguese encounter there with Adamastor is but one episode in the 1,102 stanzas of *Os Lusíadas*. Nevertheless, from our point of view this is a most significant entry of our subject into literature, in which Adamastor represented the Spirit of the Cape. Transformed into the rocks of the Peninsula, his pagan and chronically bad-tempered spectre prowls the mountains and roams the sea. Table Mountain is the laboratory where he hatches out the raging storms with which he greets those who dare disturb his solitude. The first to violate this seclusion was Dias, on whom Adamastor wrought ultimate revenge.

The fairest cape

After the initial Portuguese contacts, the tip of the Peninsula reverted to a place of geographical as much as spiritual significance, a feature welcomed by mariners as the turning point on the voyage out and the start (almost) of the 'home straight' of the return trip. What was happening ashore at the time is poorly documented. But amongst the many who must have doubled the Cape, there are those of historical interest.

Sir Francis Drake rounded the Cape on 18 June 1580. This came about more through default than design, since having become the first Englishman to navigate the Straits of Magellan at the tip of South America, Drake was unable to find a route back to the Atlantic further north (where he was busy plundering coastal towns on the Pacific coastline). He was thus compelled to sail across the Pacific and Indian oceans and finally back up the Atlantic, thereby becoming the first to circumnavigate the globe. The journey took three years, and it was no mean accolade that, of all the sights he saw, the Cape of Good Hope was the one which impressed him most. To be honest, it was not Drake himself who christened it 'the fairest cape', but his chaplain. But who would be so unromantic as to sacrifice a good story for the sake of accuracy? The second-hand account presumably reflected the sentiments, if not the exact words, of the famous knight. Whatever, they are worth repeating:

'We ranne hard aboard the cape, finding report of the Portugals to be most false, who afferme that it is the most dangerous Cape of the world, never without intolerable storms and present dangers to travellers which come neare the same. This cape is the most stately thing and the fairest cape we saw in the whole circumference of the earth.'

The Dutch descend

The virtual exclusivity which the Portuguese enjoyed was thereafter eroded by the British and Dutch. As the Cape was almost at the halfway mark to the East, attention turned to Cabo de Boa Esperança as a revictualling post, and on 6 April 1652 Jan van Riebeeck stepped ashore at Table Bay, entrusted with the task of establishing a 'refreshment station' for ships of the Dutch East India Company en route to or returning from Batavia, the Dutch East Indies.

Van Riebeeck's account of his sojourn is well documented in his diary. In it the area now the Cape of Good Hope Nature Reserve did not receive any attention. The reason for this is not difficult to understand. His primary concern was the establishment of his base at the foot of Table Mountain and attending to the welfare of the garrison. Why concern himself with the rocky and decidedly unproductive and windswept tip of the Peninsula?

Exploration of and expansion into the southern Peninsula were, however, inevitable. In November 1687 False Bay was surveyed by Simon van der Stel, Commander of the Cape. A typically windy cruise round the bay was undertaken, and salient features mapped over the few days. The sheltered corner of False Bay's western coast which subsequently was to play such an important role in the development of the region, he named Simon's Bay after himself.

Once it was recognised that it afforded shelter from the stormy blasts which plagued Table Bay in winter, this peninsular nook was elevated to a level of national strategic and military importance. The founding and expansion of Simon's Town and its maritime activities inevitably had repercussions on the present-day reserve, providing as it did a point from which people dispersed into surrounding areas. It also furnished a market for produce grown in these outlying areas at a time when Cape Town could be reached only by an energetic hike. Indeed, it is not until the establishment of Simon's Town that the southern Peninsula and the Cape of Good Hope Nature Reserve feature to any great extent in accounts of onshore activities in the Cape. The development of the reserve in the early days of European colonisation thus follows a step or two behind that of Simon's Town.

The first farmers

Although False Bay was visited on a casual basis before and after Van der Stel's survey, it was not until 1741, and following some catastrophic losses of ships, men and cargo in Table Bay, that the Dutch East India Company took action. It decreed that Simon's Bay be used as winter anchorage for their vessels between 15 May and 15 August. Here was the start of more formal utilisation of the southern Peninsula; two years later the first building was constructed at Simon's Bay, now the embryonic Simon's Town.

The environmental conditions which had limited the indigenous occupants of the southern Peninsula also imposed upon their usurpers and successors. Granted, the new settlers did construct permanent dwellings and had cereal and root crops which the aboriginals did not, but, like them, they were still dependent on fresh water. It is not surprising that what development did take place was never far from the few sources of potable water. From 1738, even before the formal establishment of Simon's Town, one Jurgen Schuster leased from the government an area of Wildschutsbrand from below Red Hill to the west coast. For the princely sum of 24 rixdollars a year, Schuster could graze his stock and kill game, 'excluding partridges, pheasants, eland and hippopotamus'!

The opening up of the area was not a speedy process. By 1786 only six families permanently resided at Simon's Town. Three of these had rights under the loan-farm system to graze land on the southern Peninsula, namely Jan Willem Hurter at Olifantsbos, Arend Munnik at Schuster's Kraal and Jeremias Auret at Buffelsfontein. Auret's area had as its centre the spring which gives the farm its name. From here his land grant extended for half-an-hour's walk in all directions. Notwithstanding the fact that this would have had Auret over his head in seawater if he had cared to keep walking for his full half-hour to the east, the area amounted to more than 1,600 hectares.

British occupation

The generally quiet and subdued activity on the southern Peninsula at this time was hardly disturbed by the upheavals of the Napoleonic wars in Europe, even when these led to the British occupation of Cape in 1795 and again in 1806, when the Dutch surrendered and the Cape became a British colony for the second time.

A significant development once the British had consolidated their military and political presence in the Cape was the promulgation of reforms which completely restructured the conditions under which land had been utilised by Dutch authority. To promote settlement and more intensive land use, 'perpetual quitrent' was introduced by the British on 6 September 1813. This allowed occupants or lessees to rent the land in perpetuity and pass it down to their descendants. This reform, and the establishment of Simon's Bay as the permanent British naval base in South Africa the following year (1814), boosted the area's attraction and, consequently, population. One of the first to take advantage of the new arrangement was John Osmond of Simon's Town. Not one to waste too much time, he wrote a letter to the Governor, Sir John Cradock, one month after the proclamation of quitrent. In it he petitioned Sir John for perpetual quitrent of 1,680 hectares at Buffelsfontein and a further 320 hectares towards Cape Point. The response, if not speedy, was at least positive, and in granting his request in 1816, the Governor stipulated that Osmond pay 150 rixdollars a year and that the area be brought into cultivation within three years.

Eleven land grants totalling over 4,000 hectares were made in 1816-17, including Smitswinkel to Petrus Hugo and Olifantsbos to Frans Daniel Roussouw, whose name is perpetuated in Russouwskop and, perhaps, Fransdam. Land between Olifantsbos and the Krom River was granted to Gerhardus Hurter, who was also obliged to cultivate it within three years; all for the sum of six shillings. At this time and subsequently, grants were made conditional upon public access to the beach. Right of way was also retained to Sirkelsvlei, the body of open freshwater in the reserve least likely to dry up in the summer months.

Limestone and livestock

One relatively dynamic landowner in the mid-nineteenth century was John McKellar who owned Buffelsfontein and a farm known as Uiterstehoek, which stretched south to Cape Point, for thirty years from 1855. As well as farming Ostriches and other livestock, McKellar supplemented his income by selling lime. George Smith, who bought Buffelsfontein in 1886 (McKellar having become insolvent the previous year), continued with lime-making, even going so far as to form his own business, The Cape Point Lime and Cement Works, with the aim of cashing in on the increased demand for cement resulting from the expansion of Simon's Town and other settlements further up the Peninsula. The main source of the lime was the calcareous rocky outcrop stretching from Buffels Bay to Booi se Skerm. At the latter site, water percolating through the rocks dissolved the lime, which was then deposited on the roofs and walls of caves where the water seeped out. This material, known as travertine, was quarried from the caves and then burnt to produce good-quality lime.

The splendidly restored kiln above Black Rocks, in which the travertine obtained from the outcrops was burnt, is of unknown creator and vintage (the notice board there commits itself to 'circa 1890'). However, it was almost certainly contemporaneous with Smith's workings and may have also been used by him. The kiln is of some interest to local historians as its construction differs somewhat from others in the Cape. It comprises an inverted cone within a buttressed cylinder. Two side openings at the bottom provided ventilation, a front opening allowed access to light the fire (or, as was the case, explode the gunpowder to set the whole thing off) and, subsequently, extract the quicklime. Two ramps lead up to the top of the cylinder, enabling the successive layers of travertine and firewood to be unloaded from carts and deposited directly into the kiln. The whole structure is about 3.5 metres high and, in its renovated state at least, solidly and attractively constructed from dressed sandstone blocks.

Lime was also obtained by burning mussel shells washed up on the beach. A less sophisticated process than extracting quicklime from limestone, shell-burning did not require such a high temperature. This made it the most popular method of manufacturing lime and was employed on the reserve before and after the kiln was built at Black Rocks. A barely recognisable trace of a kiln used by McKellar and Smith for burning shells can be seen near the shore at Buffels Bay.

As well as the limekiln, Buffels Bay supported a fishery and a whaling station. Diversity was clearly the name of the game; no one could hope to make a living from livestock or market gardening alone. This was to be brought home

An outing to Cape Point has always been popular. Visitors to Smith's Farm, now the Homestead, at the turn of the century.

even more forcibly by major developments before and after the turn of the century.

The one was the completion, in 1890, of the railway to Simon's Town, the station there being opened by Cecil Rhodes in December of that year. This allowed produce to be transported cheaply and speedily to Simon's Town from the market gardens and smallholdings on the Cape Flats east of Cape Town.

The second development to make a major impact on the reserve was also in the transport field. In 1915 a coastal road was completed from Simon's Town to the Point in the interests of national security, after the outbreak of the First World War the previous year. Further improvements were made in 1924 when the road was macadamised, opening up the area to greatly increased traffic of sightseers, picnickers and recreational fishermen.

Establishment of the nature reserve

By the early years of the twentieth century occupation of the reserve was of a recreational rather than a commercial nature. A few holiday cottages had sprung up and must have provided delightful sanctuary from suburban life. Those that owned property here were lucky indeed, a fact which did not escape notice. But when the shadow of the speculator and developer loomed across the fynbos and the beach-

es, a number of Capetonians rallied together in pursuit of an ideal which, in retrospect, was far ahead of its time. This ideal was the creation of a sanctuary, a nature reserve, at the tip of the Peninsula.

One name has, in the public eye, become synonymous with the establishment of the reserve, that of the naturalist, author and broadcaster Dr S. H. 'Stacey' Skaife. Without his contribution, perhaps less, or nothing, would have been achieved; but the securing of the reserve was very much a team effort. It would appear that Skaife was pre-empted by one man who, together with one of the landowners, was the first to recognise the threats posed to the southern Peninsula by development. This man was Brian Mansergh, a Cape Town architect. He had an abiding passion for the southern Peninsula and its wildness, arising from school days when many happy holidays and weekends were spent fishing and camping down on Smith's Farm and exploring the mountains and beaches.

In 1928 Mansergh was informed by Norman Smith that Smith's Farm might come up for sale, as Smith's mother was becoming too old and frail to stay there. The farm had been in the family since 1886 when, as Buffelsfontein, it had been taken over by his grandfather. It was reported that an up-country party had already expressed an interest in buying the land for holiday development, a fate which the Smiths, to their eternal credit, were anxious to avoid. This sentiment was strongly shared by Mansergh, who wrote to the Minister of Lands, the Hon. P. Grobler, on 8 November 1928 proposing 'The acquisition by the State of the land which spans the Cape Peninsula from False Bay to the South

Cars and charabancs at the Cape Point tea room in the early 1920s.

Atlantic and Smitswinkel Bay to Cape Point, for the establishment of a National Park or Nature Reserve to be administered and under the control of our governing bodies for all time, for the benefit of the nation'. A reply, dated 4 December, was suitably sympathetic but turned down the proposal, invoking a shortage of money for the acquisition and running of the proposed reserve.

A parallel story is recounted by Skaife in his autobiography, *A Naturalist Remembers*. Skaife was informed by his neighbour in Hout Bay, George Smith (brother of Norman), that the Smiths were willing to sell their farm on the condition that it became a nature reserve. Skaife was a man with considerable public appeal and wrote to the *Cape Times* in August 1929, extolling the virtues of the Cape of Good Hope and urging that it be declared a nature reserve. His letter was published and bolstered by an editorial. These are two versions of essentially the same story, both reflecting the strong feelings which the place engendered and the affection in which it was held.

The matter was pursued and the Cape Town City Council were approached for support. Their reactions were less than enthusiastic, however, and Smith's Farm was taken off the market. But it was a useful exercise; as well as rallying the troops, it represented a valuable rehearsal for the final performance a decade later, when in April 1938 Mansergh was informed by Smith that the family's property at Buffels Bay had to be disposed of. Mansergh wasted no time

in again writing to the Minister of Lands. In a letter of 22 April 1938 he again presented his plea, which retains its pertinence today. 'Most of our coastal belt is suffering daily loss and injury which we all deplore,' he wrote, 'and the natural beauty which is the admiration of all who visit our shores is being sacrificed.' He again met with no joy, the Minister, General Kemp, refusing to sanction the spending of state money in such a way.

In July of that year the Smiths were offered £20,000 for their farm by a Johannesburg consortium with visions of a holiday resort overlooking the limpid waters of False Bay. The Smiths, to their credit, were not keen and offered to drop their price to £16,000 if the area could be declared a nature reserve. An additional and significant development was provided by the Hare family, who offered their farm Blouberg Vlei to the state. Already managed as a game reserve, the offer required that it remain as such. This generous act must have greatly boosted the morale of the conservationists.

But Smith's Farm, the centre of the debate, remained tantalisingly beyond the grasp of those who wished to preserve its natural beauty and guarantee continued public access to this part of the Peninsula. Skaife again took up the pen and wrote to Mr Henry Hope, editor of the *Cape Argus*, subsequently generating between them renewed public interest and sympathy. An article written by Skaife appeared in the *Argus* on 16 July 1938 entitled 'Why Not a Game Reserve at Cape Point?' His most powerful line of argument rested on the likelihood of what the place could look like as a reserve against what it would turn out if the developers moved in.

The gauntlet was laid down and it was suggested to the Mayor, Councillor W. C. Foster, that the establishment of a reserve would, in addition, be an appropriate way to mark the centenary of Cape Town in 1940. It certainly had the desired effect, and a veritable army of prominent citizens rallied to the cause. Hope and Skaife found a valuable ally in G. A. Leyds of the Cape Town Rotary, and together they formed the Cape Point Preservation Society. Members of the Cape Divisional Council, particularly the chairman, C. W. T. Duminy, C. Starke, secretary G. O. Owen and engineer Tom Fox, were enthusiastic. Not so the Cape Town City Council. When its General Purposes Committee turned the proposal down, the decision was given a fiery lambasting in the *Cape Times*: 'It seems almost treasonable to this stately Peninsula of ours to think that its extreme end, now the only unspoilt part of our heritage, should fall into the hands of men who will cause it to pimple into a bungaloid acne.'

'Not enough grass to keep a scorpion alive'

The conservationists regrouped, and by early the following year (1939) were once more girded for battle. A public meeting held on 30 January was attended by 500 people, an impressive turnout even by present-day standards. At the meeting there was generally strong support for the project from all sides, barring City Council. It was reported that Councillor A. Z. Burman opposed the idea vigorously, declaring that there was 'not enough grass to keep a scorpion alive'. To this, Skaife gleefully retorted that the Councillor was not qualified to speak on the subject as scorpions don't eat grass. With public sentiment so strongly in favour of the proposed reserve, the Mayor announced that the matter would be put to the vote to enable all ratepayers to express their feelings. This they did on 9 March, with a plebiscite, the first in Cape Town's history. The rules of the game dictate that the outcome of a plebiscite is not binding, much to the relief, no doubt, of the City Council, who on learning of the six to one majority in favour of buying the land to establish a reserve, rejected the proposal. Such are the powers of democracy.

Success at last

The onus now fell on the Cape Divisional Council who, if truth be told, were somewhat relieved at the withdrawal of the City Council from the fray, as the latter's involvement would have complicated the administration of any reserve which might come into being. The matter was put before Council by Duminy and Owen at a meeting on 11 April. Their fellow councillors took the bait, and on 1 July Smith's Farm was procured for £16,000.

With a successful conclusion to their efforts Skaife records, 'Thus came to an end the long struggle to save Cape Point.' Chance would be a fine thing, but the Cape Divisional Council, the new owners, did not rest on their laurels, and set about procuring, through something of a war of attrition, other parcels of land to add to the nucleus now established. The last bit of land to be bought was, ironically, the first farm to have been granted over two centuries before. From a loan-place of 24 rixdollars per annum in 1738, Wildschutsbrand was sold in 1966 for R5,500. The entire reserve had, over the years, cost about R127,000.

The present generation of sightseers, hikers, botanists, birders, fishermen, picnickers – all those who enjoy the reserve and everything it has to offer – owes an immense debt of gratitude to those whose foresight and tenacity secured the future of this singular area. Without the remarkable sympathy and generosity of the Smith family we might now have only a 'bungaloid acne' between our two shores. Without Mansergh's stimulus and efforts, the plight of the 'fairest cape' might not have been recognised. The Hare family made an invaluable contribution, and the involvement of Divisional Council, through the offices of Chairman Duminy, was decisive. The commemorative plaque at the Field Museum and the environmental centre at Olifantsbos which bears his name celebrate the achievements of Skaife in the saga. The Smiths, Mansergh, the Hares, and Duminy, in contrast, have slipped into obscurity, a dishonourable outcome for those who did so much.

The Spes Bona Dias Birkenhead Memorial Umbrella Park

The naming of the newly established reserve was put out to tender in an unusual way. An article in the *Cape Argus* of 3 May 1939 invited readers to submit suggestions for a name, as 'it is seldom that the man in the street is asked to find a name that will be given in perpetuity . . . A board of expensively paunched plutocrats usually reserve that fun for themselves.'

The response was both swift and enthusiastic. Over one hundred suggestions were received, reflecting diverse sentiments. The historical lobby nominated Van Riebeeck, Simon van der Stel, Dias, Vasco da Gama and Sir Francis Drake to precede 'park', 'sanctuary' or whatever. The local heroes involved in the creation of the reserve were well supported, most particularly Mr Duminy. Perhaps the most unusual suggestion was 'Umbrella Park' ('in honour of Mr Chamberlain's famous umbrella'). Also suggested were 'Pixie Point', 'Elf Land', 'Sea-Girt Zoo', and 'Bok-bok Land'.

After considering all the submissions, the Divisional Council was able to announce proudly on 16 May that the name of the reserve would be 'The Cape of Good Hope Nature Reserve'. The choice was, I feel, a good one. It relives the sentiments of the early explorers and captures the spirit of the latter-day pioneers who also navigated stormy and treacherous waters in their quest for riches of 'very great though imponderable value'. 'Cape Point' is a name often used today, and it is at least economical (not least to the writers of road signs), if not wholly accurate and lacking the magic of 'Good Hope'. But where exactly is this famous Cape?

What's in a name?

Documents in the Office of the Chief Surveyor in Cape Town record that the name 'Cape of Good Hope' was officially recognised as belonging to the headland west of Cape Maclear at a meeting on 7 July 1957. No one seems quite sure who was responsible for depositing it there. It is almost as if the name was added as an afterthought when, after almost 500 years, it was found that no one spot had in fact been accorded that famous appellation.

There seems no doubt that Dias had intended his 'Stormy Cape' or 'Cape of Good Hope' to describe the whole tip of the Peninsula at least and the whole Peninsula south from Table Mountain at most.

Vasco da Gama sighted the 'Cape of Good Hope' from the west when he was still well out to sea, and was clearly referring to the whole Peninsula, or perhaps even Table Mountain, which, as the highest landmass in the area, would be visible before any other point. 'Alongside the Cape of Good Hope, to the south, lies a very great bay,' wrote Alvaro Velho who accompanied da Gama. False Bay is not south, but east, of the Cape of Good Hope; it is, however, more or less south of Table Mountain and it does lie along the length of the Peninsula. Here again is reference to the Cape of Good Hope as the whole peninsular entity and not one spot.

The first survey of the area was carried out by Simon van der Stel in 1687. His map, although crude, is unmistakably the Peninsula. Drawn primarily with the navigator in mind, 'Cabo de Bon Esprance [sic]' is one of only seven names on his sketch. It loiters coyly somewhere around Mouille Point, almost as far from the present-day Cape of Good Hope as the map will allow. At the very tip of the Peninsula, two points are lettered which warn of reefs and rocks.

We have scrutinised maps emanating from the last five centuries and found the Cape of Good Hope emblazoned in one language or another anywhere from Kimberley south to the headland which now bears the name. Many of the earlier cartographers place the name below Table Mountain at Table Bay, some drag it unceremoniously along the full length of the Cape Peninsula, others tack it on to the southern tip without indicating a particular headland. One cautious sixteenth-century mapper covers himself by inscribing 'Cabo de Boa Esperança' at both ends of the Peninsula. There's nothing like hedging your bets.

We are not the first to have found ourselves in this nomenclatural quandary. The lively and interesting account of one visitor to the Cape, J. J. Aubertin, serves to confuse the matter. On Christmas Day 1884 he finds himself at the tip of the Peninsula brooding upon the significance of the spot and its place in world history, as have many before and after him. He also speculates upon its geography: 'There are, in fact, three separate points here, but the other two are wholly inferior in character to the Cape Point. The out-side one is Cape Maclear, after the famous South African astronomer, and claims to be the real cape, geographically speaking, because its point stretches somewhat further south than the actual Cape Point.'

From this description it would appear that the present-day Cape of Good Hope is actually Cape Maclear. The latter should, therefore, hold the name 'Good Hope' by merit of prior claim. It is a shame that Aubertin does not name the middle 'point', now officially called Cape Maclear. Was it nameless in 1884? Has Cape Maclear been surreptitiously shifted a few metres to the east in order to accommodate Good Hope? Such a devious move is perhaps understandable when it was realised, doubtless to the historians' and cartographers' embarrassment, that no one place on a map had been given the name of the world's most famous cape. As it is, the name has been squeezed down the Peninsula like the last blob in a tube of toothpaste until extruded onto the remaining anonymous landmark, with a little innocent manipulation to ensure it occupied the most southerly spot. The spot christened thus, there the matter rests.

Southern lights

The strategic importance of the southern tip of the Peninsula was long recognised. With increasing shipping to the east and, more locally, into Simon's Bay, the need for a lighthouse became more urgent. With some view to the future, the granting of perpetual quitrent to John Osmond of Cape Point Farm in 1816 was made 'On condition of the owner or occupier of this land permitting His Majesty's Commissioner for the Naval Department or the Principal Officer having charge of that Branch of that Service to erect a Light House on such part of the Cape Point as may be judged most convenient for that purpose and also permitting all necessary access to such Light House when built.'

Such foresight was not matched by actions, however, and it was not until 1859 that work began on the lighthouse, on 16 March to be exact. Sites on the Cape of Good Hope massif and Vasco da Gama Peak were considered, but the highest and most conspicuous point, affording a wide sweep over both False Bay and the Atlantic seemed to be the logical choice. The result was a structure of white-painted cast-iron with a tasteful red top being erected upon the summit of Cape Point Peak, 238 metres above the sea.

Designed by Alexander Gordon, the Cape Point lighthouse was manufactured in England for the Board of Trade by the Victoria Foundry, Greenwich. Sections were shipped to Simon's Town, transferred to a smaller boat and thence transported to Buffels Bay from where a modified gun carriage was used to ferry them to a camp near the Cape of Good Hope. The final leg of the journey, up the steep and rough slope to the peak, was accomplished using a bullock-drawn sled.

Once on site, the convex iron plates which constituted

the base of the lantern were bolted together in the form of a drum. Atop this was fitted the lantern itself. Engineered by Deville and Company of London, it shone a 12-second pulse of light every minute at a strength of about 2,000 candlepower. According to a report in the *Cape of Good Hope Gazette*, 'it was visible in clear weather from a deck 16 feet high at a distance of 36 miles'.

The lighthouse came into operation on 1 May 1860. Not long into the life of the new light, misgivings were expressed regarding its position. For a disconcertingly high proportion of time, an average of 900 hours a year, in fact, the peak was enveloped in fog. Lower down the cliffs, however, the air remained clear and the visibility good. Under such conditions, the frequency of which apparently is equalled only on Newfoundland's gloomy coast, the lighthouse was rendered useless. This state of affairs, and the recommendation that the light be moved, were recorded in the Lighthouse Commission's reports of 1872, 1890 and 1906.

It took the sinking of the *Lusitania* (a Portuguese-owned steamer, not the famous Cunard liner) in 1911, with its potentially high but miraculously low loss of life, to spur the authorities into action. The driving force behind the project was the eminent engineer Harry C. Cooper, who selected a site very close to the end of the Peninsula above Dias Rock and 87 metres above sea level. This was 160 metres lower than the original lighthouse and would eliminate the problems of visibility experienced on the mist-shrouded summit. In addition to choosing the location, Cooper designed the lighthouse and supervised its construction. His choice of site was received with a certain degree of scepticism, but he managed to persuade his superiors that his proposal was feasible.

Work on the post-*Lusitania* lighthouse commenced in 1913, but it is small wonder, given the nature of the operation and the topography, that it was completed only in 1919. At the outset, a large pinnacle of rock, some 15 metres high and known as Dias Point, was blasted away with dynamite to make room for the foundations. The ridge leading to the site is narrow and exposed, the drop to the final ledges, whereon the light was to be sited, almost precipitous. To gain access, a path was cut along the ridge and an 18-inch-gauge tramway track laid. Along this ran a trolley in which materials and equipment were transported. At the end of the track a crane was installed which lowered the trolley almost 50 metres further down the cliff. Here a second trolley line ran the remaining distance to the building site. Stone for the building was quarried and dressed at or just below the site itself; sand was excavated from a cave at sea level and carried in bags up a winding path rising some 90 metres.

On 11 March 1919 the lamp was lit at sunset by Cooper's three-year-old daughter, Thurl. The light was described as a dioptric flashlight of 5 million candlepower with a range of about 38 kilometres. The fuel for the paraffin vapour mantle was drawn through a 1.6-kilometre pipe from tanks on Cape Point Peak. The light was electrified in 1936, increasing its luminosity to 19 million candlepower. Subsequently, this was reduced to some 10 million candlepower, but the Cape Point light remains the most powerful on the South African coast. It has a range of 63 kilometres, emits a group of three flashes every thirty seconds and is lit (or, at least, switched on) half an hour before sunset and is extinguished just after sunrise. It has shone every night since commissioning, with the exception of the war years when it was lit only at the request of the port captain to guide some particular vessel. Below the main light is positioned a fixed red light with a range of 18 kilometres; this covers the particularly hazardous sea area containing the Point itself and the lurking menace of the Anvil and Bellows Rocks.

The Lusitania and the light

At least 24 ships have come to grief on or near the shores of the Cape of Good Hope Nature Reserve. The remains of five of these can be inspected on the beaches, the others sank offshore or have long since broken up.

Ironically, perhaps, the first recorded victim of the Cape of Storms was Bartolomeu Dias. There have been many vessels since which have suffered similar sad fates, but not all can attribute their misfortune to the elements. Fog and poor visibility have been major factors in some of these maritime disasters, but it is noteworthy that bad weather has not played the major part in wrecking ships that it might have been presumed to, in an area with such a reputation for violent gales and mountainous seas.

The most celebrated casualty of the Cape of Good Hope (most inappropriately named in this context) is the *Flying Dutchman*. Captained by Hendrik van der Decken (alternatively Deeken), it was attempting to round the Cape sometime in the seventeenth century (the exact year differs between references), but was thwarted by heavy weather. The ship and its complement disappeared, but had no sooner done so than the legend of the *Flying Dutchman* was born. Or at least an old tale (possibly even with its roots in Dias) was remodelled for a contemporary audience. It was rumoured that van der Decken swore a blasphemous oath that he would round the Cape if it took him until Doomsday, or be damned. Adamastor and Old Nick have both been invoked as the other protagonists in this sorry state of affairs, and van der Decken seems to have lost out on the option of a fine and continues, it seems, to try and battle his way round the Cape.

The *Flying Dutchman* has been seen a number of times over the years. The most famous sighting was made by King George V when, as the Prince of Wales and midshipman on HMS *Bacchante,* he encountered the *Flying Dutchman* on 11 July 1881. Almost all subsequent recounters of this tale have omitted to mention the fact that, at the time of the sighting, Prince George was nowhere near the Cape of

Good Hope, or even South Africa. On 11 July 1881 his squadron was two days out from Melbourne, Australia!

Many countries and cultures have their own legends of 'phantom ships' or variations thereof, the nautical equivalent of the Wandering Jew. The legend may be German in origin, and one version describes how a Captain Falkenberg is fated forever to ply the North Sea, gambling his soul at dice with the devil. Perhaps the Cape's nautical ghost has survived the erosion of the years and the unromantic because of its encounters with prominent persons and, probably most significantly, its commemoration in Richard Wagner's opera *Der Fliegende Holländer*, first performed in 1843 at Dresden. This work is actually set in Norway, where the unfortunate Dutchman was on 'sabbatical', the devil having allowed him shore leave every seven years to find a woman whose love and constancy would break the curse of perpetual plying.

For the present, the name is perpetuated closer to home in the bus which ferries visitors to and from the old Cape Point lighthouse and viewing spots. Destined, like its namesake, never to round the Cape, and doubly cursed never to get out of second gear, the roaring blue beast strains its way interminably up and down the steep road, the driver doubtless uttering his own van der Decken-like oaths when American tourists in tartan shorts and a world of their own wander dreamily across his bows, requiring that the anchor be dropped rather precipitately for the sake of harmonious international relations.

Well qualified by its grisly history to haunt the gelid waters of the Cape, even more so than the *Flying Dutchman*, is the French brig *La Rozette*. On 19 August 1786 she was commandeered by six mutineers, their intention being to scuttle her and make off with the booty. Having disposed of the captain and four uncooperative crew members, hacked a hole in the bottom of the ship and taken to a lifeboat, they were disconcerted to find the vessel drifting ashore instead of disappearing conveniently below the waves. Nevertheless, they made a hasty escape from the scene of the crime and were soon enjoying the seamier side of life in the fleshpots of Cape Town. Their pleasures were short-lived, however, as *La Rozette* had meantime been discovered on the shore south of Olifantsbos Point. Having been a little indiscreet with their ill-gotten money and valuables in the local taverns, the mutineers were soon rounded up. In finding the sailors guilty of murder, the court in Cape Town sentenced four of them 'To be bound on a cross upside down and, at intervals, to be torn limb from limb, after which their heads are to be hacked off'. In a startling display of leniency, one of the others was sentenced to hang. The luckiest of them, in a relative sense, received ten years' hard labour on Robben Island, thereafter 'to be banished from these regions until eternity'. Little now remains of the 30-metre ship, although a few oak timbers are occasionally exhumed from the sand by the wind and waves.

The resting place of *La Rozette* lies close to the highest concentration of shipwrecks at the reserve. The great majority of these vessels fell foul of Albatross Rock, a notorious granitic reef which lurks only two metres or so below the surface and less than a kilometre offshore. Why so many ships should have come to grief here is not altogether clear, but in certain instances it seems a simple case of poor seamanship and coming too close to the shore. Whatever the reasons, Albatross Rock ended the days of eight vessels between 1786 and 1917.

Of the vessels which have fallen foul of Albatross Rock, one of the most interesting was RMS *Kafir*. The interest lies not only in the ship itself, or the circumstances of its demise, but in the fact that of the four Arab crew members who unfortunately drowned in the incident, one had been a bearer of Sir Henry Morton Stanley and had been present at his meeting with David Livingstone at Ujiji in 1871. He is likely, therefore, to have heard the former's immortal words 'Dr Livingstone, I presume?'

The *Thomas T. Tucker* is the most substantial wreck on the reserve and provides a popular destination for beachwalkers. The circumstances of its demise differ in certain details between accounts, but the outcome is the same. On her maiden voyage from New Orleans, the 7,000-ton Liberty ship was bound for Suez with a cargo of military hardware and supplies. When she was about 300 kilometres south of Cape Town a radio message was received warning of an enemy submarine (a German U-boat is the most popular identity, but Italian has also been mooted) in the vicinity. Scurrying for the safety of Cape Town, she made a dramatic miscalculation and ended up on the rocks at Olifantsbos Point. Or so it is said. Other versions invoke poor visibility in the fogbanks off the Peninsula for her error, and no submarine involvement at all. Whatever the case, on the night of 28 November 1942 her master reported her by radio to be aground at Robben Island, at the entrance to Table Bay. This misconception the lightkeeper at Slangkop (at Kommetjie, 10 kilometres north of Olifantsbos) soon was able to rectify. If the *Thomas T. Tucker* was heading for Cape Town, she missed it by over 40 kilometres; if her intention was to slip past the Point, then she was 10 kilometres too far north. A plea in mitigation was that the compass was found to be a full 37 degrees out, having been deviated by the almost wholly metallic composition of the cargo.

Another of the notorious granite outcrops which lurk off the coast of the reserve is the Bellows, visible to the southwest of Cape Point as a sinister swirl of water or a fountain of spray and breaking waves, depending upon the state of the sea. The most famous casualty of the Bellows was the *Lusitania*. Eyebrows are predictably raised in disbelief by visitors of an historical bent, under the impression that the ship of this name was one of the most celebrated maritime victims of the First World War. They are correct, of course, but, confusingly, that was another vessel of the same name, being the Cunard liner torpedoed by a German

Manhandling a field-gun through the fynbos. S.A. Permanent Garrison Artillery, Cape of Good Hope, 1928.

U-boat off the southwest coast of Ireland on 17 May 1915 with enormous loss of life.

The saga of the Cape Point *Lusitania* is tame in comparison, but this is certainly no bad thing, given the tragic end of her namesake. Our ship was a steamer of 5,557 tons, owned by a Portuguese company and launched in 1906. On what became her last voyage, she was due to put in at Cape Town en route from Maputo (Lourenço Marques) with 678 passengers and 122 crew aboard. At about 10.30 on the night of 18 April 1911, the lighthouse at Cape Point was sighted and a course charted to give it a wide berth. Conditions were calm but with a gathering mist. At 11.40 p.m. visibility suddenly and dramatically improved and the master, Captain Faria, found to his consternation that he was very close to the lighthouse. He turned her quickly to port and headed out to the open sea. Given the vast expanse of ocean to choose from, and the relatively tiny size of the Bellows within that expanse, it was no more than fate that brought the *Lusitania* to a grinding halt on top of that rock just before midnight.

What happened next was a model of sea rescues. In fact so straightforward and virtually without incident was the evacuation of the ship's company that it hardly merits relating. After the ship struck, there was apparently little panic on board. Not quite in the league of those passengers on

the *Titanic* who took advantage of the sudden overabundance of ice to recharge their drinks, some of the *Lusitania*'s passengers returned to their cabins to sleep after the initial excitement had died away. But not for long, as the lifeboats were lowered and distress rockets had attracted the attention of the lightkeepers at Cape Point.

The assistant 'keeper, John Allen, had hurried down to the shore and waved a lamp in the darkness in an effort to warn people against trying to come through the surf. Nonetheless, one boat made for the shore and promptly capsized and some or all of the occupants were drowned. The number of fatalities is variously recorded as none, three, four (three passengers and the Third Officer) and eight. Further attempts to reach safety this way resulted in 37 people struggling ashore, the lives of some being saved by Allen's actions. Those who stood off beyond the breakers or nearer the ship rocked gently in the waves and were picked up by rescue vessels from Simon's Town not long after. By ten o'clock the following morning, the entire ship's complement and passengers had been rescued.

Military manoeuvres

We referred earlier to shells of the explodable variety. These shells serve to remind us of military occupation of and activity at the reserve which stretch back as far as the establishment of Simon's Town, itself a major military installation and strategically important for three centuries.

The celebrations surrounding the establishment of the reserve in 1939 must have been somewhat dampened by, a mere nine weeks later, the outbreak of the Second World War. The southern Peninsula's importance in military strategy was resurrected once again and by early 1940 the Cape Point Port War Signal Station had been established, manned by the South African Naval Forces. Coastal observation posts were operative by 1941 at Cape Point and Olifantsbos. The remains of the latter, including derelict buildings and rusty barbed wire, can be seen tucked behind the cliff edge above Skaife Centre.

A signal post was reported to be operational from the west coast in the early nineteenth century. A lookout, his wife and their substantial brood of children (eight or nine, according to reports) were stationed on Paulsberg. This must have been the job in the Cape with the best view but the most boring remit. No wonder he had so many children.

An old Dutch cannon found on the since-named Kanonkop probably preceded this outlook, indicating that earlier occupants of the Cape also favoured this particular spot for a lookout. Discovered in the early years of the Second World War, the cannon now rests upon a specially built carriage, constructed to Dutch specifications. It may be admired on its rocky stanchion on Kanonkop, still aimed seawards, by any who care to undertake the gentle and very pleasant climb from the Booi se Skerm road.

During the 1914–1918 War, the Point was manned permanently by units of the Cape Mounted Rifles, who were probably responsible for the erection of blockhouses which overlooked strategic routes and buildings, notably the lighthouse and its access path.

Between the world wars the area was used for military manoeuvres and gunnery practice. Temporary camps housed the soldiers in the northern part by the Klaasjagers River. In June 1939 a permanent training camp was established at Klaasjagers following the granting of 2,400 hectares by the owner, J. F. Minicki, to the Defence Force.

Of more than local interest was the installation at Cape Point, in 1941, of South Africa's first fixed operational radar. From this strategic point the radar was used to detect enemy ships, a task first performed by Dutch and British lookouts more than a century before. It was superseded shortly afterwards by one and then another improved instrument, the third and last radar being installed on Da Gama Peak in 1944. This was manned by the Special Signal Services of the 61st Coastal Defence Corps, billeted on the slopes of the peak. The barracks have, since 1987, served as the Goldfields Environmental Education Centre and are visible on the hillside. The majority of the other buildings associated with the military have long since been demolished. Only a sounding station remains, perched most unprettily on the shore at Bordjiesrif. This detects and records vessels coming in and out of False Bay on behalf of the navy.

The wars are over, but new battles rage in the reserve – against invasions more pernicious and destructive than any foreign power. We shall return to these, and describe the management of the reserve since 1939, in the final chapter.

Winter's golden carpet of Leucadendron laureolum *(geelbos) glows on the Smitswinkel Flats.*

CHAPTER THREE

Mountain and Moorland

The Floral Riches of Inland Fynbos

A moment or two past the entrance gate as you round the bulging flank of Rooihoogte, the Peninsula stretches beyond you, and the Cape of Good Hope, symbolic and historic destination of countless travellers, lies not far ahead. You may be forgiven for fixing your sights single-mindedly on this spot as you journey on and the narrowing landmass squeezes you towards the corner of the continent. Yet, all the while, one of the most remarkable botanical feasts in the world slips by. This is the land of fynbos, the unique plant life of the Cape, ancient and enigmatic, rich and rare.

'Fynbos' is an Afrikaans word, from the old Dutch *fijn bosch*, meaning 'fine bush'. Though it is widely believed to refer to the small, narrow leaves which typify many of its plants, support is growing for an interpretation of 'fynbos' which invokes not fine leaves, but fine stems. This attribute contrasts fynbos plants with the trees of the forest, which were an important source of timber until most of them were chopped down. Fynbos plants would be much less valuable in this respect and would require a name to distinguish them.

Semantics aside, fynbos is the scrubby, heath-like vegetation which typifies much of the natural landscape of the southern and southwestern Cape. Its plants are typically sclerophyllous, that is they have large numbers of woody-walled (carbon-rich) cells near their leaf surfaces. This may serve to cut down water loss during the hot summers, but is at least as likely to be a strategy to make the leaves unpalatable to insects. The leaves of many species are small and incurled for the same reasons.

Botanists are rather coy about how exactly to define 'fynbos' from the scientific point of view. The problem seems to be that we have a word which needs a definition, rather than a recognisable and delimited situation which now needs a name. Nevertheless, a vegetation type must have certain characteristics before it can be called fynbos. These are that restioids must be present, and that ericoids and proteoids are important features. Restioids are thin, reed-like plants belonging to the Restionaceae family; ericoids are low, small-leaved heathy shrubs, many of which are in the Ericaceae (heath) family; proteoids are shrubs with quite large leaves and are members of the Proteaceae. Fynbos species grow in very nutrient-poor soils and in an environment regulated by and adapted to fire.

The Cape Floral Kingdom

Fynbos is the most extensive and species-rich vegetation type of the Cape Floristic Region. Occupying a small, roughly crescent-shaped band in the extreme southern and southwestern Cape, this region supports such a diverse and idiosyncratic flora that it has been afforded the accolade of a 'floral kingdom'. The world comprises six floral kingdoms but, with the exception of the Cape, these occupy vast areas, such as the whole of Australia (the Australian Floral Kingdom) or most of the northern hemisphere (the Boreal Floral Kingdom). The 90,000 square kilometres of the Cape Floral Kingdom support over 8,500 species, rendering it the richest floral kingdom, for its size, in the world. The density at which the plant species are packed into this small area is exceeded only in Panamanian tropical rain forest. A particularly remarkable feature is that 5,800 (68 per cent) of the Cape flora's species are endemic, that is they occur nowhere else in the world.

The Cape of Good Hope Nature Reserve is part of the Cape Floral Kingdom. Does it pale into insignificance against a background of such floral wealth? Does it reflect the richness of the rest of the Cape flora, and does it stand up to competition from other parts of the world? The answer is most definitely 'yes'. The reserve's 77 square kilometres support at least 1,080 species of indigenous plant, of which 11 are probably endemic. Its largest plant families are the daisy with 116 species, iris (80), sedge (72), orchid (67), pea (66), restio (63) and heath (49).

Proteas, ericas and restios

To assure you that the Cape of Good Hope Nature Reserve's vegetation does qualify as fynbos, some members of the protea, erica and restio families found here are illustrated on pp. 54–58.

The Proteaceae is a family of some 330 species, of varying shape, form and colour. The name is said to come from Proteus, Neptune's herdsman, who, when he was not looking after whatever animals sea gods have flocks of, avoided visitors or evil-doers by changing himself into the shape or form of his choosing. The plants which bear his name are well represented at the reserve, and the 24 species here range from the large and conspicuous flowers of *Protea repens*, through the pincushions (*Leucospermum*), cone-bushes (*Leucadendron*), diminutive *Diastellas*, fiery *Mimetes* and spidery-flowered *Serrurias*. Although these plants differ greatly in gross appearance, they are linked by certain features of their small, individual flowers which combine to make up, in some cases, the more showy inflorescences. Perhaps *Leucadendron laureolum* can claim to put on the finest displays; the Smitswinkel Flats and the slopes of Bonteberg and Teeberg glow golden in the winter months when these shrubs put on a flush of new foliage, within whose tips nestle their flowers and cones.

Our page of ericas illustrates 6 of the reserve's 49 species – a meagre few when one considers that there are an astonishing 650 species or more in the Cape flora (it is the biggest genus here), but an impressive richness for a family which is most popularly associated with the one or two species that carpet the Scottish moorlands. Certainly, the moors of Cape Point can look quite Caledonian when some of the smaller pink or purple species are in flower. For us, however, it is the individuals which shine: the strange-looking, green-flowered *Erica capitata*; the bright-red *Erica cerinthoides* which re-sprouts and flowers soon after a fire; yellow *Erica patersonia*, a floriferous and striking species which would do credit to any garden. On an historical note, William Paterson, the plant's discoverer, after whom it is named, was born in Montrose, Scotland, and came to the Cape in 1777. Sent by the Countess of Strathmore as her personal plant collector, he excelled at his task and undertook four major journeys of exploration into the South African interior in the 1770s. The account of his travels, published in 1789, is notable for being the first travel book from this country to be written in English.

The restioid component of fynbos is an important one at the reserve, because the restios themselves are so abundant. There can hardly be a square metre that does not include at least one of the 63 members of the family which have been recorded here. These range from the two-metre high *Thamnochortus*, to the densely packed, bright-green *Elegias* of the plains and their smaller kinsmen on the rocky slopes. Do take time to look closely at the restios, as they are attractive in their own way. It is in their massed stands, however, that they are such an inescapable feature of the Cape Point landscape, and provide an attractive backdrop against which more showy flowers can shine out.

A vegetation survey of the Cape of Good Hope

We know not only how many species of plant there are in the reserve, but also the distribution and composition of the vegetation types which they make up and which, together, fall under the broad umbrella of fynbos. For this information, all those who have an interest in the reserve are indebted to Hugh Taylor of the Botanical Research Institute at Stellenbosch. In 1966–7 he undertook an intensive study of the reserve, mapping the distribution of its major vegetation types and compiling a list of the species which he encountered. To add to his botanical skills, Hugh Taylor has a unique and intimate knowledge of the area, as his family had a cottage on the reserve's southwest coast for many years. Taylor was (and still is!) also a vigorous exponent of the urgent need to eradicate alien vegetation (which he also mapped as part of his study), and drew attention to the damage caused by introduced antelope, a subject which we address in our final chapter.

We have adopted Taylor's vegetation types as a convenient way of describing the reserve's terrestrial habitats. These also appear in the maps to give you an idea of their extent and distribution. Apart from the scientific information which we have gained from Taylor's work, we also obtain a clear picture of how, in simple terms, the reserve is a botanical treasure-house and an invaluable sanctuary for many rare and endangered species.

At its crudest level, the reserve's fynbos vegetation can be divided into Coast Fynbos, which we describe in Chapter Four, and Inland Fynbos. The latter can be further broken down into subsidiary units, namely Upland Mixed Fynbos which grows on the well-drained rocky hills, and Restionaceous Plateau Fynbos which grows in similarly well-drained soils, but on level ground with little or no exposed rock. A further two Inland Fynbos communities which are distinct, but rather limited in their distribution, are Tall Fynbos dominated by *Protea lepidocarpodendron*, and *Protea nitida* woodland ('Waboomveld').

The extent of these vegetation types is illustrated in the maps, from which it can be seen that Upland Mixed Fynbos is the most widespread. It occupies over 3,000 hectares, more than 40 per cent of the reserve. This is the vegetation typical of the rocky hilltops of the western escarpment which runs from Bonteberg almost to the Cape of Good Hope. Hard, bare sandstone dominates the landscape here, and the shrubs and heaths grow amongst the blocks and ridges in coarse, unyielding soils. In the oldest veld, two shrubs stand out in form and size. The yellow pincushion *Leucospermum conocarpodendron* is a domed, corky-barked member of the protea family whose grey-green foliage is enlivened in spring and summer by a mass of large, bright yellow 'pincushion' inflorescences. Another member of the Proteaceae, with much the same shape and stature (up to two metres high), is *Mimetes fimbriifolius*. This has rather inconspicuous flowers, but the young leaves are tipped red

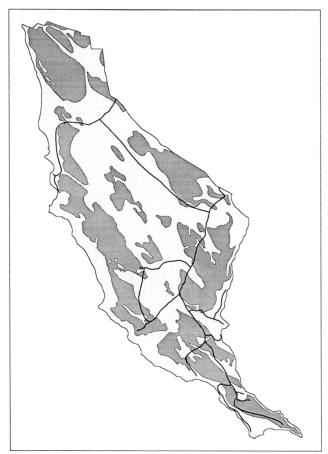

Upland Mixed Fynbos (dark shading) is the most widespread vegetation type in the reserve.

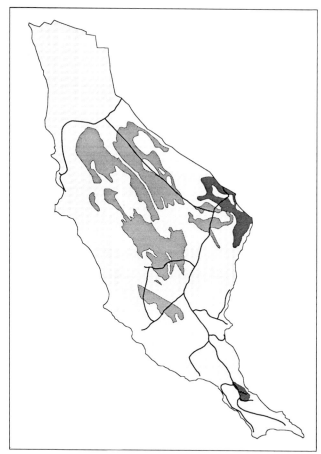

Small patches of fynbos dominated by Bearded Protea or Waboom (dark shading) occur in the south and northeast of the reserve. The mid-shaded areas show the extent of Restionaceous Plateau Fynbos.

so that the bushes blush in late winter and spring. Beneath and between these two conspicuous and almost tree-like shrubs lives an often dense assembly of restios, heaths and other fine-leaved plants.

Where particular species dominate, such as *Metalasia, Aspalathus* or the ericaceous *Salaxis*, they form mildly distinct vegetation types. The composition of these communities changes with time and from place to place, however, so it is perhaps prudent, if cowardly, to label them 'variations on a theme' and let them languish under the banner of Upland Mixed Fynbos.

Restionaceous Plateau Fynbos occurs mainly in the central part of the reserve, from Circular Drive in the south and extending northwestwards into the Smitswinkel Flats and the Krom River valley. It occupies about 1,400 hectares and is dominated by restios, from which emerges an abundance of *Leucadendron laureolum* shrubs. These are made conspicuous in this habitat not just by their relatively large size, but by their striking yellow foliage in winter. This is the shrub which forms a veritable hedge along sections of the road to Olifantsbos.

The two lesser components of Inland Fynbos are, as their names indicate, dominated by two species of protea. The one is *Protea lepidocarpodendron*, which grows predominantly, but not exclusively, on the outcrops of ferricrete at Rooihoogte and above Rooikrans. This is a winter-flowering, bearded protea, whose purplish-black-tipped inflorescences are all but obscured by its leaves. The other is *Protea nitida* or Waboom, which is confined to a very small area of the steep coastal slopes in the northeastern corner of the reserve. The Waboom is a most attractive shrub with a gnarled, corky-barked trunk and soft blue-grey foliage. The flower and leaf buds are red and the inflorescence pale yellowy-green. It is perhaps surprising that any Waboom have survived at the reserve as they were, in the absence of any other, an important source of timber for the early settlers. The wood was used for making furniture and domestic items such as butter-churners. It was also used for making felloes, the curved sections which comprise wagon wheels, hence the name Waboom, or Wagon Tree. Tannin was extracted from its bark for treating leather, and its leaves were boiled up with a rusty nail and a piece of sugar-candy to make black ink. All in all, a most useful plant. Small wonder it is so scarce on the Peninsula today.

It is important to bear in mind that what we describe here might bear no apparent relation to what you see when you visit the reserve. This is because fynbos is forever changing, and the major factor which alters it and the appearance and occupants of the landscape is fire.

Fire in fynbos

There may be times when you visit the reserve to admire your favourite pelargonium patch or carpet of ericas to find instead a scorched and blackened desert, a lunar landscape latticed with gaunt, charred skeletons and smothered with windblown dust and ash. This is not the most heartening of sights if you were a looking forward to a hillside of brilliant blooms. Comfort may be drawn from the fact that fire is a natural phenomenon in fynbos and that its plants have evolved a number of strategies by which they not only survive, in one form or another, the conflagration, but prosper in its wake.

That fire is a typical feature of the Cape is not altogether surprising, given the hot, dry summers and the flammability of much of the vegetation. Fire is, in fact, the major ecological driving force behind the structure and functioning of fynbos. Without it, fynbos would not be as we find it today, and it is unlikely that it would be so rich in plant species. Fire began its rule in the Cape almost two

million years ago, when the climate changed from one which was almost tropical, to warm-temperate, and then the present-day Mediterranean-type, with its wet winters and warm, virtually rainless summers. This set the scene for the expansion of fynbos, whose plants are adapted to long periods of drought. The summer's heat and build-up of plant material provided the perfect tinder-box, and a lightning strike or rock fall would be enough to spark off an autumn fire every few decades. Under these circumstances, it was a question of adapt or die, and those plants which could survive fire proliferated and speciated, while those that could not tolerate fire died out or were restricted to damp or rocky areas out of reach of the flames.

Nevertheless, the desert-like scene which greets you at the reserve in the first few days after a fire gives little hint of the plants' remarkable powers of recovery. The plants can survive in three major ways – as seeds, as underground storage organs or rootstocks, and as buds deep in the stems.

The seeds of many annuals can persist in or on the soil, can withstand the passage of a fire if it is not too hot, and are stimulated (most probably by chemicals in the smoke) to germinate after a fire. The seeds of many fynbos shrubs are stored in tough, woody cones which are held on the plant, an adaptation known as serotiny. The cones protect the seeds from the heat of a fire, but thereafter split to release them onto the bare ground. Although the parent plant is killed, its progeny not only survive the fire but are able to exploit the sudden abundance of sunlight and water made available by the removal of the overcanopying plants.

Erica sessiliflora
Green Heath

Opposite left: Mimetes fimbriifolius, *a member of the protea family, growing on the slopes of Bonteberg, with Paulsberg in the distance.*

Above: Seen from the summit of Rooihoogte, the broad plain of the Smitswinkel Flats sweeps across the Peninsula to the Atlantic seaboard.

Serotiny is a fire-survival strategy adopted by over 300 species of fynbos plants, some of the most well-known being species of protea and *Leucadendron*, the latter with their tight, hard cones. Of the more than 650 species of erica found in fynbos, it is curious that only one of them, *Erica sessiliflora*, has opted for this strategy, and stores its seeds in hard growths on the stem.

If the seeds are not held in a cone, or run the risk of being eaten or otherwise destroyed on the surface, what can the plant resort to? A remarkable phenomenon in fynbos is 'myrmecochory'. This is a mutually beneficial relationship between ants and plants which has evolved probably in response to fire, nutrient limitations and surface seed predation. The seeds of many fynbos plants have on them a fleshy food-body called an elaiosome. When the fat, fresh seeds drop to the ground, indigenous ants pick them up and carry them back to their underground nests. Here they eat the elaiosome but discard the seed in a midden in the nest or on the surface. Seeds may thus find themselves in a relatively nutrient-rich position (where the ants have been dumping their rubbish), or safely ensconced in the ants' nest out of reach of mice and birds and protected from fire. If the area is burnt, the ants' nest may be damaged and the seed able to germinate and grow. Myrmecochory was first noted by the pioneering botanist Rudolf Marloth in the early 1900s and has, in the last decade, received a resurgence of interest and investigation. It is now thought that almost 1,500 of the Cape flora's plants have their seeds planted or protected through the good offices of the fynbos ants.

Soil is a remarkably good insulator, so it comes as no surprise that the underground parts of many plants can survive the passage of a fire which destroys their stems and leaves above the surface. Plants that survive fire in this way include those that have bulbs or corms, such as the *Watsonias*, gladioli, irises and lilies, which are represented by so many species at the reserve. Some plants re-sprout from woody rootstocks, including *Mimetes cucullatus* (p. 54), and many of the shrubs found in coastal thicket. A shrub which is only a metre high, therefore, may have been through many fires and arise from a rootstock which could be a hundred years old or more.

The coastal thicket shrubs can also survive fire by re-sprouting from buds, known as epicormic buds, deep inside their stems. If the fire has not been too hot, these will sprout vigorously after the foliage on the outside of the plant has been burnt off. The Waboom goes one step further by encasing its stem with a thick, corky bark which provides extra insulation for its epicormic buds. Some other proteas, such as *Leucospermum conocarpodendron*, also have corky bark, but this serves only to enhance the survival chances of vital tissues in their stems, as the plant does not have epicormic buds from which to re-sprout.

These fire-survival strategies are adopted together or alone by virtually all fynbos plants, and together ensure that the desolate scene which greets you immediately after a fire is but a temporary one. Within even a few days the landscape will acquire a haze of rejuvenating green as the re-sprouters send up their leaves. Not long after, the first geophytes will emerge – orchids, tulps, *Lachenalias*, *Aristeas*, *Agapanthus*, *Moraeas* and many more – their flowers decorating the veld and gladdening despondent hearts. Come the spring, the annuals are in full bloom, with drifts of daisies and carpets of nemesias. Regrowth and regeneration continue over the years. Many plants will mature and flower only after three or four years or more; in the meantime, the annuals and bulbs have died down to await another fire and their moment of glory.

Fire is thus a natural and, at the right time, welcome feature of the reserve. It is a two-edged sword, however, and can be extremely damaging if it occurs at the wrong time of year or too closely on the heels of a previous fire. In the first instance, the seedlings which arise from seeds whose dormancy has been broken by a spring fire will die of thirst over the hot, dry summer months. In the second, those plants which need a long time to mature, flower and produce the seed that will become the next generation, may quickly become extinct if another fire goes through before they have reached this stage. Under natural conditions (inasmuch as we can visualise them today), fynbos fires occur in autumn when a lightning strike is most likely and the vegetation is dry enough to ignite and sustain a fire. Fynbos fires are also likely to occur at long intervals because of the infrequency of lightning strikes in this part of the world, and because it takes a few years (at least four) for the accumulation of enough dead wood and leaf litter to sustain a fire.

Unfortunately, the reserve, and many other fynbos areas, have been burnt too often in the past, leading, it is thought, to the near-extinction of many of the slower-growing shrubs. Frequent burning was formerly used as a management tool to encourage regrowth of plants for livestock. Fires at too-short intervals and at inappropriate times of year arise today at the reserve through malice – there is a disturbing correlation between the number of fines dispensed for motoring and other offences, and the fynbos mysteriously catching fire; the higher the number of fines, the greater the likelihood of a fire. Some plants may benefit from fires which follow in quick succession, however, and are thought to be unnaturally abundant at the reserve because a history of overburning has favoured their increase. Such plants grow quickly to maturity from seed which is stimulated to germinate by a fire, so a burn even every three or four years will result in lots of seedlings and, consequently, lots of flowers. A long time-lag between fires would, conversely, expose the dormant seed to predation by mice or attack by fungus, leaving fewer seeds to germinate when a fire does eventually occur. Our *Helichrysum vestitum* (now known as *Syncarpha vestita*) on p. 60 put on a splendid display in the summer of 1993, and we can expect good shows for the next couple of years at least. Also prolific regenerators after fire are the restios, whose great sweeps ('sweep' is made the more appropriate as they are used to make brooms) are probably also attributable to overburning.

In January 1991 about one-third of the reserve was accidentally burnt. The fire consumed fynbos ranging from 5 to perhaps 30 years old, comprising a variety of vegetation types. This was something of a blessing in disguise for us, for the following winter and spring saw a superabundance of species popping up all over the landscape. Many of these have found their way into these pages and will, we hope, demonstrate that a fynbos fire is not necessarily the destructive and depressing phenomenon that the seemingly lifeless landscape would, in the short term, suggest. Nevertheless, it does make the job of the botanists that much more difficult when, to get a truly representative picture of what is growing in a particular area, a study period of, say, 20 years, is required!

Having painted what is hopefully not too complicated a picture of Inland Fynbos, and the important role of fire in its composition and structure, we should perhaps not concern ourselves with the finer points of plant distribution. We should rather relax and take a leisurely stroll through the fynbos and enjoy whatever plants and animals we find there.

Not passing the buck

One of the first things upon which you may comment on your first inspection of this habitat is, where are all the animals? There was a time when you would have seen more large buck, but this is not so today, for the following reason. Geological and climatic history have combined to create soils in the fynbos region in which nutrients, particularly nitrogen and phosphorus, are in extremely short supply. Both of these are important in the manufacture of plant tissues. Where soils are rich and fertile, it is relatively easy for a plant to obtain nutrients to replace tissues eaten by animals, be it buck or beetle. In fynbos, however, nutrients are scarce and leaves are generally slow-growing and long-lived. The loss of even a few leaves would stress the plant considerably.

To reduce the chances of their being eaten, fynbos plants have resorted to chemical defence. They manufacture organic (carbon-based) compounds called tannins. These are very astringent, and by accumulating them in its leaves a plant essentially makes itself a thoroughly unpalatable and poisonous proposition. Tannins are often most abundant in young, growing leaves which, with their soft tissues and relatively high nitrogen content, would otherwise be highly attractive to herbivores. The effectiveness of this chemical warfare is apparent from the generally low incidence of damage to leaves of fynbos plants. There are some insects which can cope with this chemical bombardment by detoxifying the poisons in their digestive systems. Such insects can make a living off, for example, protea leaves, which are chewed along their edges by caterpillars or have the characteristic wiggly lines of leaf-borers running through them. These are the exception rather than the rule, however, and in most cases the tannins directly poison the insect or combine with gut enzymes to form indigestible compounds, rendering the ingested food valueless. Furthermore, the leaves of many fynbos plants are small and tough, making them even less palatable and more indigestible.

If herbivorous insects find it challenging to scrape a living in fynbos, how much more difficult it must be for large animals. Big, abundant grazers solve this problem by simply not occurring in fynbos. In addition to the poisonous or indigestible nature of the leaves, the nitrogen content of the plants is below the minimum required to sustain the animals in anything like a healthy state. The herds of antelope which are such a feature of the savanna do not, therefore, occur in fynbos. Some small buck are found here, but in very low numbers, and they are very choosy about what they eat. Species such as Grysbok and Steenbok are fastidious browsers, and use their delicate muzzles to rummage around and select the most nutritious parts of the plant. Great herds of animated motor-mowers would find that they could eat for 24 hours a day in fynbos without getting enough nutrition to sustain themselves. This explains to the visitor why there are so few large animals in the reserve – there simply isn't enough suitable vegetation for them to eat.

Sugarbush and sugarbird

The typical fynbos scene at the Cape of Good Hope is not, therefore, a zebra rampant or a hartebeest at bay, but a protea with a sugarbird on top. The Cape Sugarbird is one of the six bird species endemic to fynbos, and the proteas, although a relatively small family, are good ambassadors for their compatriots. To choose a protea species which is representative of the reserve is not easy. Here we can find, amongst others, the enormous *Protea cynaroides* (whose dignity is somewhat dented by having a scientific name which means 'like an artichoke'), the beautifully bearded *Protea speciosa* which sprouts so enthusiastically after a fire, and *Protea scolymocephala*, an unpretentious but very pretty species which you can see by the roadside leading down to the Cape of Good Hope. Perhaps *Protea repens* would be our choice. It's a fast-growing, serotinous species, with bright, cross-gartered flowers which brighten many a winter's day. Most important, the sugarbirds love it. This species was formerly known as *Protea mellifera*, the epithet meaning 'full of honey'. This is an evocative name for those who can remember the days of 'bossiestroop' – the thick syrup condensed from the 'Suikerbossie' nectar. In the old days, the Cape Flats and lower slopes of Table Mountain were veritable forests of this protea, and gallons of nectar were collected by simply snapping off the flowers and tipping their contents into a bucket. The 'full of honey' protea not only has retreated to the sanctuary of the few natural areas left around Cape Town, but now languishes under the name *Protea repens*, which means 'creeping'. It was discovered that this name had been given to it before it was described as *mellifera*, and the former, therefore, had prior claim. A most uncomplimentary title for this fine upstanding species, but it seems that the taxonomist Linnaeus described the species from an illustration which depicted a scrawny and prostrate specimen, so what was he to do but call it creepy?

Having selected our protea, we now must perch a Cape Sugarbird on top of it to complete the picture. There is no better place to admire this scene than the slopes of Teeberg in mid-winter. Here the *Protea repens* are in full flower, with a scattering of *Protea lepidocarpodendron* and splashes of ericas between. The painting (pp. 52–53) shows a cock sugarbird amongst his floral conquests (or the proteas with their avian conquest – it works both ways, as we shall describe).

The Cape Sugarbird's lifestyle is inextricably bound up with the flowering patterns of proteas, even to the extent of its moving around the countryside, tracking the various species as they come into flower. There is some fidelity to favoured sites, and the birds return year after year to the same patches of proteas in which we have originally ringed them. Where they go in between times has been indicated by some of the birds which we have ringed at Teeberg. These have been found subsequently almost at the tip of the Peninsula feeding from yellow pincushions, and as far afield as Kirstenbosch on the slopes of Table Mountain, which, with its great array of proteaceous shrubs, must be as near to heaven as the sugarbirds can get.

Back at the reserve, sugarbird nesting begins as soon as the *Protea repens* come into bloom in autumn, and continues over the winter. The adults are sustained by a dependable supply of nectar and an assortment of so-called satellite insects which also visit the blooms. These are the bees and beetles that congregate in and around the protea's chalice in great numbers. Rich in protein, these insects are also caught and fed to the sugarbird chicks. Of 12 hours of daylight, a sugarbird spends about 4 in flight (moving between flowers, chasing off other birds, hawking insects) and 8 hours involved in feeding, preening and other less energetic activities. Combined with the energy required to keep warm at night, these activities require an energy expenditure of about 140 kilojoules per day. While this could be met by eating, say, 9 grams of cornflakes or 5.7 grams of peanut butter, the sugarbird manages it by eating the insects caught at or drinking the nectar from over 300 protea blooms every day.

A *Protea repens* bloom lasts for about three weeks, and its maximum sugar production is attained when it is between six and nine days old. At this stage, not surprisingly, it receives most visits from the sugarbirds. The proteas are not providing all this food purely out of generosity. The bird is attracted with a definite purpose – that of pollinating the protea blooms. If you look closely at a sugarbird in a protea patch, you will see that its forehead feathers are matted with purple or yellow pollen (depending upon the species of flower it has been visiting). The pollen is picked up from one inflorescence by the feeding bird and some of it may subsequently be dislodged as the bird visits another flower. The sugarbird acts as the courier service for protea pollen and receives a meal of nectar for its troubles.

The sugarbird is not the only bird to take advantage of this copious and energy-rich food supply. Opportunism is the name of the game in fynbos, and the Teeberg protea beds can be busy with such unlikely nectar-feeders as Bully Canary and Yellowrumped Widow. They are joined at the feast by traditionally catholic feeders such as Cape Weavers, Cape White-eyes and Redwinged Starlings. When not drinking nectar, the last-named catch in flight the bright-green cetoniid beetles that drone between the flowers on warm, calm days. We have yet to find a mammal that will scuttle up a protea stem and dive head-first into the nectar bath, but it would not come as a surprise to learn that a Grey Climbing Mouse, for example, has a sweet tooth. It is thought that many of the ground proteas, such as the creeping pincushions and *Protea acaulos*, which are common at the reserve, are visited and pollinated by small rodents.

Protea pollination is also effected by the Orangebreasted Sunbird, although this species is more strongly associated with ericas. Many species of erica have long, tubular blooms which match the length and curvature of the sunbird's beak. This is no coincidence, as the two have evolved together in mutual dependence. At the reserve, the sunbird-pollinated *Ericas* include *Erica curviflora*, the sticky, purple-flowered *Erica phylicifolia* (there are nice patches at the Platboom turnoff and around the Smitswinkel view site), and *Erica cerinthoides*, which we have met before. *Erica gilva*, with its translucent, pale-yellow flowers, occurs in the densest stands, and between late summer and mid-winter its floriferous clumps beside the main and Olifantsbos roads host a great number of Orangebreasted Sunbirds. A vigorous 'skish' on your part will have them dancing around the tops of the vegetation, allowing you a good view of them as their curiosity overcomes timidity.

Devious disas

Whereas the proteas and ericas are fairly generous in their supply of nectar, and flower and bird seem satisfied with the arrangement, some plants have become both mean and devious in this respect. The orchid *Disa ferruginea*, for example, does not produce nectar, but has a bloom which resembles the iris *Tritoniopsis triticea*, which does produce nectar. This flower is one of a suite of red flowers in bloom at this time of year and visited by the Mountain Pride Butterfly. As it trundles along, the butterfly sees what it thinks is the iris (but is, in fact, the orchid), pays it a visit in the hope of a drink but gets none. The perching and probing of the butterfly are, however, all that is required to pick up the orchid's pollen sacs, and if the butterfly then visits another *Disa ferruginea*, the sacs may be successfully transferred. Pollination thus takes place at no cost to the plant but wastes a journey for the unsuspecting butterfly. It is surely no coincidence that these flowers are in bloom at the same time of year. The slopes of Rooihoogte in March are dotted with *Tritoniopsis*, while the *Disas* flower on the summit, and all around a succession of bemused brown butterflies bumbles. Alternatively, the orchid may just be taking advantage of the butterfly's indisputable predilection for the colour red, in which case it would be as well to mimic a sun hat or a Fiat Uno as, in our experience, the butterfly will visit these if they are the right colour (the disappointment must be acute).

Nevertheless, orchids may be particularly adept at the deception game, and the rare (at the reserve – it has been found only near the summit of Judas Peak) *Disa fasciata* may mimic the flowers of *Adenandra*, the China Flower. What pollinates *Adenandra* is not clear, but presumably it is an insect of some sort which may also be fooled into visiting the flat-flowered *Disa*, which does, at a pinch, resemble it.

Disa fasciata

In spring the rocky escarpment near Menskop is smothered in purple pelargoniums, the Wilde Malva Pelargonium cucullatum.

Granny's Bonnets and Heady Maidens

Orchids are a charismatic group. Nothing at the reserve grows to the size of a potted *Cymbidium* or a tropical epiphyte but, small as they are, we have here some very charming and interesting species. We found our first *Schizodium obliquum* on an isolated rocky outcrop at Circular Drive. Its kinked, thread-like stem belies the toughness it needs to withstand the wintery downpours. Close by was the first of the year's Moederkappies, *Disperis capensis* (p. 70). With the poise and elegant charm of a ballerina, this is one of our favourite fynbos flowers. The colloquial name describes an old-fashioned headgear – 'Granny's Bonnet' would be apt and literal. Many plants have this name (including a number of ornamental species such as *Aquilegias*), so the scientific qualification is required if we are to know exactly which plant we are talking about. The use of Latin or Greek names is thus not designed to confuse, or to expound the benefits of a classical education. Rather, the colloquial names of plants are ambiguous and misleading (there are lots of 'Painted Ladies' and a proliferation of 'Pypies'). Not so (necessarily) with birds, whose common names can be used with a certain impunity and clarity even if some of them are not entirely appropriate (a Cape Robin is neither a robin nor restricted to the Cape). At all times, you should pronounce the scientific name with confidence. If in doubt when asked what a certain species is, reply '*capensis*' in clear, firm tones, even if you haven't the foggiest idea what it is. On the one hand you will sound as if you know what you're talking about and, on the other, the chances are that, in this part of the world, you are right. This approach has served us well over years of guiding visitors around the reserve.

The saga of the spider orchid *Bartholina etheliae* (p. 67) would require an entire book for itself. One of the many post-fire flowers of the spring of 1991, it first made an appearance on the rocky slopes above Olifantsbos in August. Here the single leaf sat in quiet contemplation while we fussed over it, visiting it every day or two to check on its progress, or lack thereof. Just when we were beginning to wonder if it was devoid of any floral aspirations whatsoever, a tiny stem shoot appeared. The tension was all but unbearable as this grew, with painful slowness, to produce a bud and then, at last, a flower. By this time, the hillside had been so trampled by Eland and excavated by baboons that it looked as if the All England ploughing championships had been held on it. By some miracle, the orchid survived to be recorded for posterity in these pages!

Not very far to the north, another spider orchid, this time *Bartholina burmanniana*, came into flower. Near Menskop a little patch of them was growing amongst the restios, quite overcanopied and inconspicuous. Such gems, and the delightful Heady Maidens and Hummingbird Hawk Moths (p. 61) which joined us on our walk to the orchids, make the dry, dusty months and the long time searching for such rarities all worth while.

Cat's claws and kukumakrankas

The hunt for other species was somewhat easier than that for retiring orchids. August and September are superb months on the reserve, especially if there has been a fire the previous autumn and a wet winter in between. In the spring of 1991 we were captivated by the splendour of bulbs and annuals which proliferated along the escarpment above Olifantsbos and in the Krom River valley (which provided the subjects for pp. 74–75). Here were *Babiana ambigua*, from dark blue to pure white, with cream and scarlet throats, and towering tulps by the hundred, rich butter-yellow with gorgets of orange. Here is the place to find diminutive, dark-blue *Agapanthus*, pink *Lapeirousia*, yellow *Ixia* and the tricoloured *Lachenalia aloides*, a variety found here and nowhere else (p. 62).

Two of the most enigmatic flowers are the *Hyobanches* and the kukumakrankas. The former pokes its blood-red buds above the soil in mid-winter, and by September there are little groups of them dotted around the veld, like miniature carmine Christmas trees (p. 63). These are parasites, tapping into the roots of certain shrubs and siphoning off their nutrients. Because they do not need to make their own food, they do not require chlorophyll for photosynthesis and can thus afford to be something more fashionable than plain green.

We were very excited to find our first kukumakranka, the pink-and-white amaryllids of mid-summer. Their name apparently is Indian in origin, a form of which (*bramakanka*) was, somewhat mysteriously, used by the Khoi. There were reports that a species discovered a decade ago at the reserve had been declared new to science and was endemic to the area. Christened with due ceremony *Gethyllis kaapensis*, it promptly vanished and was not seen or heard of again. Driving round Circular Drive one evening, we saw a kukumakranka in full flower at the roadside. Having taken numerous photographs and recorded its location, we then sought the help of experts to identify the thing. The *cognoscenti* duly gathered and formed a respectful circle around the solitary bloom, making appreciative mumbles and musings. No one seemed quite sure what it was, but the thought of the mythical *Gethyllis kaapensis* sent little ripples of excitement through the assembled company. Resolving to pursue the matter further, we took our leave. On driving round the corner and onto the crest of the hill which overlooks the broad plain of Plateau Fynbos, we were confronted with a great meadow of kukumakrankas, hundreds of them, starry blooms stretching almost as far as the eye could see. So much for rarity! It transpired that the 'new' species was, it seems, an old one (*Gethyllis pusilla*), and *Gethyllis kaapensis* vanished in a puff of taxonomical smoke. Nevertheless, this did not detract from the beauty of these flowers (p. 71). They bloom en masse in summer only after a fire the previous autumn, and it is thought that their synchronicity is triggered by a drop in atmospheric pressure associated with cold fronts passing well to the south of the Cape but not bringing rain. After the flowers wither, the contractile roots pull the bulb back down into the soil. The sweet-smelling fruit appears a few months later – in days when they were common around Cape Town, they were eaten as sweetmeats, used as air-fresheners and infused in brandy!

The floral display of the kukumakrankas, and the other bulbs, has disappeared or diminished each spring since, and the passing years see a denser thicket of shrubs and tangle of restios. But underneath, the bulbs sit tight and await their turn.

Regal pelargoniums

A family noted more for its conspicuous flowers than the number of species is the Geraniaceae, whose major representatives at the reserve include 12 species of the genus *Pelargonium*. These hardly need an introduction, but the popular image of a spindly pot plant or a luxuriant window-box cascade is satisfied, to some extent, by the species found here. For sheer splendour, few flowers at the reserve can match the spring displays of *Pelargonium cucullatum*. This species regenerates from seed after a fire and blooms in its second year, cloaking the veld with a regal robe of purple from September to November. The escarpment above Olifantsbos and the hillsides at Platboom have put on the very finest shows in recent years. After another year or two, the plants become more woody and senescent and the purple splendour dissipates with successive springs. There will always be some in flower in spring, particularly along the roadsides where they have been trimmed by brush-cutting, and some will carry over into the summer. Do pause to pay them your respects – these are the principal ancestors of the regal hybrids which do so much to beautify the gardens, conservatories and window sills of the world.

Less flamboyant by far is *Pelargonium longifolium*. This is a geophytic species; that is, it re-sprouts from an underground tuber. Although most conspicuous after a fire, when they are easy to find in the sparse vegetation, we come across them every spring and summer in the rockiest areas or in the deeper sands among the restios (p. 73). The flower varies from almost white to dark pink, always with purple markings. The leaves are so variable that they can be spoon-shaped and almost thread-like on the same plant.

Citrus scents

Fynbos not only looks good, it smells good. Even in summer, when there are few flowers, evocative scents are wafted up as you walk through the veld. The suppliers of most of these are the buchus, long admired for their redolent and evocative airs. They belong to the family Rutaceae, which has 259 species in the Cape flora, although only 12 of these occur at the reserve. It is not easy to describe these scents other than in their own terms – 'buchu-y' is sufficiently descriptive for those familiar with them! This covers a variety of aromas, but if an overriding one is like citrus, this should not come as a surprise, as this family also contains oranges and lemons and the other citrus fruits. Our buchus bear little resemblance to these, at least superficially, being quite short, compact, narrow-leaved bushes.

Gently squeeze a leaf on the buchu plant to release the scent from the glands therein. *Agathosma ciliaris* is splendidly like liquorice; you can find it along the trail which weaves through the sandstone outcrops overlooking the Smitswinkel Flats. *Adenandra villosa* has a scent like citrus, and adds to this a mass of porcelain-white flowers with blushes of pink – if your garden contained this species and no other plant, it would never fail to provide year-round pleasure. The first hundred metres or so of the Sirkelsvlei trail from Olifantsbos leads you up a rocky hillside bedecked with *Coleonema album*, whose bright-green foliage sparkles with small white flowers in September. Even brushing the bushes as you walk releases a fine fragrance from the leaves, which lingers on your clothes long after you have returned home – a pleasant reminder of fynbos.

Some fynbos insects

In discussing insects in *A Fynbos Year*, we bemoaned the lack of information on the subject. Since then, there has been some progress made in compiling inventories of species from particular areas (including the Cape of Good Hope) by staff of the South African Museum in Cape Town, of insects found on particular plant species, and in pollination biology (notably by Steve Johnson of UCT's Botany Department). There remains, however, as the entomologists would be the first to admit, a huge amount of work to be done before we can claim to have more than a basic understanding of fynbos insect ecology.

Large and conspicuous insects in Inland Fynbos do not, with one exception, include amongst their numbers the butterflies. A list of butterflies has not yet been drawn up for the reserve, which is perhaps surprising, given the popularity of these insects with amateur naturalists and professional entomologists (only mosquitoes, being a health hazard, and bees have received as much attention). Butterflies are generally quite scarce in fynbos vegetation, largely because there are few suitable larval food plants (many caterpillars feed on grass) and the windy climate makes flying difficult.

The only large, genuinely fynbos species found at the reserve is the Mountain Pride, which we have mentioned. Its wingspan can exceed 80 millimetres, and an alternative name, Mountain Beauty, is not inappropriate. It flies in late summer and autumn, thus avoiding the wind which would handicap it earlier in the season.

The family with the greatest number of species at the reserve is the Lycaenidae, the 'blues', 'coppers' or 'bronzes'. These are generally very small, with wingspans often less than 15 millimetres. They range in colour from dirty brown, through powder-blue, to brilliant metallic blue with orange borders (as in the case of the exquisite Blue Jewel Copper). They are fast flyers, difficult to follow and almost impossible to see when they land and close their wings. Many species have little spots and protruding 'tails' on the rear of their wings. When they settle, they almost immediately turn round so that their head points downward and tail upward. In this position, the 'false eye' spots and antennae-like tails make it difficult for a would-be predator to tell, at a glance, one end from the other. So the butterfly has at least an even chance of being eaten or merely left with a tatty wing if snatched by a bird or lizard.

A number of the blues display a remarkable relationship with ants, whereby their caterpillars are 'adopted' by the ants and grow to maturity in their underground nests, feeding on their brood. Others feed on the foliage of fynbos plants, including pelargoniums. One species, the Geranium Bronze, has made itself unpopular by feeding on ornamental 'geraniums'. It has been accidentally translocated to the Canary Islands and North Africa and may yet invade Continental Europe, hunting down hanging baskets and pots full of pelargoniums! If you think the caterpillars are getting more than their fair share of your favourite garden plants, you may be right – some species are reputed to increase their bulk 30,000 times between the moment they hatch from the egg and when they pupate.

The unpalatability of fynbos vegetation is likely to limit the number of leaf-eating insects here, but the fact that over 80 per cent of fynbos flowers are insect-pollinated suggests that there must be a lot of insects (in terms of either abundance or the number of species) which feed upon nectar or pollen. The hum of honeybees is a characteristic sound of the *Protea repens* patches on a warm winter's day, and the flowering ericas can be similarly noisy as masses of small insects visit the bell-shaped blooms. Impressive as these gatherings may be, the individual flowers and their pollinators are every bit as fascinating. Many fynbos plants are peculiarly adapted to be pollinated by perhaps one group, or perhaps even one species, of insect. The pink corolla of *Saltera sarcocolla* would present a challenge to any insect other than one with an enormous snout. So it is that this flower is visited by such a creature, a tabanid fly (p. 68). Orange-breasted Sunbirds also visit this plant, although their beaks are less than half the length of the insect's snout! These flies and their relatives, the nemestrinds, are probably also important pollinators of many of the irises and lilies, amongst others, which have long corolla tubes with trumpet-shaped openings.

Work by entomologist Mark Wright has suggested that *Witsenia maura* (p. 186) is pollinated by, of all things, an earwig. Such an observation has important conservation implications, because if the pollen from one flower is unlikely to travel further than an earwig can wiggle, then genetic mixing with other *Witsenia* populations is unlikely to occur. This will ensure that any favourable genetic attributes which the isolated *Witsenia* plants may possess, and which render them well adapted to the microenvironmental conditions of their particular patch, are not disrupted by the importation of pollen from other, perhaps slightly different, *Witsenia* populations. The same situation may prevail with another reserve rarity, the False Heath, which is visited by small nitidulid beetles. These tend not to gather much pollen, or travel very far with it. Such genetic isolation again leads to the small, widely separated groups, or even individual plants, becoming uniquely adapted to the very specific conditions in which they are found.

We frequently encounter Meloid blister beetles at the reserve because they, like us, are attracted to flowers. The petals of gladioli, irises, *Roella* and other showy blooms are eaten by these insects. This habit does not endear them to gardeners or botanists, but may be a deliberate sacrifice on the part of the plant – you can eat my petals if you transfer my pollen. The beetles are black with bright red or yellow spots, a pattern and coloration which announce to would-be predators that they, the beetles, are distasteful. If this is not a sufficient deterrent, the beetles call up reinforcements in the form of a strategy called autohaemorrhaging, or reflex bleeding. This involves excreting a liquid, usually from the knee joints, which contains the poison canathardin. In avoiding being eaten, the beetles sacrifice up to 15 per cent of their body weight in fluid loss, and have to drink copiously thereafter to replace this.

Wood-boring beetles come in a variety of shapes, sizes and colours. *Ceroplesis* is boldy marked black and red, which, like the blister beetles, may serve to ward off predators. It also emits a somewhat disconcerting squeak if alarmed, which may also surprise a predator – it certainly surprised us! Wood-borers lay their eggs in dead wood, and the larvae may take three or four years to develop into an adult, presumably because there is so little nutrition in a dead fynbos shrub. Look for them around the trunks and branches of old burnt-out pincushions.

Pipits and plovers

The birds of Upland Mixed Fynbos are themselves a mixed lot and, like the plants, vary according to the number of years which have elapsed since

Bladder grasshopper
Physemacris variolosus

the last fire. To a bird, and most likely to the human observer as well, the recently burnt fynbos looks pretty much the same across the board. There is no difference in the vegetation, largely because there is no vegetation, and an abundance of rocks is the only feature which will distinguish Upland from Plateau Fynbos. In this largely uniform habitat, a few Crowned Plovers take up temporary residence and pace around amongst the re-sprouting restios. LBJs (Little Brown Jobs, a convenient generic term for any bird which is just that) take the form of Plainbacked Pipits. These remain for two or three years or until the vegetation has become too high or dense for effective foraging (the pipits feed by walking along the bare ground and snatching insects from its surface). An additional feature in the rocky burnt-out areas is the arrival from time to time of small flocks of seed-eating birds, such as Rock Pigeons, Cape Siskins and Cape Canaries. These are probably important seed-predators in post-fire fynbos and, unlike mice, can quickly move in to burnt areas and exploit any seeds which have been exposed by the fire or released from splitting cones.

The presence of Orangebreasted and Malachite Sunbirds soon after fire is attributable to the speedy re-sprouting and re-flowering of *Erica cerinthoides* and *Saltera sarcocolla*, whose red and pink blooms glow like dying embers amongst the fynbos charcoal. The plants tend to be very scattered, but it is possible to see and hear Malachite Sunbirds approaching from some distance and quite a height, then dropping steeply down to perch on and probe a flower. The peregrinations of their pollinators are presumably important to the success of the plants.

In 'middle-aged' (about five years old) Upland and Plateau Fynbos there is generally a dearth of birds. An avian limbo prevails, from which the open-country species have departed, but at which the birds typical of mature fynbos have not yet arrived. The *Mimetes* and pincushions have not yet matured, so there are no sugarbirds or sunbirds; and only a sprinkling of Greybacked Cisticolas and the seed-eating Yellowrumped Widows stand between the birder and ornithological purgatory.

A modicum of respite is provided in the oldest vegetation, areas which have not been burnt for at least 15 years, where the heaths and restios are fairly dense and the proteas sizeable and, in season, floriferous. The birds of this habitat generally comprise two factions. The one is a small number of resident insect-eating species, notably Cape Robin and Greybacked Cisticolas, but even here their combined average density may not be much over two birds per hectare. An influx of sugarbirds and sunbirds when the pincushions and *Mimetes* come into flower forms the other faction, and makes a most welcome sight.

Fynbos is not, you will have gathered, the most exciting place for birds. But the reserve as a whole can boast a fairly impressive list. While you walk through the veld, it is as well to keep half an eye heavenward, as your chances of seeing a Peregrine here are very good. One of their favourite pastimes seems to be to display over the Cape Point car park! A pair of Black Eagles also nests here, and may be seen gliding overhead on the hunt for dassies and tortoises.

Grazers, browsers and hunters

Although their presence at the reserve is something of a contentious issue, no one could deny that Bontebok are handsome antelopes, with their coat of many colours, or at least browns, white and a bloom of purple (pp. 178–179). There are about 200 here, and they are not difficult to see, in particular the ones that gather on the lawns in front of the Homestead. This habit indicates their preference for grass, although they will also congregate on areas of recently burnt veld and nibble the re-sprouting vegetation there, as you are likely to find around Circular Drive.

Bontebok are social animals, but tailor their herds into groups comprising bachelor males, and nursery herds of females and their lambs (which are born in spring). Adult males occupy and defend territories, chasing off intruding males. The occupier of each territory attempts to entice and keep within it as many females as it can with a series of prances, tail curling, muzzle pointing and other beguiling displays. The females, in response, come and go as they please. If you disturb a herd of Bontebok, you may notice that one animal lingers as the others move off. This is the territorial male, and, in what has been interpreted as symbolic gesture of defiance, he turns broadside on to a perceived threat and then urinates before moving off.

The Bontebok is not considered to be a species in its own right, but a subspecies of the Blesbok, and they do indeed look very similar. Whatever its taxonomic status, the Bontebok is the rarest antelope in southern Africa and perhaps merits a place in the Cape of Good Hope on that basis until such time as suitable areas can be found for them elsewhere. Historically, they were recorded no further west than Caledon, and were never found in the scrubby and nutrient-poor fynbos vegetation, but rather in grasslands. In fynbos they suffer from chronic copper and cobalt deficiencies, and attempts to improve the grazing by establishing artificial pastures at the reserve led to overgrazing and intolerably high levels of parasitic infestation.

At the latest count the Eland herd numbered 59 animals. Very rarely are they seen by visitors, apart from the hikers who make forays along the trails. The Eland herd was a regular visitor in the late afternoon to the vlei at Skaife, and they made a superb and dignified sight as they trooped down the hillside. In all our time at the reserve, I think we have seen them from the roads no more than five times, so they could hardly claim to provide much in the way of public spectacle. They also tend to be rather nervous, and gallop

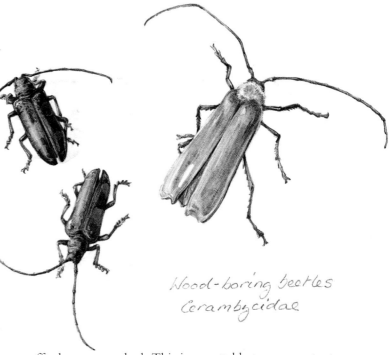

Wood-boring beetles
Cerambycidae

off when approached. This is regrettable to some extent, as they are magnificent animals and, after all, Africa's biggest antelope. Males can grow to almost two metres at the shoulder and weigh 700 kilograms; the older animals take on a 'blue' appearance as their hair thins out and their skin begins to show through their coats. Their twisted horns can be a metre long and are carried by both sexes.

Before European settlement, Eland occurred widely in South Africa, and on the Peninsula were described as 'common' along the Salt and Liesbeek rivers near Cape Town and at Hout Bay. Their remains have been found in prehistoric middens at the reserve, although it is likely that, as with the case of many other large mammals, they made only brief visits to the end of the Peninsula before moving on in search of more suitable food. Eland are predominantly browsers, although they will graze fresh grass.

More at home here, but generally solitary and not at all easy to see, are three species of small antelope – the Grysbok, Steenbok and Common Duiker. The last-named is particularly scarce, and we have encountered them only in the northern sector of the reserve in the Krom River valley. The other two species, which are only about 50 centimetres at shoulder height, may be seen more often and almost anywhere in the reserve, as they are active by day. The western arm of Circular Drive seems to be a good place for Steenbok, but as the vegetation grows they will doubtless become increasingly difficult to observe. The name 'Steenbok' means 'brick-coloured buck', which describes its rich, brown tones. 'Grysbok', on the other hand, means 'grey buck', and refers to the white hairs which give a grizzled appearance to their coats.

Described as 'Roebuck' by early settlers, the Grey Rhebok is not dissimilar in build to that European deer, but is greyish-brown on top and almost pure white underneath. There are a few small herds on the reserve, but they are

Mid-winter at the Cape of Good Hope – geelbos and blombos in full flower near Russouwskop.

retiring and not easy to see and, even when close to the roads, they blend into the rocky background. Rhebok feed selectively by browsing fresh growth, buds and flowers from fynbos shrubs, the most popular being *Metalasia muricata* and *Aspalathus*. The latter, interestingly, is able to 'fix' atmospheric nitrogen and therefore has a higher nitrogen content in its tissues than most other fynbos plants. It is a favoured food of buck and is, in consequence, one of very few fynbos plants which have spines to deter browsers. The reserve's Rhebok also eat a few grasses, but these make a relatively small contribution to the overall diet, which comprises at least 77 plant species.

The distribution of the antelope species is influenced, to one extent or another, by fire, providing as it does fresh plant growth. Burning also has more radical effects on mammals, and is a key factor in regulating the numbers and distribution of mice at the reserve. The study by Professor Jenny Jarvis has provided insight into the rise and fall of the rodent empire. The 1991 fire resulted, not unexpectedly, in a sharp drop in their numbers. This is attributable not just to mortality, but to the removal of food and shelter, which obliges the mice to move out. Fire survival is highest in rocky areas, where the mice can escape the flames by retreating under stones. In 1992 a dramatic increase in the numbers of Pygmy Mice was recorded. This species has a high breeding rate, and its tendency to wander results in its being one of the first to colonise areas of regenerating vegetation. Two years after the fire there was an increase in

vegetation productivity, possibly a function of the nutrients which had been released by the fire now being incorporated into the regenerating plants. This, in turn, was reflected in a rise in the numbers of small mammals, particularly Striped Mice, which had by this stage increased by 80 per cent from their immediate post-fire levels. Small mammal recovery is, therefore, a relatively speedy process and, in general, the post-fire period witnesses a succession from a Pygmy Mouse pioneer community to a Striped Mouse climax community.

Fire is not the only hazard which the rodents face in fynbos. A variety of predators, including birds of prey such as Rock Kestrel (p. 77) and Blackshouldered Kite, and carnivorous mammals such as genets and mongooses, is constantly on the hunt for them. Although we have seen a Caracal bring down a Grysbok, the bulk of its diet at the reserve is probably made up of mice and other small animals. For a cat traditionally considered to be nocturnal, we are surprised at how often we have seen them by day, not least the one which paced nonchalantly along the roadside near the Homestead, unbothered by the traffic. Some of the reserve staff have been lucky enough to see Caracals and their kittens walking along the roads in broad daylight! When it stalks prey, the highest points of the Caracal are its shoulders and hips, with the body slung between like the span of a suspension bridge. The burst of speed which terminates a protracted stalk is unnerving, particularly for the victim.

The Caracal is the top predator at the reserve and probably does quite well here in the absence of potential competitors such as Leopard and Black-backed Jackal, both of which occurred in the past. Some dietary overlap is likely with the few Cape Foxes which live here, although the fox eats insects as well as small mammals. It is not known how many Caracal there are, but the population, like that of most other animals, is self-regulating: if there is enough food for them, they will thrive; if times are lean, their numbers will decline correspondingly.

Agamas and Cape Crocodiles

A final group of animals to look for in Inland Fynbos is one whose members will certainly see you, even if you don't see them. These are the lizards. On warm days at any time of year, almost every rock will have an extra ridge on it, in the form of an Agama or a Black Zonure Lizard (also known as the 'Kaapse Krokodil'). These are the most conspicuous of the reserve's 11 lizard species. The others are either subterranean (such as the

Lobelia pinifolia

Golden Sand Lizard) or extremely fast-moving and not likely to linger while you watch them. The Agama, or 'koggelmannetjie', in spring is a most striking reptile. The male's head can be brilliant turquoise, and a narrow stripe of this colour runs down his back. This is his courtship and nuptial dress; at other times of year (and at all times in the case of the female) it is the colour of the sandstone.

The Black Zonure Lizard shares the same rocky habitat as the Agama, and often the two will perch side by side with no apparent antipathy. The former does indeed look like a diminutive, black, scaly crocodile, but as they only grow to about 20 centimetres, the resemblance is a distant one!

This brief foray through Inland Fynbos has, we hope, given you a taste of what you can find here. Although not apparent at first, it is an immensely rich and exciting environment and worthy of more than a cursory glance from a speeding car as you head for the Point. The secret of enjoying fynbos is: take time and think small.

Cape Sugarbird Promerops cafer
on the protea-and erica-covered
slopes of Teeberg.

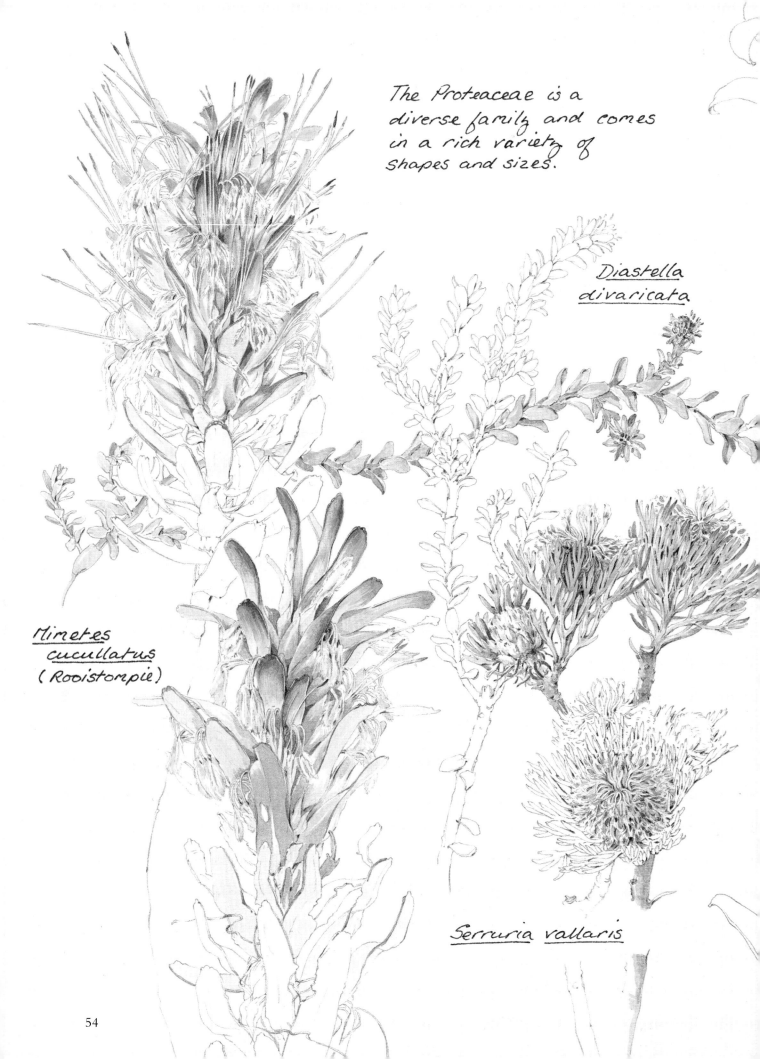

The Proteaceae is a
diverse family and comes
in a rich variety of
shapes and sizes.

Diastella
divaricata

Mimetes
cucullatus
(Rooistompie)

Serruria vallaris

54

Leucadendron coniferum ♀

Protea repens
(Suikerbossie)

55

Erica decora
(Klokkiesheide)

Erica
patersonia
Mealie Heath

Erica spumosa
(Swartbekkie)

56

Erica curviflora
Water Heath

Erica capitata
(Kapokkie)

Erica cerinthoides
Fire Heath

Six of the almost
forty species of Erica
found on the reserve

57

Restios and sedges
are widespread and
abundant on the reserve.
Many species flower in
winter.

At least seventy members
of the pea family, Fabaceae,
grow on the reserve.

Aspalathus sp.
flowers and
ripening fruits

Fountain Bush
Psoralea pinnata
(Bloukeur)

Rafnia sp.

Phaenocoma
prolifera

(Rooisewejaartjie)

Edmondia
sesamoides

(Strooiblommetjie)

Drifts of white everlastings,
like snow in summer,
blanket the landscape.

Helichrysum vestitum
Cape Everlasting
(Sewejaartjie)

60

Many moths flittering
around on this
warm October day.

Heady Maiden
Syntomis cerbera

African Hummingbird Hawk-Moth
Macroglossum _trochilus_

One of six blue spider orchids
Bartholina _burmanniana_
tucked in amongst restios
by the Olifantsbos road
at Menskop.

61

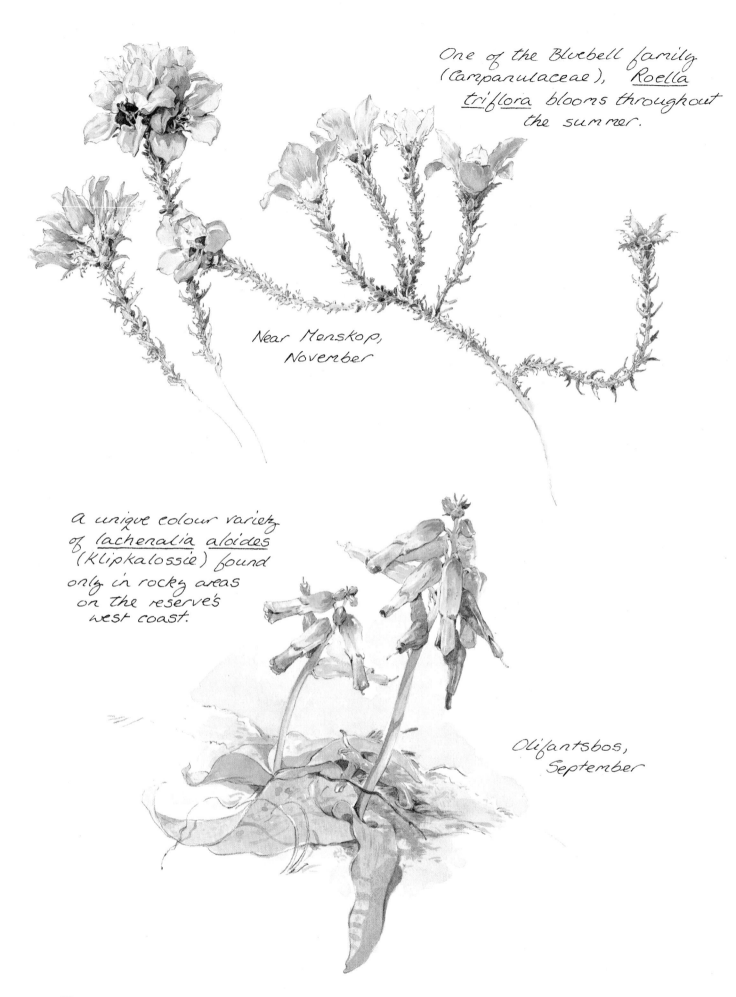

One of the Bluebell family (Campanulaceae), _Roella triflora_ blooms throughout the summer.

Near Menskop, November

A unique colour variety of _lachenalia aloides_ (Klipkalossie) found only in rocky areas on the reserve's west coast.

Olifantsbos, September

The curious Cat's Claws
<u>Hyobanche</u> <u>sanguinea</u> is a
parasite which obtains all its
nourishment from the roots of
other plants.

Klein Blouberg,
August

Reserve boundary, north
of Klaasjagersberg.

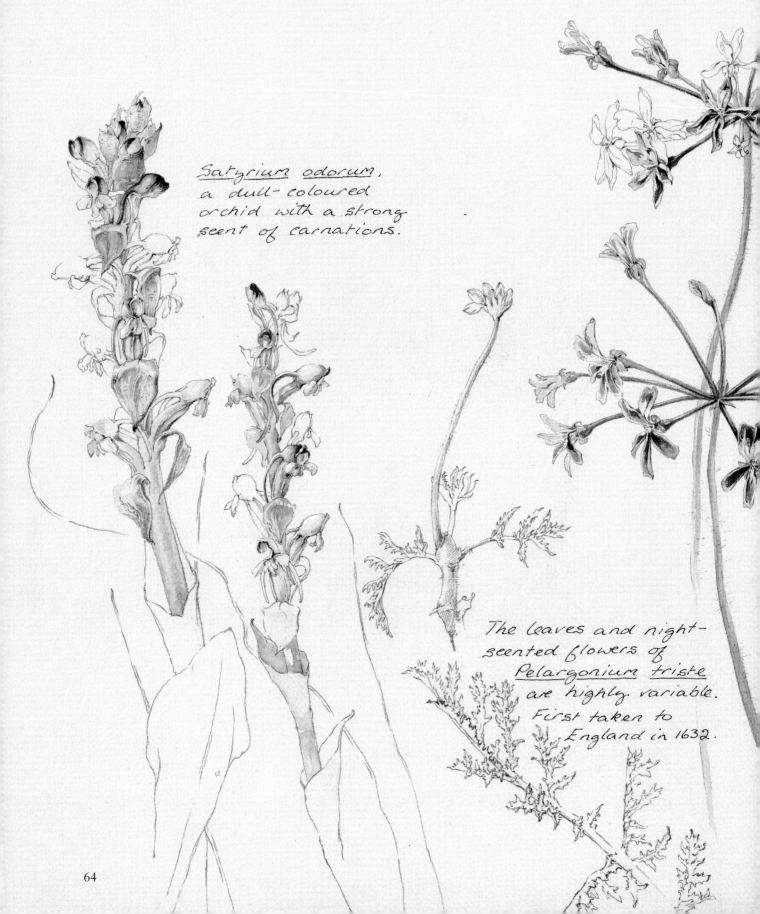

Satyrium odorum,
a dull-coloured
orchid with a strong
scent of carnations.

The leaves and night-
scented flowers of
Pelargonium triste
are highly variable.
First taken to
England in 1632.

Satyrium coriifolium
flowers from august to
December. It grows up
to 75 cm in height.

Disa cornuta occurs
widely in southern Africa.
This spectacular orchid
can grow up to a metre high.
Circular Drive, October.

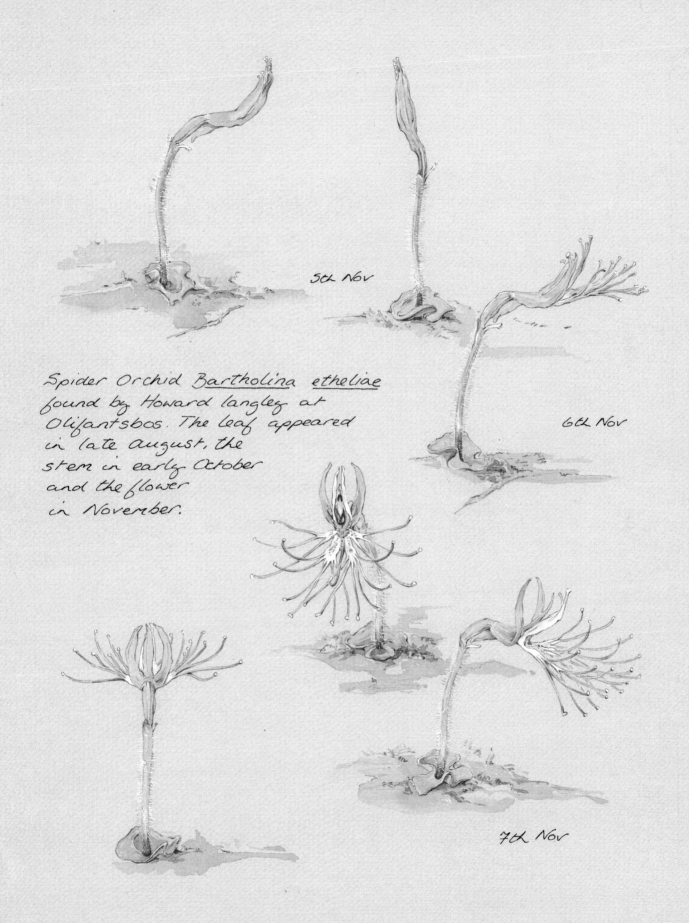

5th Nov

6th Nov

Spider Orchid _Bartholina_ _etheliae_
found by Howard Langley at
Olifantsbos. The leaf appeared
in late August, the
stem in early October
and the flower
in November.

7th Nov

The sticky flowers of
Saltera sarcocolla
(vlieebos) are visited by
sunbirds and long-
proboscid flies.
  Dias Monument, July.

Acrolophia bolusii
An easily overlooked
orchid. Theefontein,
October.

Two of our favourite
spring orchids, the tiny
Schizodium obliquum
and _Disperis capensis_
(Moederkappie)
Circular Drive, August.

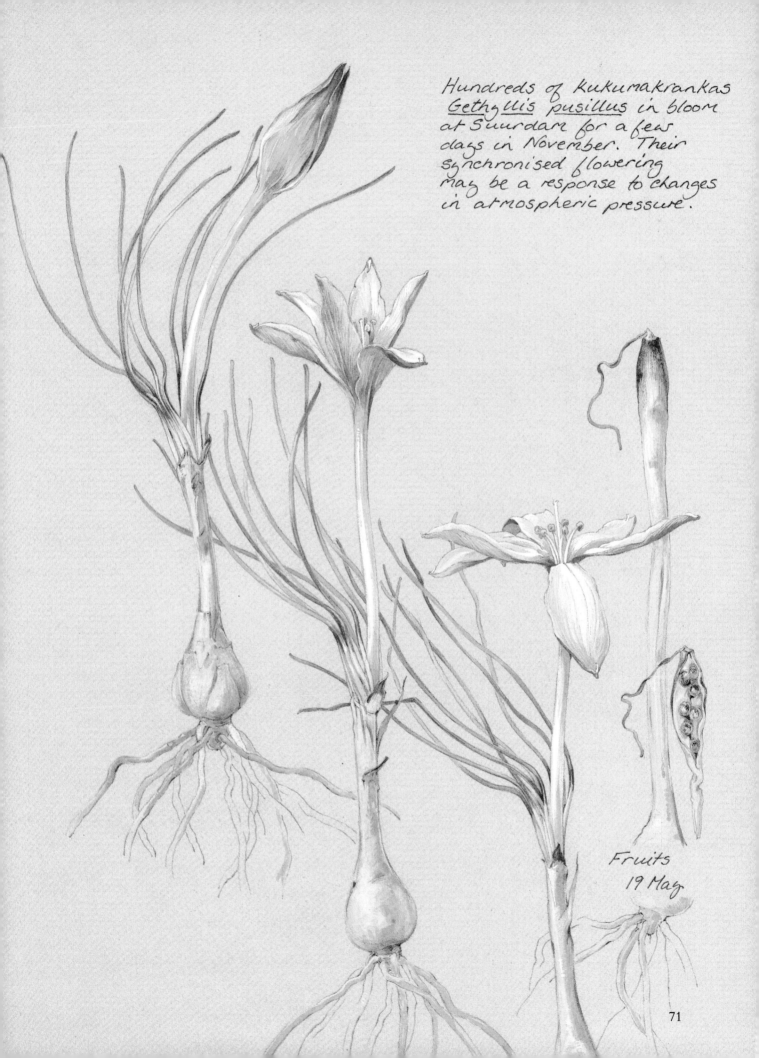

Hundreds of kukumakrankas
Gethyllis pusillus in bloom
at Suurdam for a few
days in November. Their
synchronised flowering
may be a response to changes
in atmospheric pressure.

Fruits
19 May

71

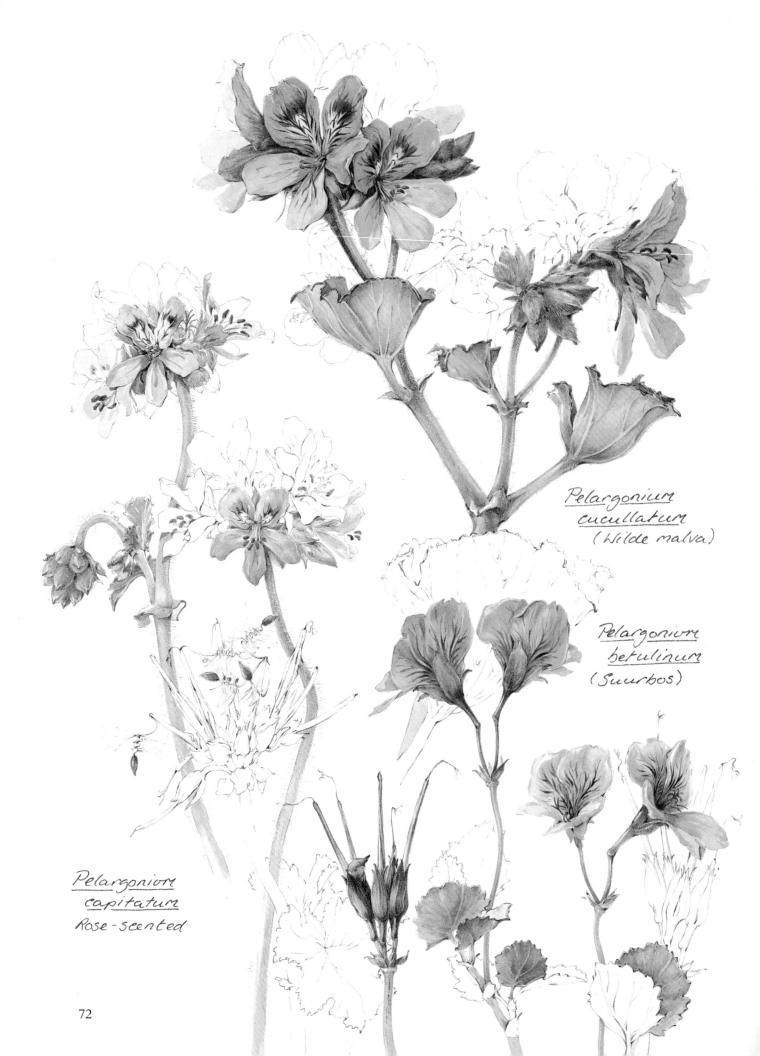

*Pelargonium
cucullatum*
(Wilde malva)

*Pelargonium
betulinum*
(Suurbos)

*Pelargonium
capitatum*
Rose-scented

72

Pelargonium longifolium amongst
restios. A summer flowering species,
particularly numerous after fire
when it resprouts from an underground
tuber.   Dassiefontein, November.

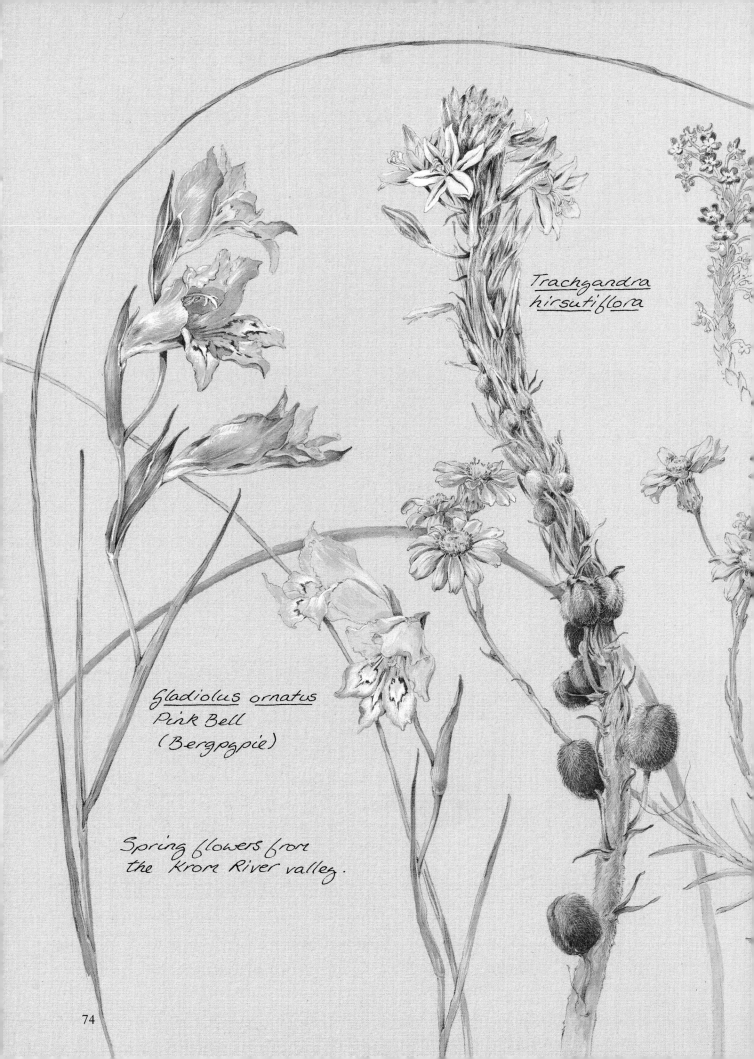

Trachyandra
hirsutiflora

Gladiolus ornatus
Pink Bell
(Bergpypie)

Spring flowers from
the Krom River valley.

74

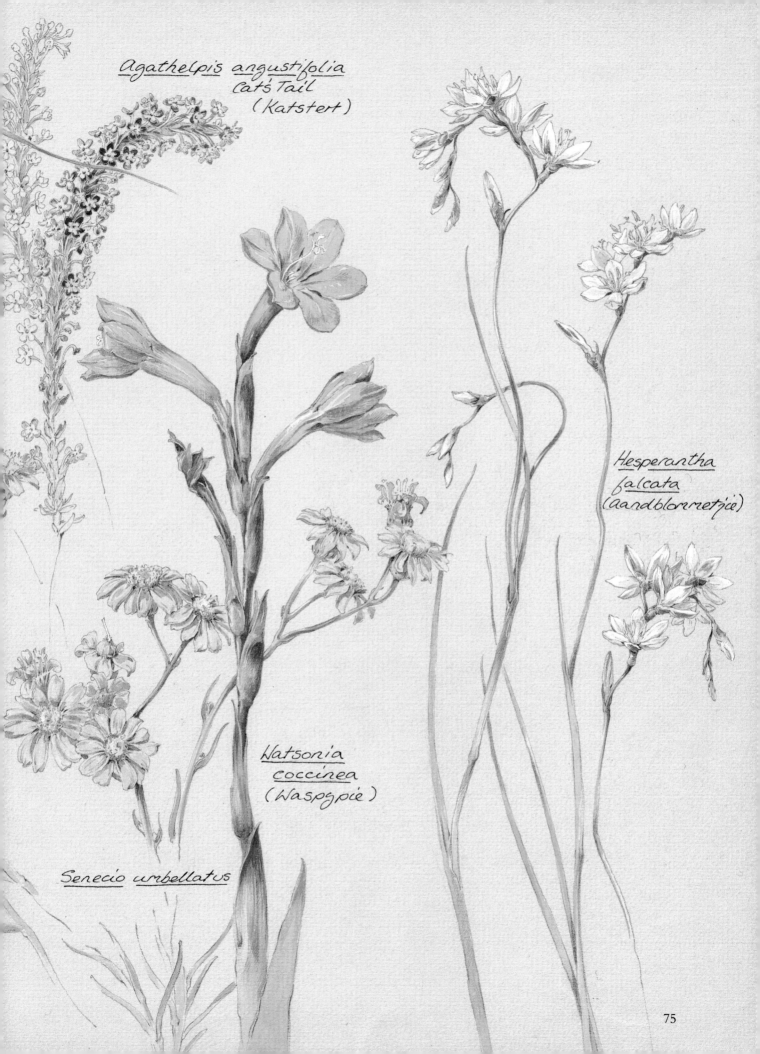

Agathelpis angustifolia
Cat's Tail
(Katstert)

Hesperantha
falcata
(aardblommetjie)

Watsonia
coccinea
(Waspypie)

Senecio umbellatus

Yellow Ixia or Geelkalossie
<u>Ixia dubia</u>. One of the iris
family, flowering in spring
and early summer.

A burnt-out pincushion
bush provides a convenient perch
for this Rock Kestrel
Falco tinnunculus
(Kransvalk)

Above: A Candelabra in flower on the old dunes between Buffels Bay and Bordjiesrif.
Below: Dune Fynbos on the west coast near Klein Rondevlei with Olifantsbos Point in the distance to the south.

CHAPTER FOUR

Bulbuls, Berries and Baboons

Plants and Animals of Dunes, Thicket and Forest

In this chapter we describe some of the wildlife you can find in 'Coast Fynbos'. The visitor who drives straight to the Point and back again will not experience a great deal, if any, of the plants and animals of this habitat. A little time spent walking along a coastal trail, or even simply driving to the Cape of Good Hope, Buffels Bay or Olifantsbos, will, however, allow you to enjoy many of its natural charms.

We have chosen also to describe here the reserve's 'woodlands' and its only (and very small) natural forest. The former are, more accurately, thickets. They occur in small coastal strips and pockets bounded by Coast Fynbos along their seaward edge, and Inland Fynbos on their landward. In their broadest sense, the thickets and their associated plants may be collectively termed strandveld. As 'beach bush', this is as good a name for it as any and has, like many Afrikaans words, become part of the Cape's English lexicon.

Together, the Coast Fynbos and thickets occupy 1,385 hectares, or about 18 per cent of the land area of the reserve. Their combined distribution is illustrated on the accompanying map. In your exploration of them you will also visit some of the most scenic areas of the reserve – the view from Gifkommetjie, for example, is magnificent; the coastal walk to Olifantsbos Point, one of the prettiest in the Peninsula. A flavour of these habitats will complement your enjoyment of Inland Fynbos, and further emphasise the richness and beauty of the Cape of Good Hope Nature Reserve.

Wild Rosemary and the Gorgon's Head

Coast Fynbos is not simply vegetation found at the coast. It occurs on dunes built of sand that has been blown from the beaches which we see today, or from beaches which existed many thousands of years ago when the sea level was lower. Coast Fynbos can be found in predictable places, such as the hummocky dunes at Platboom and the coastal strip at Olifantsbos, and the more unusual, notably inland on the old, hardened dune which stretches northwest from Buffels Bay.

Coast Fynbos, like its inland counterpart, is made up of a variety of plant communities. The most extensive of these is classified as '*Eriocephalus* Coast-shelf Fynbos and Dune Mixed Fynbos'. It is found along almost the entire length of the reserve's west coast (with the exception of a brief interruption at Gifkommetjie), and on the east coast it occurs at the Meadows and from Buffels Bay north to about Venus Pool. Its soils are composed of shell-sand, as one would expect, and vary in texture. The amount of humus is low in the younger dunes but higher in the older, inland dunes. In some areas the southeaster has whipped off the thin top-soil to expose limestone underneath.

Below: Fynbos and Broad-leaved Thicket occur around much of the reserve's coastline and on the old dune which runs across Rietveld from Buffels Bay.

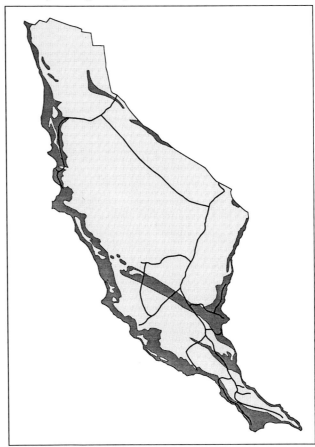

Dried umbel and germinating seeds of the Candelabra Flower.

The qualifier of Coast-shelf Fynbos is *Eriocephalus*, the Wild Rosemary, a shrub with grey, aromatic foliage and cascades of pretty white flowers in winter and spring. The seed heads comprise soft, fluffy pappi which are gathered by birds to provide a warm lining to their nests. Spotted Prinias are great gatherers of this *kapok*; after their chicks have fledged, the nest deteriorates and the seeds fall to the ground. This is an ingenious way of dispersing seeds.

To see just how splendid are the Wild Rosemary and fellow members of this vegetation type, visit the *Thomas T. Tucker* coastal trail at Olifantsbos Bay. Just to the south of the car park, the path leads through a delightful rock-garden cum shrubbery, with wind-clipped rosemarys hugging the boulders and stately stands of *Thamnochortus* reeds lining the route. Blombos and Gonnabos crowd together here, and winter's purple patches of flowering Tortoiseberry are laden with luscious fruits in summer (pp. 96–97). This fruit is eaten not only by tortoises, but by birds such as Cape Bulbuls and Redwinged Starlings. It was doubtless also enjoyed by the original human inhabitants of the reserve, but the first written appraisal of it comes to us from Simon van der Stel. In his journal of 1685 he wrote that the plant 'bears a sort of cherry, pleasant and clean tasting, cooling to the health, thirst-quenching and very welcome to the traveller'. A description which would do credit to a wine as much as a berry!

Another splash of orange is provided here in late summer by the Pig's Ear, a fleshy-leaved member of the crassula family whose pendulous blooms are visited by Lesser Doublecollared Sunbirds. The sunbird clings to the vertical stem and extracts the nectar from each floret with its curved beak (p. 101), and at the same time has its forehead feathers dusted with pollen. The male is very striking in breeding plumage; his mate at all times is a subdued grey-brown.

Further along, the path reaches an old raised boulder-beach which, like the shrubbery, Capability Brown could not have designed more beautifully. The awkward angles of individual rough-cut stones combine to make a crazy-paving that somehow does not jar the eye, even if it does wobble the knees. Over and through the rocks creep the solid, stunted boughs of trees with lofty yearnings but no defence against searing salt-spray. Milkwoods and Hottentot's Cherry are among the would-be noble trees doomed to the horizontal for a hundred years and more.

Taking us back much more than a century, to Greek legend, is a curious plant growing amongst the rocks and beside the path. This is the Gorgon's Head Euphorbia (p. 103), a succulent species with thickened, knobbly stems. Its whorl of red buds and small, pale flowers around their tips must have reminded someone of Medusa's serpentine locks. The euphorbias flow with a poisonous milky latex when damaged, an exudate which is reputedly highly irritable to mucous membranes. So it is surprising that the squat clumps of Gorgon's Head are champed enthusiastically by the Eland with no apparent ill effects.

The limestone outcrops at Black Rocks, which represent an uncommon constituent of Coast-shelf Fynbos, support some interesting plants. A selection of these is illustrated on pp. 98–99. The brilliant red flowers of Cancer Bush (so called because of a traditional belief that it cured this disease) develop into inflated sausage-like seed pods. These split in the sunshine, an action which catapults the seeds from their parent, or else the pods break off and are buffeted around in the wind, scattering the seeds. Its scientific name, *Sutherlandia*, commemorates James Sutherland who, at the turn of the seventeenth century, was the first superintendent of the Edinburgh Botanic Garden.

The grassy coastal foreland below the Booi se Skerm caves is the place to see the April Fool Flower. This is a member of the genus *Haemanthus*, which has over 20 species, two of which occur at the reserve. The enormous leaves appear in winter, but wither into sizeable popadums over the summer. The rhubarb-like spotted stalks emerge in autumn, and the flowers bloom in March and April (p. 104). When the watery fruits ripen, the stem leans over until it all but lies on the ground. This did not seem, to us, to be caused simply by the weight of the crop. An Angulate Tortoise eating fruits which had been lowered to the ground in this way seemed to provide an explanation for the phenomenon. If it is a deliberate strategy, there cannot be many plants which have adopted the slow, but presumably reliable, tortoise as a seed disperser. After the fruits have been eaten or the unlucky ones have rotted away, new leaves appear. The uninitiated person who finds these leaves and waits expectantly for a flower to pop up in a day or two will have a long vigil. Hence the April Fool!

Dune flowers

The popular impression of dunes, as dry, sandy and unstable, does not portray them as the most friendly places for plants. But dunes come in various shapes and sizes and, what is important, age. Dunes which have been recently formed are very loose, have very little humus in them, and are unable to support much plant-life. A walk across the dune plume at Platboom will demonstrate this convincingly. Here is a dune which is still on the move, creeping up the valley and extending outwards along its edges with the perpetual addition of wind-blown sand from the beach to the southeast. In some sheltered spots, however, the fringes of such juvenile dunes are colonised by various grasses, whose stems and leaves are often half-buried with fresh sand. But this is the first step in stabilisation, and if this process continues successfully, other species can move in. An efficient stabiliser is the succulent Sour Fig (p. 105), which forms thick, fleshy mats that trap and bind the wind-blown sand. So effective is it in this task that it and its near-relatives have been introduced to countries around the world where drifting sand is a problem.

Dunes which have thrown up the travel bug and settled down, as it were, support a distinctive and much richer flora than the young dunes. The ancient, hardened calcrete-topped dunes of the reserve have often retained their typically hummocky aspect, but have accumulated a good depth of soil, often with a high compost content, and been colonised by plants which are collectively termed 'Dune Mixed Fynbos'. A low, fine-leaved shrubby vegetation with spikes of restios emerging from the bushes, it is characterised on the coast by Blombos, Waxberry and *Phylica ericoides*. Our favourite pelargonium also occurs here, and we visit the coastal flats around Die Mond each spring to pay it our respects. This is *Pelargonium betulinum*, the Birch-leaved Pelargonium (*betula* being the birch tree of northern climes), and its large, purple flowers (p. 72) make the most splendid sight when a hundred or so plants are in full bloom together. An equally attractive white-flowered variety occurs, but we have not yet seen it at the reserve. As a garden plant, *P. betulinum* has few rivals and is far superior, in our estimation, to the ornamental pelargonium hybrids (it does cross naturally in the wild with *P. cucullatum*). It is visited by long-nosed tabanid flies and, occasionally, by Orangebreasted Sunbirds, although the latter are unlikely to be effective pollinators in this instance.

Where the old dune ventures cross-country, traversing the reserve from the Homestead to Rietveld, there is a gradual transition from coastal to inland plant species. A characteristic plant here is *Thamnochortus erectus*, a tall reed still harvested (not at the reserve!) for thatching. Also common, but preferring deep sand, is the conebush *Leucadendron coniferum*. As you drive over the extended humps, the old

Wild Rosemary
*Eriocephalus
africanus*

dunes, on the southeastern section of Circular Drive, you pass through a little forest of these attractive members of the protea family. These are nicely proportioned, rounded shrubs growing up to three metres high and with bright-red seed-cones ripening in autumn.

The dunes provide a lovely display of flowers in springtime. Annuals include senecios, gazanias, nemesias, oxalis and Bokbaaivygies (Livingstone Daisies). These and many more put on a particularly good spring display after fire. At this time the bulbs can also be impressive – the Rietveld dune is a good spot for the strikingly elegant *Moraea tripetala*, the blue-and-white starry *Lapeirousia corymbosa*, and the exquisitely perfumed *Babiana ambigua*. We are not the only ones to enjoy the fine qualities of the last-named species. Its scientific name, *Babiana*, is unusual in being the only botanical one to be drawn from Afrikaans. *Bobbejaan* is a baboon, and the flower is popularly known as the Bobbejaantjie in recognition of the baboons' liking for the bulbs.

Creeping along in this habitat is the prostrate protea *Leucospermum hypophyllocarpodendron hypophyllocarpodendron*, whose common name, Green Snake-stem Pincushion, is not much less intimidating. This has an attractive growth form, creating little low-growing mats and clumps, from which snake out serpent-like shoots and small branches topped with upright leaves. In spring the bright-yellow pincushion-like inflorescences burst from hard, purplish buds. The flowers are yeasty-scented and may be pollinated by mice, although they are also visited by ants. Another creeper, though less robust than the

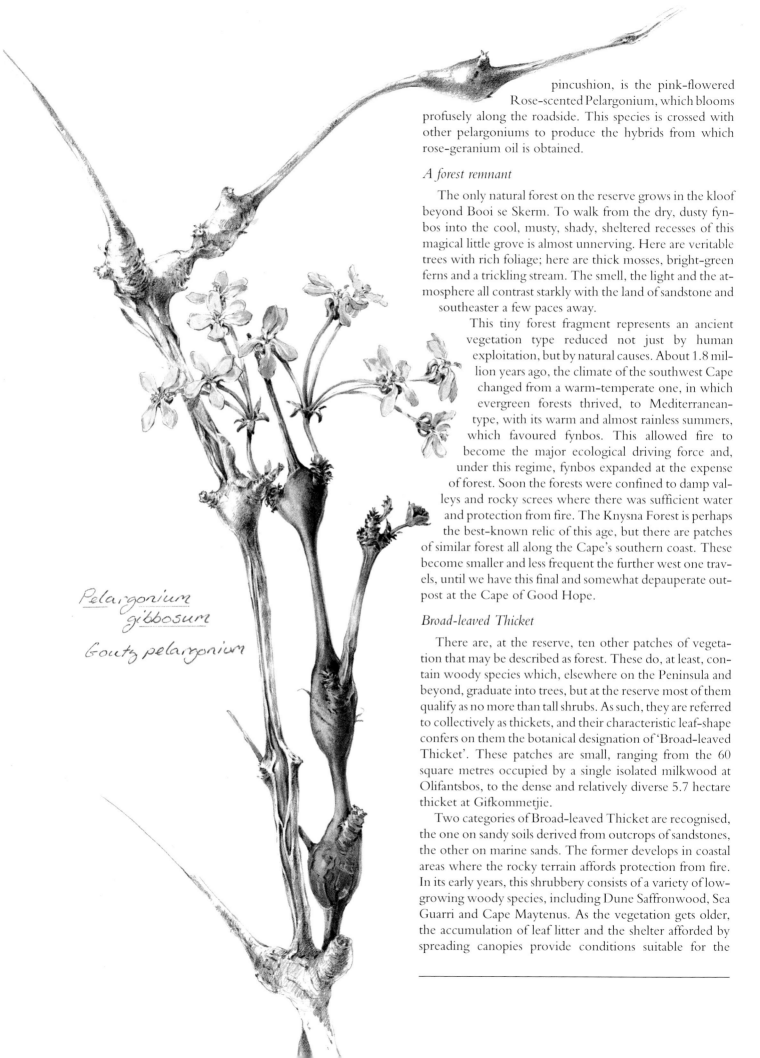

Pelargonium
gibbosum

Goutg pelargonium

pincushion, is the pink-flowered Rose-scented Pelargonium, which blooms profusely along the roadside. This species is crossed with other pelargoniums to produce the hybrids from which rose-geranium oil is obtained.

A forest remnant

The only natural forest on the reserve grows in the kloof beyond Booi se Skerm. To walk from the dry, dusty fynbos into the cool, musty, shady, sheltered recesses of this magical little grove is almost unnerving. Here are veritable trees with rich foliage; here are thick mosses, bright-green ferns and a trickling stream. The smell, the light and the atmosphere all contrast starkly with the land of sandstone and southeaster a few paces away.

This tiny forest fragment represents an ancient vegetation type reduced not just by human exploitation, but by natural causes. About 1.8 million years ago, the climate of the southwest Cape changed from a warm-temperate one, in which evergreen forests thrived, to Mediterranean-type, with its warm and almost rainless summers, which favoured fynbos. This allowed fire to become the major ecological driving force and, under this regime, fynbos expanded at the expense of forest. Soon the forests were confined to damp valleys and rocky screes where there was sufficient water and protection from fire. The Knysna Forest is perhaps the best-known relic of this age, but there are patches of similar forest all along the Cape's southern coast. These become smaller and less frequent the further west one travels, until we have this final and somewhat depauperate outpost at the Cape of Good Hope.

Broad-leaved Thicket

There are, at the reserve, ten other patches of vegetation that may be described as forest. These do, at least, contain woody species which, elsewhere on the Peninsula and beyond, graduate into trees, but at the reserve most of them qualify as no more than tall shrubs. As such, they are referred to collectively as thickets, and their characteristic leaf-shape confers on them the botanical designation of 'Broad-leaved Thicket'. These patches are small, ranging from the 60 square metres occupied by a single isolated milkwood at Olifantsbos, to the dense and relatively diverse 5.7 hectare thicket at Gifkommetjie.

Two categories of Broad-leaved Thicket are recognised, the one on sandy soils derived from outcrops of sandstones, the other on marine sands. The former develops in coastal areas where the rocky terrain affords protection from fire. In its early years, this shrubbery consists of a variety of low-growing woody species, including Dune Saffronwood, Sea Guarri and Cape Maytenus. As the vegetation gets older, the accumulation of leaf litter and the shelter afforded by spreading canopies provide conditions suitable for the establishment of Hottentot's Cherry and Fine-leaved Iron-wood. It is these two species which characterise and ultimately dominate this community, and which can be seen to best effect at Gifkommetjie. Here a hiking trail leads you down the slope out of the fynbos and into the coastal thicket.

Gifkommetjie supports the highest number of 'forest' species (15) at the reserve. So dense is the vegetation that some of the paths are completely overcanopied. In this dark and gloomy setting there is little ground cover, apart from a dappling of small glades where the sun can penetrate and in which a few grasses and flowers grow. Entwining the branches are climbers such as Haakdoring and Monkey Rope, while scrambling along the lower levels is the Gouty Pelargonium. This is an odd pelargonium, not at all like the other members of its group. Along its woody stems are swollen nodes, whose function, it has been postulated, is either to store water or to act as chocks that lodge the scrambler in the branches of the supporting shrub. For many years this particular pelargonium perplexed and intrigued us. It was an easy plant to find, but it took us an age to discover one in flower. It is not a showy flower, at least compared with other pelargoniums, but the colour is unusual, and a pleasant scent is released after sunset, presumably because its pollinators are nocturnal insects. The painting here is of this first flower that we found.

The venerable milkwood

The Broad-leaved Thicket which grows on marine sands is dominated by White Milkwood. A milkwood thicket is the pinnacle of a long and laborious development. Where the Dune Fynbos, with its restios and Birch-leaved Pelargoniums, is not burnt and replaced by an infant version of itself, it is gradually usurped by strandveld shrubs such as Cape Sumach, Coastal Olive and Cherrywood, with Bitou and Blombos dotted amongst them. With the passing years these are, in turn, invaded and ultimately overcanopied by milkwood. The very oldest milkwood thickets comprise almost pure stands of this species, with only a few straggly Coast Cabbage Trees to break the monopoly, and very few plants growing on the shaded floor.

The handsome, slow-growing, evergreen milkwood is one of South Africa's most celebrated trees. It is almost exclusively coastal in its distribution, and occurs from the Cape Peninsula east and north to Zimbabwe. At the reserve it rarely exceeds the proportions of a large shrub; elsewhere it may attain 10 metres. It seems to have a somewhat erratic flowering and fruiting schedule, although these generally take place in the first and second half of the year, respectively. Not all plants bloom at the same time, however. The flowers are rather insignificant and greeny-white in colour. What the milkwood in full bloom lacks in terms of spectacle is compensated for with a powerful pong. Insects, particularly kelp flies from the nearby beaches, throng to the malodorous flowers; insect-eating birds, in turn, do likewise. The fruits are green at first, ripening to an attrac-

tive purplish-black (p. 174).

Some stunted milkwoods grow at a scattering of inland sites, a kilometre or two from the coast. Here these almost bonsai-like shrubs are cramped into rocky crevices and crannies, protected from fire, and below perches where frugivorous birds have offloaded their seed-packed droppings. Indeed, the birds might be responsible not only for delivering the seed, but for fertilising the soil with the droppings which accumulate below a traditional perch or roost. This so enriches the impoverished fynbos soil that it is able to sustain the strandveld species. Once these species are established, the leaf litter begins to build up and more birds come to strip the fruits and deposit their droppings, thus creating and perpetuating little islands of strandveld in an ocean of fynbos.

More typically, milkwood is a coastal species, with thickets providing shelter and shade for picnickers at Buffels Bay, Bordjiesrif and Platboom (the wind-cropped bushes are the inspiration for the last-named – 'Flat tree'). Some fine old specimens grace the dunes by the Buffels River. Old and gnarled, they carry the scars of past fires and the woodman's axe, but have survived. Most of the reserve's milkwoods have not been so lucky, and the historical majority have probably been felled. The wood is tough and solid (*Sideroxylon*, its scientific name, is Greek for 'iron wood'). Those trees unsuitable for timber would have been used as fuel for the limekilns or domestic fires, and any regeneration

Ruschia Sarmentosa

thwarted by frequent veld fires and browsing by stock. Given the opportunity, however, milkwoods can live to a great age. Perhaps the oldest, and certainly the most famous, South African milkwood, and one which we may mention for its connection with the Cape of Good Hope, is the venerable 'Post Office Tree' at Mossel Bay on the Cape south coast. In 1500 the spot was visited by the surviving ships of Pedro Alvares Cabral's ill-fated fleet. One of the sailors wrote a letter describing the loss of Dias off the Cape and 'posted' the message in a shoe tied to a milkwood tree. The message was addressed to João da Nova, and it was he, we are told, who discovered it there the following year. Subsequently, the tree was adopted as poste restante by generations of passing seamen. The tree is estimated to be 600 years old and has been declared a National Monument.

The milkwoods at Olifantsbos are a relic of what must have been an extensive thicket, cleared to make way for cultivation. The remaining bushes have a low, humped appearance. From a distance, and with a little imagination, they resemble a herd of large animals. At least this is the only explanation we can offer for the name Olifantsbos, being Elephant Bush or Forest. There do not appear to be any records of elephants from the reserve in the period since European contact, although they were reported from further up the west coast where, unlike Olifantsbos, the Olifants River can ascribe its name to a herd of these animals.

Forest fires

Coastal thicket owes its existence largely to the protection from fire afforded it by the rocky escarpments and outcrops and the succulent nature of the smaller plants which form its lower layers or grow around its fringes. Its constituent species do not, in general, burn easily, but they do take a long time to graduate from the sapling stage to a size at which they can survive the passage of a fire. (This they do by re-sprouting from stem buds and from underground rootstocks. The multi-stemmed nature of many of the old milkwoods, for example, is evidence that they have been through a fire or two.) Furthermore, many fire-free years are required to establish the conditions (such as a deep, peaty seed-bed) necessary for some species to colonise an area. Given the early history of exploitation and frequent burning of the reserve, it is not surprising that this vegetation type should be so scarce.

More was the pity, therefore, when the fire of 1991 roared over the escarpment and blazed through the thickets at Gifkommetjie, Olifantsbos and elsewhere along the west coast. The resultant scene was a gloomy one, with many fine old milkwoods and Hottentot's Cherry transformed to blackened skeletons, and most of the smaller woody shrubs reduced to ashes. Visiting Olifantsbos two weeks after the fire, we were startled to see a large and unscorched shrub suddenly burst into flames. This was caused, we discovered, by the thick layer of peat which had continued to smoulder and, every now and then, became hot

Flowering vygies amongst the milkwood at Olifantsbos Bay.

enough to rekindle the flames and incinerate yet another bush. The loss of this deep compost, with its nutrients and water-retaining capacity, was particularly worrying in terms of the re-establishment of the thicket. Over the following months we followed the recovery, or otherwise, of the plants. Quite a few bushes re-sprouted vigorously with the onset of the winter rains, but the fire had been so intense that many of the largest milkwoods had been so damaged that neither their rootstocks nor stem buds had survived.

A bird in the bush

The shrubs and small trees were not the only casualties of the fire, of course. All the animals which live in the thicket had not only lost a home but, in many cases, had doubtless also succumbed. This habitat is relatively rich in birds, but these at least would have been able to escape the conflagration by flying off. One of our Olifantsbos-ringed Fiscal Flycatchers made an appearance five kilometres away at Scarborough shortly after the fire, but the majority of our ringed bush-birds have not been seen again.

An idea of the kinds of birds which inhabit coastal thicket, and the densities at which they occur, was obtained from observations we made over two years in a study plot at Olifantsbos. At the time, the vegetation was at least thirty years old, and comprised fairly dense growths of typical shrubs such as Cape Myrtle, Taaibos, Bastard Saffronwood, Hottentot's Cherry and White Milkwood. To find any birds at all was pleasure indeed after the ornithological starvation of burnt-out Inland Fynbos. In the coastal thicket we discovered that not only were there more birds (which, at an average of 15 per hectare, is 136 times more than in old Restionaceous Plateau Fynbos!), but a different suite of species was involved. Here we never saw those denizens of the proteas and heaths, the Cape Sugarbird and Orange-breasted Sunbird, but found instead mousebirds and bulbuls, shrikes and doves, robins and warblers. The razor-sharp demarcation which we noted between the birds of fynbos and those of thicket was two-edged, and it was necessary to climb for only half a minute or so onto the escarpment above Olifantsbos to leave behind one avian realm and enter another. While the sugarbirds flittered around in the pincushions and proteas, in the thicket below the Bully Canaries could be heard twittering and the Boubous *boo-boo*-ing, but never would they or most of their cronies venture the few metres out of their chosen habitat and into the fynbos.

The most numerous bird at Olifantsbos was the Lesser Doublecollared Sunbird; our plot invariably contained one or two on each of our visits. Here the sunbird was not fulfilling its traditional role as a nectarivore, but feeding for the most part on insects and other invertebrates (an old Afrikaans name translates as 'spider hunter'). Many other species here are insectivorous, including Spotted Prinia and Fiscal Flycatcher. One of the most important food sources in coastal thicket is, however, fruit. Some of the typical shrubs which supply this bounty are illustrated on pp. 94–95. In addition to the specialised fruit-and-veg eaters, such as Speckled Mousebirds, other species with more catholic diets would arrive to feast from the berry-laden branches. Scores of Redwinged Starlings would descend, and up to a dozen Cape Bulbuls at a time would install themselves in a bearing milkwood. The presence of fleshy fruits and fruit-eating birds is one of the most notable ecological distinctions between fynbos and strandveld.

Birds and berries

Coastal thicket, as we have seen, displays a high incidence of shrubs which produce berries and, consequently, attracts a relatively high abundance of birds which feed on these. This contrasts strongly with fynbos vegetation, where berry-bearing plants are extremely scarce and frugivorous birds likewise. The fleshy fruit is a strategy adopted by plants to spread their seeds. To tempt the birds, the fruit must be conspicuous and wholesome in the health-shop way. A bird will not eat a fruit which is of no food value; conversely, a plant does not want to invest in its fruit more than the minimum amount of precious resources necessary to attract the

bird and persuade it to eat the fruit. Two soil nutrients – potassium and phosphorus – are important in the production of fleshy fruits. These elements are relatively abundant in strandveld, and the shrubs incorporate them into their fruits. In fynbos, on the other hand, potassium and phosphorus are not generally available in quantities great enough for the plant to produce a fruit which is sufficiently nutritious and saporous to attract birds. Is this what makes berry-bearing, bird-dispersed plants scarce in fynbos?

White Milkwood does grow in fynbos areas where protected from fire, as we have noted. Indeed, we have found quite a variety of fleshy-fruited shrubs, including Taaibos, Hottentot's Cherry and Sea Guarri, secreted in the most inhospitable cracks and crevices in the rocks along much

Protected by rocky outcrops, Broad-leaved Thicket at Olifantsbos has survived a fire, while the vegetation in the open has been burnt.

of the escarpment and inland on the plateau. It appears, therefore, that frequent fires are at least as much responsible for limiting the colonisation of fynbos by this group of plants as a shortage of nutrients.

Despite the abundance of berries in strandveld, we have been surprised by the often complete failure of birds to exploit this cornucopia. One is tempted to think that their absence is a consequence of the birds switching their attentions to the fruits of the alien Rooikrans, a situation which we contemplate in the last chapter. But whatever the reason, there have been times when the fruit-laden bushes at Olifantsbos have stood silent and ignored while their crops rotted on the branches.

A birder in the bush

The coastal thicket is the most attractive of the reserve's dry-land habitats to birds and, therefore, most profitable for birders. After an energy-sapping day trudging through the fynbos in search of anything feathered (a single bird in seven hours, and an LBJ at that, was our record), it was refreshing to pause awhile and enjoy the relative riches of strandveld. At Olifantsbos, little parties of Cape White-eyes *preepreep* their way through the foliage, gleaning insects and tweaking off berries. Boubous and Bokmakieries, those vociferous shrikes, sing from the thickets, scolded by Greybacked Cisticolas and Spotted Prinias. Causing greater consternation were the Redbreasted Sparrowhawks and African Goshawks, which glide overhead, on the hunt for an unwary dove. Certainly, strandveld is a noisier place than fynbos, at least as far as bird song is concerned. At Skaife, the Cape Robin was 'trumpet to the morn', and would signal the dawn and almost imperceptible lightening of the sky well before the sun had managed to drag itself out of bed and over the horizon. The robin has a rich, fluty song, much of it its own, but shamelessly borrowing phrases from other birds. Our resident robin not only mimicked about every other bush-bird that occurred in his patch, but did an impressive rendition of the African Black Oystercatcher's *klee-kleep* and the Greenshank's *teu-teu-teu*.

As the first rays strike the tops of the bushes, the Speckled Mousebirds clamber up branches and, with legs akimbo, orientate their 'furry' bellies towards the sun to absorb the warmth. With eyes half-closed, these crosses between a solar panel and a teddy bear bask in endothermic bliss until the pleasures of heat are exchanged for those of food, and off they fly.

A popular destination for the mousebirds is the Slangbessie. The buds which sprout from its dry, threadbare frame in autumn are eaten by the mousebirds and Bully Canaries; the flowers are probed by Lesser Doublecollared Sunbirds (and the not-much-smaller Hummingbird Hawk Moths and carpenter bees); and the brilliant fruits are relished by bulbuls and Redwinged Starlings, with the Bully Canaries coming in for a second course. The scientist who named this plant *Lycium ferocissimum* presumably did so on the basis of a nasty experience – the thorns are fiendishly (nay, ferociously) sharp.

Although the 30 species of birds we found in our Olifantsbos plot were an improvement on fynbos, we appreciate that coastal thicket further east along the coast is much richer. Milkwood thicket at De Hoop Nature Reserve (on the coast about 200 kilometres east of Cape Point) supported almost 50 species of birds, of which 17 were not found at Olifantsbos. Interestingly, however, the density of

birds at the two sites did not differ substantially. The habitats can, therefore, support the same numbers of birds; but with an increase in species richness (as found at De Hoop), the numbers of each individual species must decrease in order to accommodate the same overall total. The trend for species to drop from east to west along the coast, culminating at Cape Point, is a phenomenon that applies to trees as well as birds, and there is a general decline in species richness in the forest patches as one moves towards Cape Town along the south coast. Of the many true forest trees recorded at Knysna, for example, only one species (the Cape Beech) is found at the Cape of Good Hope Nature Reserve.

The most unusual avian visitor to our strandveld was a pair of Greater Scimitarbills, metallic-blue birds with sharply decurved beaks. These birds put in a somewhat fleeting appearance in October 1984, a mere one thousand kilometres south of their usual range, and not quite the species we had expected to see near the tip of the Peninsula. In a more local class of rarity, we have seen the likes of Barthroated Apalis and Longbilled Crombec here. In common with quite a few other birds, these are numerous and easy to see to the north of Cape Town and beyond, but are exceedingly rare at the reserve. Indeed, the apalis, which we have recorded only twice (including one bird caught and ringed at Skaife in October 1984, and last seen mobbing a Puff Adder at Olifantsbos the following April), qualifies for the same rarity league as the two scimitarbills! Such are the idiosyncrasies of Cape Point birding.

Serpents in the sand

Mention of a Puff Adder brings us conveniently to this and other reptiles. The snakes have not been studied in the same detail as the birds or the plants of the reserve, so we are unable to offer details of their distribution and abundance. Nevertheless, they are wide-ranging and it is unlikely that any species occurring in coastal areas are wholly confined to them. One is, however, much more likely to find a Mole Snake here than in the rocky inland areas. This is because this large, shiny, black species specialises in capturing Cape Dune Molerats, and enters their soft-sand burrows for this purpose. We have often come across a metre or so of Mole Snake protruding from a fresh mole heap, while the business end, oblivious of our spectating, patiently waits for the return of its quarry. Mole Snakes are not venomous (although the bite inflicted if you handle them carelessly may go septic) but kill their prey by constriction.

The Mole Snake is probably the largest of the snakes found at the reserve, and may exceed two metres. (Only the Cape Cobra approaches this length in this part of the world.) A particularly large, beautifully polished specimen frequents our mist-netting site at Olifantsbos. We have seen it innumerable times, but it still gives us the willies every time we stumble across it stretched out languorously amongst the grass. The species is viviparous, that is it gives birth to live young (as opposed to eggs). Some 30 to 50 snakelets, 20 or so centimetres long, are born in autumn.

The Cape Cobra may be mistaken for a Mole Snake, as both are dark-coloured. The cobra, however, comes in a variety of other shades. Those at the reserve range from pale golden-brown, yellowish with black mottles, through to the colour of rooibos tea or darker. This is a fast-moving reptile, always anxious to get out of your way, but potentially dangerous if encountered unexpectedly or if its escape route is blocked. Cobras may be seen anywhere on the reserve, although we have come across them (or they have come across us) most often in alien thickets and along the coastal belt.

Cape Cobras may come across you by accident, but the species which you are most likely to bump into involuntarily is the Puff Adder. We have reason to be grateful for the one at Olifantsbos which, despite my apparent single-minded determination to get bitten, has yet to even hiss in displeasure. My first encounter with this Puff Adder was when I joined her on a cliff ledge beside Die Kloof. I was there to investigate an old Hamerkop's nest, she to sunbathe. There might have been room for both of us if she had moved over a bit but, as the snake had prior claim, I didn't feel I could make an issue of it. On another occasion, I was pulling out aliens when the mottled form in the shade of the plant I was heaving transformed itself into the Puff Adder. Often since, we have confronted each other at more respectable distances, and she was once, and without any protest on her part, skilfully captured by Dr Terry Oatley to be admired and then released. Sadly, we have not seen her since the big fire, and fear she may have succumbed in that. Puff Adders are mainly nocturnal, when they hunt for rodents and amphibians, but are quite commonly seen crossing any of the reserve roads with their curious caterpillar crawl, or basking on the warm tarmac in the morning or late afternoon.

Notwithstanding our own experiences with a mild-mannered Puff Adder, which seem to contradict popular impressions of it as a bad-tempered beast, this is a dangerous snake and one for which visitors should be constantly on the lookout when walking through the veld. Its camouflage is effective, and if you are unfortunate to stand on one and get bitten, its venom is haemotoxic, with a dash of neurotoxicity, and potentially lethal.

A final species worth noting, and probably more at home in strandveld than fynbos, is one which is only occasionally seen above ground. This is the Dwarf Garter or Spotted Harlequin Snake (p. 102), a small, brightly coloured relative of the cobra and, like it, poisonous. Its diminutive gape

Lycium berries and stink bugs.

makes it unlikely that it could bite you or inject much venom, but one should not take chances. When confronted or pestered, it does not strike but wriggles furiously, a strategy which may serve to confuse a predator with a kaleidoscope of colours. It feeds on other small snakes which it captures underground. The spectacle of one swallowing a Delalande's Blind Snake hardly smaller than itself was morbidly compulsive.

The petal eater

The Angulate Tortoise is abundant at the reserve and, like most of the snakes, occurs in fynbos as well as coastal areas. We have gained the impression that these tortoises are more numerous in strandveld, though this may be a reflection of their greater conspicuousness here as they amble around the roads and feed on the verges. They are active on warm days at any time of year, seeking shade if the midday heat becomes oppressive. In spring they are faced with more fresh and succulent food than they know what to do with. This is the time of plenty, and although they will eat leaves, stems and fruits, it would appear that flower petals are most favoured. Yellow seems to attract the tortoises more than any other colour, for whatever reason, so the gazanias and other daisies with blooms of gold receive most attention (p. 96). In summer, the tortoises' diet must inevitably comprise mainly dry plant material. In February we have seen them eating dead grass at Olifantsbos, which looked singularly unappetising. But then dried grass is, after all, only hay and, as any horse will tell you, perfectly good food as long as you eat enough of it. The tortoises also eat dead animals and often make a meal of baboon droppings. The latter have a high nitrogen content and may appeal to the tortoise for this reason. One tortoise on the Link Road was seen to chew gravel chips which had loosened from the tarmac; presumably these also contained some desirable trace element or mineral.

Angulate Tortoises grow up to about 30 centimetres, the males being the larger of the sexes. Procuring a mate can be quite a vigorous affair, the males using their gular shield (that part of the shell which projects below their necks) to ram and overturn rivals. The victor will then pursue the female and, having finally caught up with her, seduce her with nudges and nibbles before mating takes place. The eggs (one or two per clutch, and up to six each year) are laid in pits excavated by the female, who moistens the soil with urine if it is dry or hard. The eggs take anything from 100 to 200 days to hatch, and the hatchlings weigh about 15 grams. These tiny creatures are vulnerable to predation by ants, birds (such as Fiscal Shrikes and Whitenecked Ravens) and mongooses.

Mongooses and other mammals

Your chances of seeing a Cape, or Small, Grey Mongoose in the reserve are good. It is a common species here and, because it hunts by day, is often seen running across the roads or open areas of veld. Its grizzled, salt-and-pepper pelage and long, unkempt tail make it instantly recognisable, the more so because the only other animal with which you are likely to confuse it, the Large Grey Mongoose, or Ichneumon, does not occur here (though it may appear in the not-too-distant future, having recently expanded its range into the Cape Town area). A reputation as a fearless killer of snakes is justified to some extent, but the Cape Grey Mongoose is primarily an insect-eater, being particularly fond of grasshoppers. Mice and small birds are also eaten, and it will scavenge dead animals and waste food from rubbish bins. Investigating the source of a high-pitched, persistent squeak one day at Russouwskop revealed two tiny baby mongooses curled up in a small rock crevice. The entrance was hardly big enough to get a hand through, but the chamber inside was more spacious, and provided a safe, dry den.

We know of the presence of predatory mammals in strandveld mainly through occasional chance sightings, tracks and droppings, and a marking scheme carried out by Professor Jenny Jarvis and her zoology students from UCT. Every April, cage-traps are set in the Olifantsbos area, and these rarely fail to catch genets and mongooses. Each animal is fitted with a metal ear-tag for individual identification, and many have been re-caught in subsequent years at their original site of capture, adding to the scant information about the longevity and site-fidelity of these animals.

Large-spotted and Small-spotted Genets both occur at the reserve, but can hardly be promoted as a drawcard for visitors, because they are nocturnal. This is regrettable, as they are most attractive little mammals, with their spots and stripes and long, ringed tails. Their diet is varied and includes mice, birds, small snakes, frogs and insects. Fruits are also eaten, but probably only when other foods are in short supply.

A common feature of the coastal plains is the numerous earthy heaps, often of impressive dimensions, thrown up by Cape Dune Molerats in the excavation of their tunnels. These can extend to a hundred metres long and penetrate a metre below the surface; they are dug with the animal's powerful front feet and the enormous incisor teeth, which actually grow outside the lips, enabling the animal to burrow without filling its mouth with sand. The moles are vegetarian and eat the subterranean parts of plants (roots and bulbs), as well as pulling down their stems and leaves from above the surface. The Cape Dune Molerat is the largest animal in the world that lives exclusively underground.

Another vegetarian which is rarely seen but leaves telltale signs is the Porcupine. It was quite a thrill for us to find our first porcupine quills, and we came across them at the rate of one or two a month until we had accumulated quite a nice collection. The collector's zeal was, however, somewhat dampened by the discovery of a dead Porcupine, which presented us with something of an *embarras de richesse*, and porcupine quills experienced an inflationary spiral. We saw live Porcupines very rarely; every now and then one would trot past Skaife at dusk, shuffling and snuffling through the long grass. Roots and bulbs are their favourite food and, like the baboons, they leave evidence of their activities in the form of a landscape dotted with small craters and the shredded remains of geophytic and other plants.

The Chacma Baboon

The animal most popularly associated with the Cape of Good Hope Nature Reserve is the Chacma Baboon. For many visitors, the sight of a troop foraging, or at play, is the highlight of a trip here. The baboons range over the entire reserve, from tide-line to hilltops. They spend a high proportion of their time in the rocky areas of the central plateau, but because you are perhaps more likely to see them on the coastal forelands, we include them in this chapter.

'Chacma', 'choachamma' or 'choa kamma' was the name, probably an onomatopoeia, given to the baboon by the indigenous peoples at the Cape, and was introduced to general usage in 1819 by the French zoologist Baron Cuvier. The Chacma Baboon occurs in Africa as far north as the southern parts of Angola and Zambia. It is a fairly large, dog-like ape. The sexes differ greatly in size, the males averaging 1.5 metres long (including a 72-centimetre tail), the females 1.2 metres (including their tail of 60 centimetres). The biggest males can weigh over 40 kilograms, but 30 is more usual; females are about half this. The size and colour of the baboons depend upon their age. The basic colour is a dark brown, but adult males have a tinge of yellow, most noticeably on the forehead. New-born youngsters tend to have relatively dark fur which lightens with age. Adult males are easy to distinguish by their size, heavier muzzles, thick hairy mane and very large canine teeth (up to six centimetres long). Females may be distinguished from similarly sized subadult males by their well-developed and, when in season, brightly coloured ischial callosities, the 'horny epidermal thickenings on the rump' – otherwise known as a big pink bottom. Males mature at about eight years old, females at three or four. Baboons are gregarious, living in troops of up to a hundred animals.

Studies of the reserve's baboons were carried out in the 1950s and early 1960s by the late Professor K. R. L. Hall of the universities of Bristol and Cape Town and, in 1975, by Christine Davidge of UCT's FitzPatrick Institute. The following account borrows from their results and from the observations of Carl Nortier, whose obligation, as the reserve's Law Enforcement Officer, to admonish miscreants is not confined to only one primate species.

The Cape of Good Hope baboons are unique in two ways. Firstly, they are the world's most southerly-dwelling primate (other than humans) and, secondly, they eat shellfish and other sea-life which they procure in the intertidal zone. There are presently five troops here, the centres of their home-ranges being roughly at Olifantsbos, Gifkommetjie, Cape Point, Buffels Bay and Bordjiesrif. The average size of each troop is 40, and although it is not easy to determine the exact number of baboons in the reserve, the population was recently estimated to be in the order of 190 animals. This figure comprises about 25 adult males, 70 adult females and the remainder subadults. The population is boosted temporarily by the two troops based just outside the reserve, on the west and east coast respectively, which make occasional sorties through the boundary fence, thus avoiding the entrance fee.

The baboons' territorial system is a fairly loose one, and the troops often 'trespass' on their neighbours' domain. Furthermore, a few individuals from adjoining territories sometimes join up to form splinter troops. These seem to be temporary arrangements only, however, and the prodigals return to their original troops after a short while.

The baboons have, in one respect or another, all been corrupted by human interference – visitors still feed them despite fifty years of being firmly but politely asked not to do so. This has resulted in many sad situations and seemingly insoluble problems, from which the baboons invariably emerge as the losers. Of all the troops, the Olifantsbos one has had least contact with visitors and goes about the daily round much as it will have done before the tourist arrived on the scene. For this reason, it was the troop chosen for study. From his observations, Hall soon realised that there was no merit in describing baboon behaviour in human terms. The labels which we affix to them – aggressive, domineering, autocratic and totalitarian, amongst others – are unjustified and inaccurate. Nevertheless, there is always a temptation to anthropomorphise and interpret and judge the baboons' actions according to our own standards. The problem with baboons is that they are just too human, and display many of the less appealing and unsavoury traits of that species.

Baboon behaviour

A prerequisite for baboon life is a safe place in which to sleep at night. The cliffs behind Skaife were one of nine sites used as a roost by the Olifantsbos troop. Baboons start heading for their roost at about four o'clock in the afternoon, and seldom get up before about seven in the morning. The first to rise are the adult males, and the whole troop spends some time (anything from a few minutes to three hours) in social activities, including playing, mutual grooming and mating. The baboons then leave the roost site to forage.

Feeding is the major activity between mid-morning and mid-afternoon. The search for food takes place within a home-range which, in the case of the Olifantsbos troop, covers some 3,700 hectares and extends north to the boundary fence, east to about Rooihoogte and south to Gifkommetjie. Within this, the baboons walk up to nine kilometres each day, generally stretched out in a long, straggling line and getting together only at concentrated food sources or when they are relaxing towards the end of the day.

In his study of baboon diet, Hall suggested that it would be easier to list those items which they don't eat! Their diet does, in fact, comprise 95 per cent plant material. At the reserve, 114 species of plant are eaten. Certain parts of the plant are preferred, and the baboon will, not surprisingly, target those flowers or fruits which are in season. Summer will find them eating the pincushion flowerheads of *Leucospermum conocarpodendron* on the escarpment and feasting on Tortoiseberries at the coast. In winter and spring they concentrate on re-sprouting bulbs as the first leaves emerge from the soil. Berries are the obvious choice on woody strandveld shrubs. The flowers of over 20 plant species, ranging from ericas to Wild Sage, are nipped off and eaten. A multitude of iris, gladioli, orchid and watsonia bulbs are dug up and their tough, fibrous skins stripped off. (The progress of a troop of baboons can be traced across the veld by following the small craters pockmarking the ground, like a miniature artillery practice

Cape Tiger Moth
Dionychopus similis

Green Drab
Ophiusa tirhaca

range.) The 5 per cent animal component of their diet includes grasshoppers and ants. Intertidal foraging was not, in fact, observed as often as its notoriety would perhaps suggest. On the beach the baboons ate Shore Crabs and Cape Rock Crabs from the rockpools. The tops of Granular Limpets adhering to the rocks were bitten off and the contents scooped out with the tongue. Stranded kelp was lifted to expose Beach Hoppers and isopods. A young baboon was seen to pick up and play with a clutch of oystercatcher eggs, which were later discarded undamaged!

There does not seem to be a clearly defined breeding season at the reserve, but most young are born in July–November following a six-month gestation. The baby is weaned after six to eight months, during which time it gets more adventuresome and playful, and risks being cuffed by the long-suffering adults and adolescents should they become over-familiar. Every visitor likes to see a baby baboon riding jockey-style on its mother's back. This is an advance on the first few days after birth, which the youngster spends hanging under its mother's belly.

Social dominance is not as clear-cut amongst baboons as is popularly believed, but the most conspicuous member of the troop is generally a large, old male. He is the one who will place himself between the troop and a perceived threat, and he customarily leads the troop to the roost in the afternoon. Most of the members of the troop keep on the lookout for danger, but the old females appear to be the most vigilant. When another baboon troop appears, the adult males are the ones to assert their authority and chase off the transgressors. This may be a noisy and dramatic spectacle, with the males barking loudly and everyone else squealing. Very rarely do the combatants come into physical contact, however, and injuries as a result of territorial disputes are almost unknown. More fighting takes place within troops, rather than between them. When a skirmish breaks out between two or three males, it can lead to general mayhem, as all the baboons pitch in. The contestants in these fights can receive nasty bite wounds. Some males pool their resources and gang up on a more dominant male; if a baboon finds himself on the losing side, however, he will make a convenient switch of allegiance and turn on his erstwhile allies.

The parallels with politicians and football supporters go on and on, but it is nice to record that baboons do have, to us, some endearing qualities. When they have finished foraging for the day and are making their way slowly to the roost, they spend time grooming one another, playing and sitting quietly contemplating their position in the universe (pp. 92–93). This is all immensely therapeutic and pleasurable for baboon and human observer alike. Mutual grooming, in particular, looks very affectionate to us, but whether fondness can be invoked in the quest, on the one hand, to rid oneself of fleas and ticks and, on the other, to supplement one's diet with such parasites and a sprinkling of salt flakes and dry skin, is debatable.

Rhinos and satyrs

There is virtually no information available on the insects of strandveld. The baboons, doubtless, have a better appreciation of the kinds of insects to be found here and their habits (essentially, which ones make good eating and which ones are to be avoided). Our own encounters with strandveld insects are limited to the large bumbling beetles and bees which become entangled in our mist-nets when we are trying to catch birds, and the unwelcome attentions of biting flies.

The bumblers include the dung and rhinoceros beetles, which are both members of the Scarabaeidae, an enormous family which contains over 19,000 species worldwide. Dung beetles are famous for their dung-rolling. Most of the animal dung at the reserve comes virtually pre-packed – the droppings of Bontebok, for example, come in convenient little balls which require little reshaping. The dung balls are a source of food for the adult beetles and their young (the eggs are laid on a ball of buried dung); they are also used in courtship and honeymoon feasts.

The horn which gives the rhinoceros beetle its name is found only on the males of the species. It appears to be used as a weapon in clashes between rival males. We have not recorded this beetle very often at the reserve, but like so many other insects here, further study and diligent searching would doubtless reveal a rich and fascinating fauna.

To extract carpenter bees safely from our nets requires a measure of manual dexterity well beyond that demanded by a bird. 'Safely' as much for the extractor and the extracted – the bees have a powerful sting and do not hesitate to use it. Carpenter bees excavate their nest chambers in dead wood. This is a surprisingly scarce commodity in the coastal thicket, as few of the shrubs attain the age of decay. The limbs of shrubs killed, but not completely burnt, by fire provide additional habitat, and the old oaks and other introduced trees also benefit the bees.

The carpenter bees which sting only when provoked are much less of a hazard than the biting (or piercing) flies. On warm, calm days the tabanid flies, with their hypodermic-needle-like snouts, are abundant. The proboscis can reach alarming lengths (up to 60 millimetres in some species), and the jab inflicted in their efforts to obtain blood from an unwilling victim serves to concentrate the mind to a degree. The resultant itchy bump is similarly painful. Consolation may be had from the fact that the tabanids are important pollinators of many flowers, these being species with characteristically deep corolla tubes. Other biting, or injecting, members of the Tabanidae are the familiar horseflies. In our experience, the horseflies find the colour blue irresistible. Blue shirts or trousers are, therefore, avoided when we walk the reserve on fine summer days. The bloodsucker of the horsefly family is the female; an innocuous beast, the male feeds on pollen and nectar.

As well as those insects which make their presence felt in an often painful way, some are conspicuous by their sheer abundance, others by their size and beauty. In pole position at milkwood flowering time are the kelp flies. Tap a branch and the flies will rise like smoke from the flowers, but quickly settle again. Kelp flies are likely to be important pollinators of strandveld shrubs. Many of the shrubs here have small, inconspicuous, highly scented blooms, a combination of characteristics which would favour pollination by these insects. The small, trumpet-shaped *Lycium* flowers, as we have mentioned, attract carpenter bees, sunbirds and day-flying moths. Honey bees also visit these flowers, and one suspects that these are the efficient pollinators; certainly, the carpenter bees seem to cause more damage to the flowers than good, and chew through the base of the petals to obtain their nectar, rather than going through the front door where they would be brushed with pollen.

The Pride of Table Mountain butterfly, whose predilection for red we have already described, makes sorties down to the coast to feed from Candelabras at Buffels Bay (pp. 182–183) and the April Fools at Black Rocks and elsewhere. This is the only butterfly we have recorded at these flowers, but other insects, notably ants and bees, were numerous at the April Fools. The Candelabras were also visited by Malachite and Lesser Doublecollared Sunbirds,

the combination of red plants and iridescent birds being quite dazzling.

Although the weather may be warm and bright, a sure sign that summer is at an end is given by the Autumn Brown butterflies. In March and April these are very common over coastal swards where their caterpillars feed on various grasses. Very rarely did we encounter them away from this habitat. The Autumn Brown is member of the Satyridae, a family which takes its name from the Satyrs, sprites of woods and fields and typically drunk and lustful. The slow, wavering flight of the butterflies might suggest some level of intoxication, but presumably they are no more licentious than any other butterfly.

These and a great variety of other insects may be encountered in your rambles through the thicket. It is a shame that so little is known about even the common ones, but this should not detract too much from the pleasure of watching a preying mantis on the prowl, or the striped beauty of the pyrgomorphid grasshoppers (so detested by gardeners, but here enjoying their floral feast with impunity). Here are stick insects, bladder grasshoppers, hunter wasps, glow worms, monkey beetles, cotton stainers, twig wilters . . . The list is almost endless, and with every step you can find something of interest (if it doesn't find you first).

Rhinoceros beetle
Dynastinae

Peaceful moments for the
baboons at Olifantsbos.
Time to reflect upon the
meaning of life and rid
oneself of fleas.

93

Rhus glauca
(Bloukoeribos).

One of six species
on the reserve, they
often hybridise.

Maytenus, a member of
the saffron family
(Celastraceae). When ripe
the fruits split to expose
the arillate seeds.

Strandveld fruits
Olifantsbos, July - August.

Chrysanthemoides
monilifera (Bietou)

Cassine peragua (lepelhout)
The berries ripen from
red to deep purple.

The weatherbeaten carapace of a long-
dead Angulate Tortoise _Chersina angulata_.

This youngster ignored the
berries but had a
predilection for yellow
daisies.

The Tortoiseberry *Nylandtia spinosa*
flowers during the winter and its
fleshy fruits ripen in summer.
 The berries are eaten by birds
such as Cape Bulbuls and
 Redwinged Starlings as
well as tortoises.

A ruin for many years,
the kiln was beautifully
restored in 1990.

_Zaluzianskya
villosa_

Dipogon lignosus

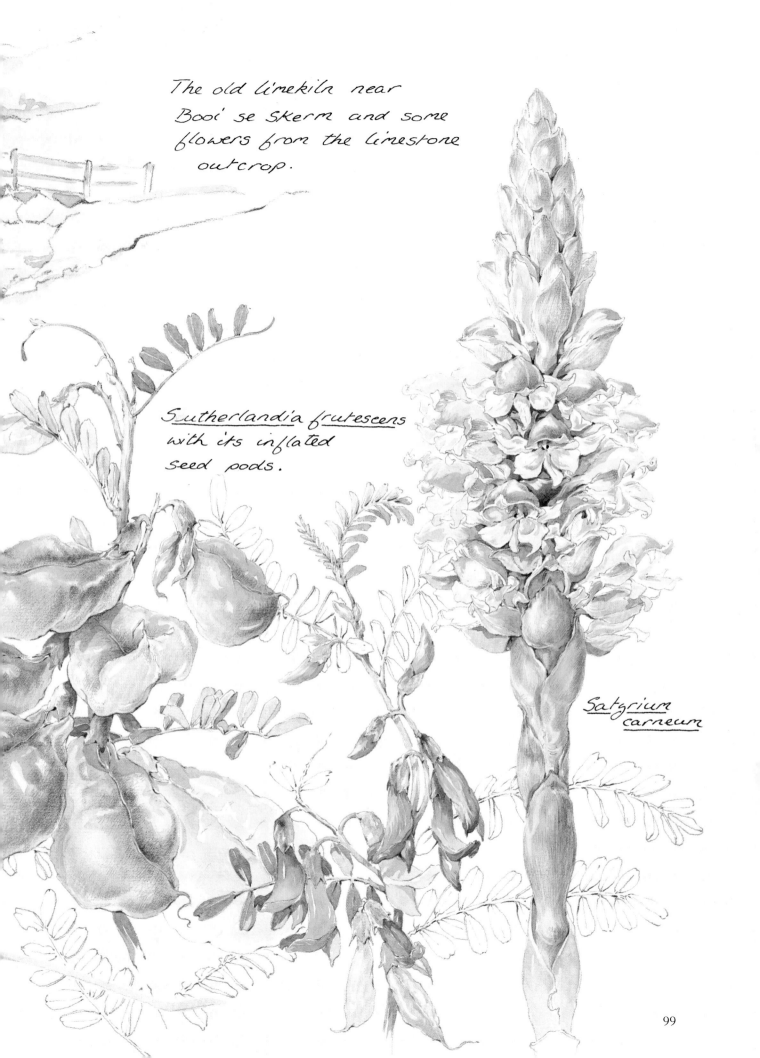

The old limekiln near
Booi' se Skerm and some
flowers from the limestone
outcrop.

Sutherlandia frutescens
with its inflated
seed pods.

Satyrium
carneum

99

a male Malachite Sunbird
Nectarinia _famosa_ in the
Olifantsbos Wild Dagga
patch.

100

Lesser Doublecollared
Sunbird *Nectarinia chalybea*
feeding from the flowers of
Pig's Ear *Cotyledon orbiculare*

A Garter or Spotted Harlequin-Snake
Homoroselaps _lacteus_ making
a rare appearance above ground
at Olifantsbos.

Euphorbia caput-medusae
The Gorgon's Head Euphorbia
survives even on the windswept,
salt-sprayed boulder beach at
Olifantsbos. The mythical
Gorgons had snakes for hair
and boar's tusks for teeth.

⅟₁

Haemanthus coccineus
April Fool (Bergajuin)

The flowers appear only after
the enormous leaves (which can
be 700mm long!) have withered.

Black Rocks, March.

Sour fig Carpobrotus edulis (Suurvy). Most common near the coast and widely used for stabilising sand. The fruits are eaten by baboons (and humans!)

A patch of diminutive spring-flowering Bladderwort in the marsh below Die Boer.

CHAPTER FIVE

Ducks and Disas

Blackwater Lakelets, Streams, Marshes and Lagoons

Freshwater is not a conspicuous feature of the reserve. The few waterbodies that do occur are, for the most part, small and indistinct. Furthermore, they do not support the numbers or variety of wildlife (such as waterfowl) traditionally associated with such habitats. The ecological interest and importance of the Cape of Good Hope's streams, lakelets and marshes do, however, lie in their very gloominess and inhospitality.

There is, in fact, more freshwater on the reserve than meets the eye. This is because most of it takes the form of underground seepage and soil-water which, although not apparent to our eyes, occupy a pivotal position in structuring plant communities and determining the distribution and abundance of certain animal species.

Seeps and groundwater

The most common underground water feature is the seepage zone, more cosily know as a seep. Seeps are formed in the following way. The plateau which dominates the reserve's topography is composed of a series of gently tilted steps or terraces. Where these come near the soil surface, they impede the percolation of groundwater, with the result that marshy areas with a good depth of moist peat have formed behind them. These seeps are permanently damp and can be recognised by their tall and relatively luxuriant vegetation, contrasting with that of the sparser, well-drained areas.

Open water

A scattering of permanent lakelets, or vleis, is dotted across the reserve from Sirkelsvlei in the northwest, to Suurdam, the Homestead ponds and one or two others in the south and east. The qualification 'permanent' is used advisedly; occasionally these vleis do dry out, but only in the hottest summers after the driest winters. The vleis receive their water mainly from surface trickle along their shorelines in the wet winter months and from seepage from the high water-table of the marshy areas around them.

Sirkelsvlei is the largest freshwater body, extending over 6.3 hectares and with a maximum depth of 1.4 metres. It is a paradoxical pond, situated as it is on a plateau which is higher than the surrounding landscape and which offers only the tiniest of catchments. There is no obvious inflow, apart from some surface trickle in winter, and yet Sirkelsvlei rarely dries out. The secret, it is thought, lies in underground springs, or in water fed from the adjacent marshes and channelled by the two sandstone ridges between which the vlei lies.

Vleis which dry out as a matter of course each summer, but fill up in winter, are widespread in the reserve. Indeed, the combination of shallow soils on impervious rock in a level landscape allows even the gentlest of depressions to become a wetland of varying lifespan if it rains hard enough. Some of these, such as Groot and Klein Rondevlei, are predictable to the extent that they feature on official maps. As Large and Small Round Pond, these demonstrate accurate, if not overwhelmingly imaginative, naming on the part of those who christened them. These ponds lie in the hollows between the old dune ridges on the west coast, filling up with the first winter rains and holding their water perhaps into mid-summer. There is a multitude of other smaller and even less long-lived vleis, particularly on the Smitswinkel Flats. Although temporary, they remain in existence long enough to support their own discrete plant communities. At the smallest level, the dimples and scoops in the weathered sandstone blocks can harbour interesting invertebrates and plants, as well as providing ablution and drinking facilities for birds and other small animals. These bird baths can be up to 30 centimetres deep and, where overhung or permanently shaded, can persist into the summer months.

Many of the other waterbodies are entirely or partly artificial, having been excavated from already marshy areas to create open water for livestock in the last century and early part of the present, and to attract game animals as part of management in the late 1960s and early 1970s. These vleis are smaller than Sirkelsvlei but, like it, tend to be shallow. Gilli Dam, for example, which lies next to the main road at the southern junction of Circular Drive, is about 300 square metres in area and 1.5 metres deep when full. It is

A profusion of Berzelia *marks a permanently wet seepage zone, or 'seep', on the Smitswinkel Flats.*

also fed by seepage and surface trickle, and has no outlet apart from overflowing occasionally at its lowest corner when topped up by the winter rains. The average temperature of the vleis is 18 or 19°C, although at the surface in summer this can be considerably higher (Gilli Dam can reach 30°C) as a result of the absorption of the sun's warmth by the dark-coloured water. In winter, the water can be as cool as 11°C. The deeper the water, the greater the difference in water temperature between the top and the bottom, with a maximum of 9°C difference recorded for Suurdam, on Circular Drive. Here the water is deep enough to develop discrete layers, each with its own temperature and other physical and biological characteristics. In the shallower pools, the strong winds mix the water around, and such layers, or strata, are unable to develop.

Rivers and streams

Running water is, like the vleis, a thing of impermanence. None of the reserve's rivers are very large and most of them dry up in summer. Indeed, 'river' is a generous accolade; 'stream' would be more apt, as most can be negotiated with a long step or a short jump. The biggest stream or river is the Krom, sometimes known as the Hout River. It collects water from the Klaasjagers River and innumerable creeks and runnels, flows past Theefontein and thence across the gentle flats to the sea at Die Mond ('The Mouth', a common estuarine name). The Krom River is virtually permanent, although many of its tributaries dry up in sum-

mer. The Krom thus relies on seepage from the great subterranean reservoir of the Smitswinkel Flats. Slowly and inexorably the water creeps through the ground; that which is not drawn up by thirsty plants, or lost to the desiccating winds and heat of summer, meanders microscopically through the rocks and soil until it drips down the peaty banks.

The one east coast stream of note is the Buffels River. This drains the southern flank of Kanonkop and the basin in which Smith's Farm nestles. Although this is a small catchment, the river never seems to run dry. Its upper reaches have been much modified; it is blocked by the Bordjiesrif road and has been impounded at two places to form the Homestead ponds. From the lower of these, the Buffels slinks shamefaced into a tangle of scrub (which includes a vigorous growth of Castor-oil Plants) and disappears beneath the dunes. Here it seems to regain its self-respect to emerge bright and sparkling. Where the valley bottom levels out, some marshy pans have developed, filled with Reedmace. A brief barrier of dunes is all that now stands between the river and the sea. Only after the wettest winters does the Buffels River put up much of a fight and flow swiftly over the beach and into the waves; at other times it sinks submissively into the sand.

At Olifantsbos Bay, the stream which tumbles down Die Kloof has cut a deep and narrow channel across the coastal plain. It becomes very sluggish near its estuary, and a deep, evil-smelling trench is the product of still waters and decaying seaweed. This organic input increases its attraction to wildlife, and makes the little lagoon at the top of the shore an attractive one for birds. We return to estuaries and lagoons in due course, but their relative richness contrasts with the 'inland' vleis and rivers, which hold little appeal to birds.

Water chemistry

The chemical characteristics of fynbos freshwater are not so much a consequence of the rain which falls into them, but of the substances that it picks up from the terrain into and through which much of it flows. This landscape is harsh and the plants which grow in it are exposed to a chronic shortage of nutrients. As we have discussed, the plants cling on to any goodness which they can obtain from the soil by manufacturing chemical deterrents to discourage herbivorous insects. With the eventual death of the plant, these poisonous cocktails find their way back into the soil and groundwater, thence into the streams and vleis. Here they have just the same effects as they did in the living plant – they suppress microbial activity and limit the growth and abundance of animals further up the food chain.

These chemicals, the humic acids or polyphenols, not only make the water mildly toxic but render it a deep amber, a colour particularly apparent in shallow pans and rocky-bottomed streams. Deeper vleis are decidedly dark, nay black; hence the general classification of fynbos waterbodies as 'blackwater lakelets'. This blackness prevents light from penetrating very far into the water, exacerbating the already limited colonisation and growth of water plants.

The processes which lead to this state of affairs have been investigated by recording what happens to fynbos vegetation when it drops into fynbos water. When *Berzelia lanuginosa* leaves and *Elegia thyrsifera* stems were immersed in freshwater collected from Suurdam, it was found that the breakdown of the plant material started with the release of soluble material from the plant cells. This is a physical process, and does not involve the activities of microbes such as bacteria (which, under favourable conditions, play a major role in the decomposition of dead plant and animal matter). The escape of polyphenols from the plant cells in this way resulted in a darkening of the water and a rise in acidity. After 30 days it was found that very little biological decomposition had taken place – only 8 per cent of the weight of the *Elegia thyrsifera* was lost this way, and 13 per cent of *Berzelia lanuginosa*. This simple experiment provides important insight into the processes and conditions which are at the root of fynbos functioning.

The forbidding darkness and acidity of fynbos water, and the very slow rate of decay of dead plants or animals dropping into it, are, therefore, the consequence of toxic chemicals, the polyphenols, leaching from fynbos plants. Polyphenols are organic compounds, the simplest of which is phenol itself, otherwise known as carbolic acid. Carbolic acid is a disinfectant and is used in weedkillers and other chemical nasties. No wonder that so little can live in the blackwater lakelets!

The chemical composition of fynbos freshwater is not static. Rainfall may dilute some substances but increase the input of others through flushing them from the surrounding soil, for example. The water in the vleis, therefore, becomes paler in winter as a result of increased flushing and a decrease in the input of humic substances at this season (fynbos plants are evergreen, but some leaves are lost during summer and autumn). Burning of fynbos vegetation also influences water chemistry, notably by increasing the levels of nitrates during the first winter after a fire.

The summer southeasters and the winter northwesters carry salt-laden sea-spray into and over the reserve. This inevitably finds its way into the groundwater and the vleis. The amount of sodium and chlorine in Sirkelsvlei, in fact, makes it almost indistinguishable from seawater. A high rate of evaporation in the hot and windy summers also serves to concentrate these salts. It is interesting that Sirkelsvlei has a higher salt concentration than the recently constructed artificial vleis, such as Suurdam and Gilli Dam. This presumably is a consequence of its longer exposure to the briny zephyrs. Waterbodies in the southwestern Cape as a whole are characterised by their strong saltiness, and it is not until one penetrates fairly far inland to the northeast of the region that the water shows a tendency towards the chemical composition required to classify it as 'freshwater' at an international level.

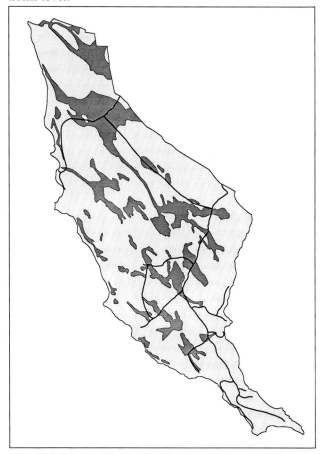

The shaded areas show the distribution of the permanently wet seepage zones and the seasonally flooded Restionaceous Tussock Marsh.

Berzelia
abrotanoides

It is hard to say if the present chemistry of some of the reserve's waterbodies is altogether natural, as they have received numerous 'artificial additives' over the years. During the Second World War, for example, Sirkelsvlei was used as a target for bombers, strafing by low-flying aircraft, and by field-guns sited at Klaasjagersberg. In later years, some of the small ponds were laced with copper sulphate and had hundreds of shell-cases dumped into them in an attempt to boost the mineral intake of the introduced buck, which were experiencing acute shortages of trace elements. Truck-loads of military hardware were subsequently removed from Sirkelsvlei, but what effect its addition, and subsequent extraction, had on water chemistry can only be speculated upon. The building of concrete dams, linings and drains has also modified the water's natural properties. Despite this interference, aquatic life has persisted, although some, including the reserve's most important animal, the singularly rare frog known as the Cape Platanna, have suffered as a result. Before describing it and its cohabitants, however, we begin with the plants which characterise seeps, vleis and rivers.

Freshwater flora

The reserve wetlands support a distinct and attractive flora. At their humblest and smallest, these are the mosses and spring-flowering ephemerals which grow in and around the monkey-stone pools. At the other end of the scale, a substantial area of the reserve supports a vegetation type known as Restionaceous Tussock Marsh. This occurs on the flats which, in winter, are flooded like rice paddies by water overflowing from the small streams that run through them. The soil becomes waterlogged, and there is some

surface water as well. As you can see from the map, this vegetation type is widespread, occupying about 1,600 hectares, or 21 per cent of the reserve's land area. Although bone-dry in summer, tussock marsh owes its existence to freshwater, hence its inclusion in this chapter. At a relatively uncomplicated and basic level, some of the tussock marshes look for all the world like a field of unripe cereal crops, comprising, as they do, dense and almost uniform stands of tall, bright-green, black-spiked *Elegia cuspidata*. There are few other species here, but around the edges smaller restios and a sprinkling of heaths can be found.

Lower-growing tussock marsh characterises much of the area bordering the northern section of Circular Drive. Here is a greater variety of restios, with layers of low shrubs and a good selection of annuals in spring. Some attractive heaths grow here, including *Erica bruniades*. Close inspection of its tiny flowers reveals a furry bloom of pink and red, like a frosted Christmas-tree bauble. Many other ericas thrive in these damp areas. Most are low-growing, forming carpets and clumps of pure white to the deepest purple.

Tussock marsh is also distinguished by a lack of tall shrubs. The seeps and riverbanks, on the other hand, host a variety of densely clumped bushes, and stand out in the landscape on this account. These habitats boast deeper soil and a more reliable water supply than the marshes, and support many plant species which combine rarity and good looks.

Prominent among these is *Mimetes hirtus*, a member of the Proteaceae family and one which is very particular about its choice of abode. In its limited range it is found almost exclusively in low-lying coastal areas, and invariably in seepage zones. Here it grows quickly (from germination to first flowering may take only two years), reaching its peak at five to ten years and old age at fifteen. It is certainly one of the most attractive members of its tribe, with its striking red and yellow florets. It is not illustrated in these pages, but graces the cover of *A Fynbos Year* for those who wish to admire it.

Also conspicuous in this habitat is the Marsh Daisy. Growing sometimes to almost two metres in height, its straggly stems are topped by white, daisy-like flowers for much of the winter and spring (p. 122–123). You can discern the lines and extent of the seepage zones and stream banks at this time of year, as they are pricked by little constellations of Marsh Daisy flowers, shining from a background of deep greens.

A third plant which jostles for position in this veritable jungle is *Berzelia abrotanoides*, a curious species whose clustered flowers begin as marble-like buds, from whose hard and almost glassy surface there appears a multitude of tiny white or creamy flowers to form woolly floral pompoms. These are much favoured by beetles, bees and flies and, like the Marsh Daisy, contrast strongly with their sombre background.

These species, together or alone, may be admired conveniently from the roadside at many points in the reserve.

There are particularly nice patches of *Mimetes hirtus* on the seaward side of the road just short of Olifantsbos Bay, on the western flank of the slope below Anvil Rock, and in the south at Gilli Dam (where a mass of *Watsonias* also greets you in spring). The banks of Suurdam and Gilli Dam combine vlei and seepage zone flora, with a fine stand of scrub dominated by *Berzelia* and Marsh Daisy. At Suurdam the fine, black, silty soil and deep peat support a healthy growth of sedges around the pond's margin, while a floating carpet of the sedge *Scirpus prolifer* creeps out from the shores and ventures across the open water. On the northern side of the Link Road are seeps with some fine stands of *Psoralea*, whose blue, miniature sweet-pea-like flowers are delicately scented. A great bank of *Aspalathus* there turns the landscape yellow in spring, saturating the air with a strong, yeasty odour and the drone of insects harvesting the crop of nectar and pollen.

Seep heaths include the tall, straggly *Erica curviflora*, with its long, tubular blooms, and the more compact Swart-bekkie. The latter's common name addresses its protruding black stamens; its scientific epithet *spumosa*, the frothy or foam-like flowers (pp. 56–57). The wetlands are also home to a brace of exceedingly rare heaths, *Erica eburnea* and *Erica fontana*. Although presently considered to be endemic to the reserve and species in their own right, they are a source of some confusion and debate because they hybridise with other closely related ericas, giving rise to plants which vary in size and flower colour.

More traditionally associated with permanent wetlands is the familiar Reedmace, also known as the Bulrush. This tall (up to 2.5 metres) plant, with its cigar-shaped seed spike, occurs in small, but very dense, beds at the Homestead ponds, in a marsh near the limekiln, and in shallow pans at the mouth of the Buffels River and at Olifants Bay. There is also a tiny, isolated patch on a seep by the Link Road. It may seem remarkable that the Reedmace has managed to colonise such a remote spot, in the midst of what, to this moisture-loving species, must be a veritable desert. A wander through a Reedmace bed on a windy day will demonstrate how this comes about. When the cylindrical fruits are ripe, they 'unfurl' and release their downy, dancing seeds to the breeze. Most of these inevitably fall on stony ground; some unfortunate ones are even blown out to sea. Such are the vast numbers released, however, that chance dictates that, sooner or later, one will land in suitable habitat and germinate there. Although the seeds can travel great distances, and Reedmace is found almost throughout the world, there is some debate whether it reached the Cape under its own steam or was, like so many plants, brought here by early settlers.

Fires and flames

The high water-content of the soil allows the tussock marsh, seeps and other wetland communities to recover relatively quickly from the effects of fire. Within two or three years they are well vegetated and lush, and many species will have matured and flowered in this short time. This contrasts markedly with the many years which elapse before the plants that characterise mature Upland Fynbos recover their pre-fire state. Tussock marsh also boasts a number of bulbous plants which re-sprout after fire. The flats south of the Link Road can be ablaze with brilliant orange-red *Watsonias* in the first spring after a fire. The yellow-flowered *Bobartia indica*, with its long, restio-like leaves, also blooms profusely in response to fire. You can admire this species in springtime on the flats near the Brightwater Road. Commonly known as Flames because of its colours, *Gladiolus bonaespei* could earn this name by the enthusiasm with which it emerges after flames of the consuming kind have swept over it. From July to September these flowers glow and flicker on the damp slopes and flats in the central and northwestern part of the reserve.

Prominent among the many intriguing species which sprout and bloom amidst the charred stems of Marsh Daisies and blackened stumps of *Mimetes* are the orchids. In the spring of 1991, many species which had not been seen for many years on the reserve, and some which had never been

Flooded by winter rain, a marshy pan is brightened by a flowering Watsonia coccinea.

Gladiolus
bonaespei
Flames

of a mystery. It has been suggested that the stickiness of some erica flowers (notably, at the reserve, *Erica phylicafolia*, whose purple blooms often have insects adhering to them) may be an adaptation with this in mind, but the phenomenon awaits investigation.

The following spring we revisited the seep below Die Boer. There were few orchids, but we noted the healthy recovery of other species. In the deepest, dampest peat, the yellow-flowered *Villarsia capensis* was in bloom. The leaves are evergreen, and the long flower stalk comes directly from the root and is known as a scale. The fringed petals are an unusual and attractive feature of this gentian (p. 122). The restios had put on tremendous growth, and were looking fresh and healthy despite the tangling tendrils of the parasitic dodder and the attentions of numerous leaf-mimicking grasshoppers. When alarmed, the grasshoppers invariably take up position flat against the restio stem on the opposite side to the perceived threat. If you circumnavigate a restio, the grasshoppers will move correspondingly, always 180° ahead of you, hugging the stem and aligning themselves in such a way that their cryptic coloration and patterning are put to best effect. Like so many fynbos insects, these grasshoppers are very poorly known. A strategic sweep with a butterfly-net is as likely to procure for you a specimen new to science as one which has already been described. Your main problem lies not so much in finding your insect, but in finding a tame taxonomist with the knowledge and resources to identify it. One new species of restio-mimicking grasshopper has been found at the reserve, and many more doubtless wait to be discovered.

Disa delights

Our *Disa racemosa* (p. 125) flowered profusely following the 1991 fire. There were dozens of plants, and their tall, slender stems and hooded flowers made an impressive display. A year later there were far fewer in bloom, and their numbers diminished yet further after another year. The plants are still there, of course, but they will remain dormant until the next fire. Hopefully, this will not be for another decade or two. *Disa racemosa* is one of the loftiest members of its genus, growing to a metre high, and is widespread in the southwestern Cape. It is crossed with the more celebrated Red Disa by orchid enthusiasts to create vigorous and attractive hybrids.

At this small, but perfectly formed, drainage basin just to the south of Skaife the surrounding hills provide a catchment from which the groundwater emerges almost at the foot of the slopes. Here it forms surface trickle and spreads out into a lush seep. This, in turn, is compressed into a small riverlet which flows into a vlei tucked behind the dunes. Known as Matroosdam, it has, in the past, been enlarged to provide drinking water for stock. Shortly before the area was incorporated into the reserve, however, much of the peat was extracted and sold. This made the vlei bottom very leaky, and until the peat builds up to its previous thickness,

recorded here before, were found. Most of them were discovered by Bill Liltved during fieldwork for his exhaustive study of the Orchidaceae of the Cape Floral Kingdom. Such was the rate at which Bill found unusual species, and so infectious was his enthusiasm for them, that there was, for a while, a danger of *Between Two Shores* becoming a book of orchids. The line was drawn, as it were, at a selection from the seep below Die Boer and the *Disa racemosa* from near Skaife (being a large and conspicuous species, we actually discovered this one for ourselves). Those from the former site reflect the remarkable richness of the orchid family at the reserve. The six illustrated were only a few of the many species growing here, and it was possible to find a dozen or more within an area the size of a tennis court.

The orchids were not the only springtime splendours of this marshy spot. The blackened peat glittered with oxalis, their white petals candy-striped with brilliant red. Amongst the charcoal and sodden wood-ash, little patches of Bladderwort were huddled. These diminutive plants have delicate lavender-and-yellow flowers on the thinnest of hair-like stems. 'Wort' is Old English for plant, and is the suffix for many of their names. There were also thousands of sundews, little uncurling spikes of pink flowers on stems rising from a glistening rosette of red leaves. Their scientific name, *Drosera,* means 'dewy', and accurately describes the stickiness of the leaves. These trap and digest insects to supplement their nutrient supply. Why more plants have not adopted this strategy in this notoriously nutrient-poor environment is something the area of open water will remain smaller, shallower and shorter-lived than previously. Nevertheless, it still constitutes an important and interesting wetland. Indeed, the whole basin is a model illustration of the variety of vegetation types, and their ecological requirements and characteristics, which the reserve can boast and which can occur within such a small area.

From the clifftop above Skaife you can see the sharp transition from Inland Fynbos on the rocky plateau to Dune Fynbos at the foot of the escarpment, where the rocks give way to smooth, sandy slopes. These slopes are the product of material eroded from the rocks above and, to a greater extent, input of marine sand from below. As the ground levels out and the water-table reaches the surface, there is a sharp demarcation between the Dune Fynbos of the slopes (with its Blombos, Coastal Olive and ground pincushions), and a lush crescent of tall seepage vegetation. Beyond the Marsh Daisies, *Psoralea* and *Berzelias* at its edge, the *Disas* grow among the tall restios. On an open delta of sparsely vegetated and crow's-feet-runnelled black peat, there is a scattering of sundews and oxalis. The vlei is bounded by a thick growth of sedges; beyond its rank margin are sand dunes topped with coastal thicket, a windcropped crew-cut of milkwood and taaibos. A few strides further takes you over the summit and down to the high-tide line. All this diversity is contained in the few hundred metres of coastal strip from clifftop to the ocean. Not only is this a textbook display of the environmental factors (topography, soil, water content, proximity to the sea, and so on) which determine the plants' distributions, but it is ideally placed for visiting botany students who, should they be so inclined, can enjoy the pleasure of studying plant ecology from the comfort of Skaife stoep.

Freshwater fauna

The paucity of nutrients and the darkness of the reserve's freshwater have a constraining effect on animal life from the lowest to the highest levels. The antiseptic properties curtail bacterial growth, which in turn limits the amount of decaying matter that would provide food for other organisms. These factors also restrict the growth and development of phytoplankton, the tiny, unicellular organisms which harness the energy from sunlight to make their own food, in the same way that plants do. Perhaps surprisingly, it is not so much the inability of sunlight to penetrate even the murky shallows which limits the numbers of these microscopic plants, but chemical factors. Because they require nutrients, trace elements and a more alkaline water for healthy life, as well as sunshine, they do not fare well in the Good Hope vleis. Their animal counterparts, the zooplankton, are also in very short supply.

In his study of the blackwater fauna at the reserve, Dr Tony Gardiner could find only between 12 and 16 species of zooplankton in the vleis. This represented less than half the number of species recorded at Rondevlei, a shallow, relatively clear, nutritious and alkaline lake on the Cape Flats not far to the north. The zooplankton populations of the reserve also tended to be dominated by individual species, rather than being an even mixture of many species. In Gilli Dam, for example, a cyclopod rejoicing in the name of *Metadiaptomus purcelli* accounted for 97 per cent of the vlei's zooplankton. It occurred at densities of up to 99,000 per cubic metre. This may sound a lot, but it is a tiny beast. Cyclopods are crustaceans, and so called because of the single eye in the centre of their heads. In many species, the males are smaller than the females, and have an antenna modified for grasping their partner during mating. They feed on particles suspended in the water, as do many of their kin. At Sirkelsvlei, the cyclopod made up an average of 53 per cent of the plankton population, with the rotifer *Brachionus plicatilis* coming into second place at 34 per cent. At certain times of year, however, the latter was more numerous; during one January their numbers peaked at over 310,000 per cubic metre of water, but at other times they were very scarce. Rotifers are also known as 'wheel animalcules' and around their mouths have a ring of cilia, or hairs, which they beat to waft food particles towards them. The biggest rotifers reach two millimetres in size; most are less than one millimetre long. Other species of zooplankton, including waterfleas (*Daphnia*) and waterbears (Tardigrades), were recorded in very much lower numbers at the vleis.

In terms of abundance, Sirkelsvlei came out tops overall, with an average of just over 105,000 zooplankton per cubic metre of water. Gilli Dam recorded just half this number, and Suurdam was singularly depauperate, with a mere 1,800. Most of its occupants were also very small compared with the zooplankton in the other two vleis. Why Suurdam should be so inimical for zooplankton was not altogether apparent, but the relatively high toxicity of its water may have been an important contributing factor.

Zooplankton populations are known to fluctuate in response to environmental conditions, such as temperature and day-length. At the reserve, however, such responses tended to be limited, and seasonal variation was, generally, not great. If, under salubrious conditions, however, the numbers of one species soar to very high levels, a species which feeds upon it undergoes a population boom in response, and gobbles them up. This was the case with *Metadiaptomus purcelli* at Gilli Dam. Here it experienced a crash in numbers when its youngsters were eaten by a proliferation of the nymphs or larvae of Notonectids (more catchily known as backswimmer bugs) in early summer.

Pirates and predators

Insect larvae are an important component of the blackwater lakelet communities. Many are ferocious predators, often attacking and devouring animals much larger than themselves. The juvenile stages of dragonflies, and water-

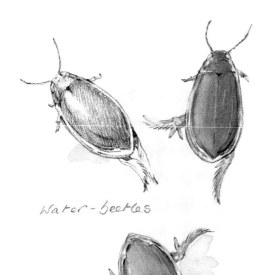

Water-beetles

bugs andbeetles, are found in freshwater vleis, but they bear little resemblance to the more familiar adults. The brilliant dragonflies, which dart, dip and hover around the water's edge, spend their early lives as subaquatic nymphs, a period of development which can take three years or more. This process begins with the female laying her eggs in a narrow slit which she cuts in a leaf or stem, above or just below the water. Her mate often circles around menacingly to see off other males. When the nymph hatches, it drops down into the water, if it is not already therein, and soon undergoes the first of many moults which will see it through to the final stage before emerging from the water for the last time. The nymphs employ a combination of stealth and camouflage to secure their prey, which can vary in size from waterfleas to tadpoles.

The backswimmer bugs do just what their name suggests. They are stoutly built little bugs, distinctly boat-shaped and with a prominent keel along the back. They lie on their backs and propel themselves through the water with a pair of long, oar-like legs fringed with hairs. Backswimmers are keen hunters, ambitiously attacking prey many times their size. Tadpoles are much favoured.

Our diving beetles were inadvertently netted at Gilli Dam by zoology students in pursuit of frogs. They are accomplished subaquarists – they swim with remarkable speed and agility and can jig, swerve and cruise backwards as well as forwards. The perfectly streamlined body is propelled by powerful hind legs; when the beetle stops swimming, it floats to the surface and takes air aboard through two tubes, the spiracles, which protrude from its rear end. The water-beetle larvae are veritable Nimrods, consummate and confident hunters, using their hefty mandibles to disembowel their prey. Their reputation is such that in some parts of the world (it is a widespread family) they are known as water tigers! Diving beetles are not only good swimmers, but good flyers as well. Most of the reserve's vleis, how-

ever remote, contain a beetle or two, and they simply move house when the water dries up.

Less charismatic, perhaps, than the diving beetles, but of considerable ecological interest, are the shrimp-like amphipods which occur in almost any body of freshwater. They are also, as my pitfall traps demonstrated, quite numerous in the seasonally inundated tussock marshes in winter. (The pitfall traps, not quite the pinnacle of scientific design and technology, are jam jars set into the ground and flush with its surface, and into them the invertebrates plunge.) We have even found amphipods swimming around merrily in monkey-stone bird baths, perched on blocks of rocks three metres high and far from the nearest freshwater. How they get there is something of a mystery.

In common with so many fynbos freshwater invertebrates, the amphipods are poorly known. It was of interest, if not altogether surprising, therefore, that a specimen recently found at the reserve by Dr Barbara Stewart and Dr Pete Cook proved to be new to science. Christened *Paramelita magna*, it was collected from a tributary of the Krom River and from the Buffels River. It is a member of the superfamily Crangonyctoidea, which sounds like an ancient and distinguished branch of the Central European aristocracy, and at least confers an air of some importance on this humble animal. The specific epithet *magna* means large, and refers to the exceptional size of the adults. At 22 millimetres, they are twice as big as some other members of their family. Amphipods are not particularly strong swimmers, and in fast-flowing water they shelter under stones to avoid being washed away.

A perennial problem is that of food. Wherever they occur, the amphipods feed mainly by scavenging decaying plant and animal matter, which must make life in the monkey stones, in particular, rather frugal. Perhaps they and the other small animals which share their habitat fare better in the rivers, but even here food is likely to be a limiting factor. In the northern hemisphere, falling autumn leaves provide a rich source of energy and nutrients for stream invertebrates. In the Western Cape there is no such mass provisioning by river-bank vegetation, but only a low-key, rather protracted input. Any build-up of leaf debris and nutrients in the low water-levels of the summer and autumn is, however, likely to be flushed out by the scouring floods of winter. At this season, in particular, the invertebrates are likely to experience an acute shortage of food. How they cope with this is unclear. One potential source of food is the spate-generated foam which accumulates behind any barrier or below any little cataract in the fast-flowing streams. After a winter downpour, the deep, froth-topped pools of the Krom River have the appearance of a well-drawn Guinness and, like that celebrated beverage, may contain much goodness.

The rivers' foams and froths range from almost pure white and the smooth consistency of whipped cream, to mucky brown and bubble-bloated, the product of some over-enthusiastic cappuccino maker. In whatever form, the foams act as filters, extracting detritus from the water which flows through and splashes up into them. Chemical analysis of the foam has revealed comparatively high concentrations of nutrients in an environment which is notoriously nutrient-poor. Whether this cornucopia is accessible to the invertebrates and they, in turn, gather at them is, as yet, unknown. If they are as appetising as the results suggest, these fluvial bubble-baths will be much welcomed by the reserve's impoverished freshwater fauna.

Frogs, fish and a small brown snake

Altogether, 14 species of frogs and toads have been recorded at the reserve. The potential for extending this list is probably not high, but a new species (Weale's Rattling Frog) was found here as recently as 1989.

The majority of frogs and toads are, as one would expect, inextricably linked with water. The Sand Rain Frogs, however, can't swim, and avoid water like the plague. Even their eggs are laid in underground chambers, and the tadpoles hatch and develop within these. Another fossorial species, the Cape Sand Frog, does at least lay its eggs in water, but in the non-breeding season frequents dry, sandy areas. Occasionally we have inadvertently scuffed one up from its hiding place in the freshly excavated sand thrown up by a dune mole. The frog makes an impressively hasty retreat, digging with its hind feet and shuffling backwards to safety.

The remaining frogs and toads are animals of the wetlands. With the onset of the winter rains, the marshes and vleis become amphitheatres echoing to the persistent and determined clicks, chirps, squeaks and rattles of the batrachian chorus. Any pan or puddle amongst a good growth of restios will harbour a multitude of Clicking Frogs staking their claims to territories and mates. The monotonous chipping call of this species is one of the characteristic sounds of the reserve's reedy flats and marshes. A near-relative, the Banded Stream Frog, is very difficult to spot if it remains motionless in its favoured stream-side vegetation, its markings making it all but invisible. This species is a remarkable jumper and, stretched to full length in full leap, displays a body which is as skinny as it is athletic. A distinguishing feature is its extraordinarily elongated middle toe.

In the lower reaches of the Olifantsbos stream and around the Homestead ponds, the deep, throaty grunt of the Cape River Frog resonates in the Bulrush beds in spring and summer. Their muscular hind legs (which would be an inadvisable accoutrement in France) serve to launch them to impressive heights and distances if they are threatened or when they leap to catch flying insects. They will also eat their own tadpoles with enthusiasm, which makes it just as well that a female can lay up to 15,000 eggs at a time.

Not as agile as the Cape River Frog, but much more handsome, is the Leopard Toad. At rest (which, from our experience of a captive animal, seems to be most of the time), the toad is a portly gentleman (p. 177). In pursuit of prey, however, it executes movements of surprising grace; deliberate, perhaps, but in mid-leap it qualifies as a languid ballerina of unexpected elegance. Insects and earthworms are gulped down enthusiastically, but the toad will lunge at anything that moves and ask questions of palatability only in retrospect. It is the largest of the region's toads, and may exceed 10 centimetres in length. Males tip the scales at 60

The peat-stained water and bubbling froth of a typical fynbos stream.

grams and females at 120 grams. If their cryptic patterning does not render them invisible to predators, they can exude an irritating fluid from the blister-like bumps on their upperparts. It is also said that they can spit a noxious fluid a metre or more. They cannot, however, give you warts. As the late Walter Rose, the distinguished Cape Town naturalist and doyen of herpetologists, pointed out, this superstition is no more than that, and in handling a toad, he added, 'you would be just as liable to acquire its bandy legs'.

Leopard Toads are found at Klaasjagersberg, not far from the dark perennial pools of the river there, and they visit houses to catch insects attracted to lights at night. They are likely to occur elsewhere in the reserve in suitably damp habitat, but their exact distribution has not been determined. They occupy traditional hideaways under stones or logs, and may be found in the same place year after year. Some do shift abode every now and then in response to local conditions (a case of the Leopard Toad changing his spots), and in springtime they gather at their breeding sites. Here they engage in what is known as 'explosive breeding'. That is, they assemble at suitable ponds to mate and lay eggs for only a very short time, in this case three or four nights in August or September. The males call from a concealed position among the water-side vegetation, and the females select from this chorus the mate of their choice. That the Leopard Toad's call is described as 'a deep, slowly pulsatile snore' makes one wonder what nuance renders one male any more attractive than another. Once the two meet up, the male grasps the female in a fairly powerful embrace, known as amplexus, and fertilises the eggs as she lays them. The males recorded at these breeding congregations were found to be between one and three years old, whereas their mates ranged from two to six years old. Such statistics may seem of academic interest only, but they do represent the earliest age at which any of

Banded Stream
Frog

the world's two thousand or so species of frogs and toads have been found to reproduce.

We have already mentioned the reserve's most important animal. Important, that is, in terms of rarity. This is the Cape Platanna, a species which will never walk off with any prizes at a beauty contest (p. 176), but is of considerable interest to biologists. It is a small-headed, large-bodied amphibian, measuring only about five centimetres from snout to vent, darkly striped on the back and mottled underneath, and as slippery as an orange pip. One of a number of species first discovered by Walter Rose, it was colloquially known as the Sago-belly Platanna (from *plathander*, meaning flat-handed), but is now more conservatively referred to as the Cape Platanna. It was given the scientific name of *Xenopus gilli*. *Xenopus* is Greek for 'strange foot'; the epithet, Rose explained, being 'in recognition of the unfailing assistance offered to us at the South African Museum by the Director, Dr E. L. Gill, and his staff'. A generous gesture, as was typical of Rose. The reserve's Gilli Dam, in turn, is named after the platanna.

At the time of its discovery, the Cape Platanna was known only from the Cape Flats, but has since been found at a sprinkling of sites along the southwestern Cape coast. Its stronghold is the Cape of Good Hope Nature Reserve. It displays a remarkable ability to cope with conditions in the blackwater lakelets and is, in fact, one of the most acid-tolerant of all known amphibians.

It shares a few of the Cape Point ponds with a near-relative, the Common Platanna. This is a much larger species, but displays many of the features of its cousin: it has no tongue, eyelids or ears, and has relatively enormous webbed back feet with the characteristic claws on three of its toes – an alternative name for the platanna family is the clawed toads. It eats any animal matter, stuffing its prey into its cavernous mouth with its short fingers. The Common Platanna is a relatively recent arrival to the area, its spread having been facilitated by human disturbance of the environment and, in the fynbos region, changes to the water chemistry of the blackwater lakelets. Destruction of the natural vegetation and its replacement by alien trees and shrubs have reduced the acidity of the water. This has allowed the Common Platanna to colonise waterbodies at the reserve and elsewhere in the southwestern Cape from which it was previously excluded by its inability to survive in acidic waters. Having got here, the Common Platanna is now wreaking havoc with the Cape Platanna through cannibalism and competition and, most sinister, interbreeding to produce new generations of hybrid platannas. In this way, the Cape Platanna will vanish into a genetic melting-pot. There is thus a great danger that the 'Sago-belly Platanna' will become extinct just 70 years after it was first discovered. Only about 20 per cent of the Cape Point vleis now contain only Cape Platannas; the remainder are inhabited by both species and hybrids. The Cape Platanna presently qualifies as one of the world's rarest and most endangered amphibians.

There is only one species of freshwater fish which occurs naturally at the reserve. This is the Cape Galaxias, a small, pale, sickly-looking thing, which is almost transparent. It makes up for its insipid looks with an interesting lifestyle which allows its eggs to survive in dried-out river beds. This is a wise move in an environment which experiences such low rainfall. The Cape galaxias is absent from many of the vleis, but does occur in the Klaasjagers River. They have also made unexpected appearances in the wheel-rutted puddles of dirt roads some distance from the more secure encampment of the rivers.

The students who caught our waterbeetles have, on occasions, been alarmed by the appearance in their nets of a snake. They need not worry, as such an animal almost invariably turns out to be the mild-mannered Common Brown Water Snake. This is a constricting species, throwing its coils around frogs and tadpoles, which are seized after a rapid chase through the water. The prey is then brought ashore and swallowed head first.

Another aquatic member of the reptile group is the Cape Terrapin. Inhabiting a few of the reserve's ponds, the terrapin is a withdrawn little animal, and its only appearance may be in the form of a snout and two rheumy eyes peering at you from the black water. Such fleeting glimpses may be had if you sit quietly on the rocky shore at Sirkelsvlei. Although it is difficult to judge their size here because of the opaqueness of the water, terrapins grow up to 280 millimetres long and can weigh 2.5 kilograms. Terrapins excavate a small chamber in damp earth in which to lay their clutch of 10–30 papery-shelled eggs (which differ from the hard-shelled eggs of terrestrial tortoises); these hatch after 90–100 days. Cape Terrapins feed on frogs, tadpoles, carrion, in fact anything they can get their jaws around. They also stalk and seize birds which come to the water's edge, although this is unlikely to be a major source of food at Sirkelsvlei, where birds are rather scarce.

Wetland mammals and birds

As far as we can tell, the only mammal which displays a preference for open freshwater, as opposed to seeps and marshes, is the Water Mongoose. While other mammals may visit water to drink or, in the case of genets, occasionally hunt along the river banks, this mongoose never ventures far from open water. This is a large species (about 80 centimetres long), a bit wild and woolly in aspect, and something of a smelly beast, such that we more often detect one by scent than sight. Water Mongooses live in the Bulrushes at Olifantsbos, Skaife and elsewhere, and create their well-worn runs and tunnels through the thick vegetation. Their droppings and prey remains indicated a liking for frogs, although birds' eggs (notably of African Black Oystercatcher) and small mammals are also eaten.

The small, brown, hairy bullet which hurtles across your path in the marshy areas is likely to be a Vlei Rat, with or without a Water Mongoose in hot pursuit. This is the commonest rodent of the damp areas, and probably one of the most widespread and abundant in the reserve. If you don't manage to see the animal itself (p. 127), its presence is revealed by little heaps of neatly snipped and chewed stalks of restios and other plant material. These are the accumulated remains of this herbivore's meals, and are often dotted with droppings. The latter are eaten once more to get a second chance of extracting nutrients. The species clearly takes recycling commendably seriously.

The Vlei Rat is active by day and, although found predominantly in wet areas, is not aquatic to the extent that it will swim by choice. They grow to about 24 centimetres long and weigh up to 120 grams. Like many of their kin, they are favoured food of snakes, small carnivores, and birds of prey such as the resident Rock Kestrels. The African Marsh Harriers and Marsh Owls which make an occasional appearance in the reserve's wetland areas are also likely to hunt Vlei Rats.

In the quest for birds, it was not long before I discovered that the reserve's wetlands were not exactly an ornithologist's paradise. Observations over subsequent years have not dispelled this notion. A mere 10 species were recorded over a two-year period in my tussock marsh study-plots. These species were represented by a maximum of about 0.4 of a bird per hectare (even translated to four birds in ten hectares, this still doesn't amount to much). In its earliest post-fire stage, and in common with the other vegetation types early in their histories, tussock marsh attracted opportunist open-country birds such as Crowned Plovers and Plainbacked Pipits. The only typically wetland species recorded was an Ethiopian Snipe, a singleton with whom I became on quite friendly terms, as I recorded it almost daily in winter at a particularly muddy corner of one study-plot at Circular Drive.

Within only a year of the fire, some of the restios were almost waist-high, and the plovers, pipits and snipe had disappeared. This rapid recovery of the vegetation was reflected in a correspondingly speedy return of the marsh's characteristic birds; or, to be more accurate, bird. The only species upon which I could depend to put in an appearance during my counts was the Levaillant's Cisticola, a jaunty little warbler, noisy and pugnacious. The Afrikaans name, 'vleitinktinkie', is nicely descriptive, telling you all you need to know about its habitat preferences and its liveliness and sharp call. In a five-year-old tussock marsh plot at the Blouberg gate, the tinktinkie was occasionally joined by Grassbirds and Greybacked Cisticolas, with an Orangethroated Longclaw or Yellowrumped Widow adding a welcome splash of colour every now and then.

If the marshes are all but birdless, the seeps are marginally more appealing, at least at certain times of year. When the *Mimetes hirtus* comes into flower, the Cape Sugarbirds and Orangebreasted Sunbirds arrive in force to feed on the nectar. The flat-topped stem provides a convenient landing pad for sugarbirds, which lean over and systematically probe each storey of florets. These contain their greatest amount of nectar when partially open, a time at which pollen is also most abundant on the freshly exposed pollen presenters. The plant thus provides its biggest bribe (the nectar) when a visit by the sugarbird would be most conducive to the transfer of pollen between flowers. Sunbirds, on the other hand, tend to feed from underneath and do not come into contact with the plant's pollen presenters. They are probably not good pollinators and, unlike the sugarbird, get their nectar without fulfilling their side of the bargain.

Because they are so noisy and conspicuous when chasing other birds, the impression is given that the sugarbirds spend as much time embroiled in disputes with other birds as they do feeding. Observations of Cape Sugarbirds at *Mimetes hirtus* patches have shown them to be most aggressive early in the morning. At this time nectar availability is greatest. This behaviour allows the birds to drink the nectar they require in only a few visits to flowers; the rest of the time can be spent fending off boarders. Later in the day, the *Mimetes* florets hold less nectar; more visits are thus required by the sugarbird to get his ration, and less time can be spent seeing off intruding sugarbirds and Orange-breasted Sunbirds.

The seepage thickets attract birds other than nectar feeders. Typical species include Spotted Prinias, Cape Robins and Bokmakieries. Yellowrumped Widows are also fond of this habitat. The males use the tallest shrubs as song posts; from here they undertake defensive sorties against intruding males and courtship pursuits of potential mates. In nuptial dress, the cock Yellowrumped Widow resembles an overgrown bumble-bee, an impression reinforced by its rotund little body and bee-like flight.

Yellowbills and Blacksmiths

Neither the temporary nor permanent waterbodies succeed in attracting much in the way of waterfowl. Most common, in a relative sense, is the Yellowbilled Duck. As soon as they begin to fill up with water, seasonal vleis such as Groot Rondevlei are visited by a pair or two of this familiar species (p. 121). Nesting has been recorded at a number of sites along the west coast, with broods of ducklings appearing from July onwards. That the eggs and youngsters escape the depredations of mongooses does credit to the care provided by the parents.

The vleis' frogs are hunted by one or two Hamerkops (which venture into all corners of the reserve in search of suitable hunting grounds) and parties of Little Egrets. The latter's gleaming white plumage contrasts starkly with the darkness of the water, but does not seem to handicap the egret's hunting skills, as proven by the satisfied swallowing after swift jabs into the shallows.

Blacksmith Plovers forage in a variety of habitats at the reserve, but prefer the seashore, where they catch Beach Hoppers and kelp-fly maggots, and the grass lawns, where they procure insects and worms. In the nesting season they make their modest scrapes beside a temporary vlei or in a marshy seep. From April to August we have found numerous nests at the reserve, not because of any particular skill on our part, but because a Blacksmith Plover is highly conspicuous. If the incubating bird is disturbed, it will quietly slip off the nest and trot away, leaving the cryptically coloured clutch exposed. One to three eggs are laid, and the incubation period is about a month. Hatching is synchronised, and the young leave the nest almost immediately to forage under the watchful eye of the parents. If danger threatens, the chicks crouch motionless and almost invisible while the adults utter their distinctive *tink tink* alarm call (p. 126). The resemblance of this to the bucolic and now seldom heard sound of the blacksmith's hammer striking his anvil has given the bird its name.

Although it is a more dependable aquatic environment, Sirkelsvlei is even less attractive to waterbirds than the seasonal pans. An attempt was made to persuade ducks to nest there by constructing rocky islets in the centre of the lakelet. The problem was not nest sites but, as is now appreciated, water quality. It is not surprising that the islets were not colonised, although they are used as a transit lounge by Egyptian and Spurwinged Geese. The ponds at the Homestead are also somewhat birdless, but their rating in the birders' eyes is elevated by the roost of Blackcrowned Night Herons, which is a feature of the water-side Camphor Trees. These birds can be admired from the car park by carefully scanning the trees to the back of the pond. Keen eyes, best aided by binoculars, will soon pick out the birds in the dappled shade (p. 120). At night the birds move down to the coast to fish in the rock pools if the tide is right; otherwise they hunt around the edges of the ponds and are welcome to as many of the alien fish therein as they can catch.

The Krom River takes a lazy route through the coastal plain, carving a deep, muddy channel towards its mouth. Shortly before it spills out over the beach, the river widens to form a modest marsh, thickly vegetated with reeds and sedges and sparsely blotched with black, muddy pools. This has the appearance of a rich and productive environment, but the curse of nutrient-poor blackwater strikes again. A similar habitat enjoying an inflow of nutritious water would be very attractive to birds. Here we have to content ourselves with, in the wader department, the odd Blacksmith Plover and, in summer, a few Greenshanks and the occasional Common Sandpiper. Small flocks of Yellowbilled Duck frequent the marshes in winter, feeding on seeds and emergent plants. Black Ducks, in contrast, prefer the swiftly flowing upper reaches of the river; one pair seems to be resident on the Krom River and has bred there.

Estuaries and lagoons

The word *krom* means curving or bent. In terms of a river, this could be interpreted as meandering, which the Krom does to some extent as it flows gently across the coastal plain. This would seem a satisfactory explanation of the name in terms of the river's anatomy today. Formerly, however, the river took a right-angle turn at the beach and flowed and expanded south to form a long, narrow lagoon behind the dunes as far as The Fishery. On a hike along the reserve's coastline early in 1962, José Burman described the lagoon as being 'separated from the sea by a sandbar about 200 yards wide' and that it 'turns south and enters the sea about a mile lower down the coast'. A lagoon extending north to Dassiesfontein and south past The Fishery is depicted on the Department of Surveys map of the area.

This was the situation, it would seem, until the early 1980s. I can still remember my first visit to Die Mond in early 1984. Feeling suitably exploratory and quivering with the expectation of a bird-thronged wetland, I found instead the Krom River flowing feebly straight across the beach and into the sea, without so much as a puddle on the shore, and not a bird to be seen. Once or twice over the following winters, the outflow would close up and a modest pan result, but for much of the time the area comprised a broad windswept beach with but a trickle of water running over or through it. Any chance that the lagoon would attain once more the expanse indicated on the official map was scuppered by the storm in May 1984. This obliterated the extensive and well-vegetated dune system behind which the lagoon lurked. Over the following decade, we witnessed the irregular expansion and contraction of the lagoon, but only once did it manage to creep more than a few score metres to the south. The gradual re-establishment of the dunes may allow the lagoon to regain something of its former proportions but, if it happens at all, it is likely to take many years.

The lagoon which does come into being every now and then varies not only in size, but in lifespan, its persistence depending upon marine and river conditions. The waves which can unblock the outflow and release the water can, conversely, also shore it up. Similarly, increased inflow from the river in winter might, in the first instance, lead to the creation of the lagoon through an accumulation of sediments at the outflow, but would ultimately lead to the dam collapsing under the sheer weight of water. When this happens, to the accompaniment of an unnerving roar, Die Mond lagoon is transformed from a sheet of tranquil water to an expanse of damp sand within a few minutes.

At best, the lagoon persists for a few months. During this time it is topped up with freshwater from the river and seawater which spills over the sandbank at high tide. Under such conditions, the salinity and temperature of the water are constantly changing. Nevertheless, many animals can survive in this unpredictable and fluctuating environment. Not long after the lagoon has established, small volcano-like heaps of sand erupt all over the bottom. These indicate the burrows of sandprawns, which feed on suspended matter extracted from the water and detritus in the sediments. The invertebrate fauna of Die Mond remains largely unknown, but worms and snails are amongst the other small animals which are likely to make the lagoon their home at this time. Sometimes a shoal of mullet is trapped in the lagoon; life for these fish must be somewhat precarious as the water level drops – this exposes them to predators and, if worse comes to worst, they succumb if the lagoon dries out altogether. More likely to occur sooner, however, is the collapse of the sandbank and the draining of the water and all its contents into the sea.

When the lagoon is full, it may host a respectably sized flock of Avocets (282 is our highest count), which swim and swish with delicate grace in search of prey. As the water level drops, the exposed shores attract the occasional Curlew Sandpiper and Sanderling in summer. On his 1962 visit, José Burman noted that 'there are plenty of wildfowl to be found in the vicinity of this lagoon'. Whether the place really is less attractive to birds today than it was 30 years ago can only be speculated upon. If 'wildfowl' is extended to include gulls, terns and cormorants, then there can be many birds present, as it is a popular place for bathing and roosting. In its strictest sense, however, the word means gamebirds, which at the lagoon would be ducks and geese. In this case, a scattering of Yellowbilled Ducks and a pair or two of Egyptian and Spurwinged Geese are the best we can do nowadays.

The much smaller and even more ephemeral lagoon at Olifantsbos Bay is, perhaps paradoxically, rather more attractive to birds. Here there is considerable organic input from beached kelp, which enriches the water and the malodorous mud. Here the Sacred Ibises probe and the wagtails flitter, and the Curlew Sandpipers scurry about energetically amongst the preening postprandial gulls.

The narrow muddy margins of the steep-sided channel just before the beach are popular with plovers. This is the best spot on the reserve to find Kittlitz's, and about the only place where one can depend upon seeing Threebanded Plovers. Both are attractive species, and both also nest at Olifantsbos. Their chicks are the quintessence of cuteness!

Blackcrowned Night Heron
<u>Nycticorax nycticorax</u> (gewone nagreier)
A dozen or more roost in the
Camphor Bushes by the Homestead
Pond. This is an adult with its
black head and long plumes.

The species is not known
to nest at the reserve, but
brown immature birds
are often seen with adults.

A Yellowbilled Duck
Anas undulata at
Groot Rondevlei, and Gymnodiscus
capillaris flowering alongside
the path to the water's
edge.

July.

Villarsia _capensis_, a member of the Gentian family, flowering in summer on the Smitswinkelvlakte.

Restios entwined with fruiting Dodder _Cuscuta nitida_ (Vrouhaar)

The Swamp Daisy
Osmitopsis
asteriscoides

(Belskruie) is a
characteristic plant
of seepage zones.

123

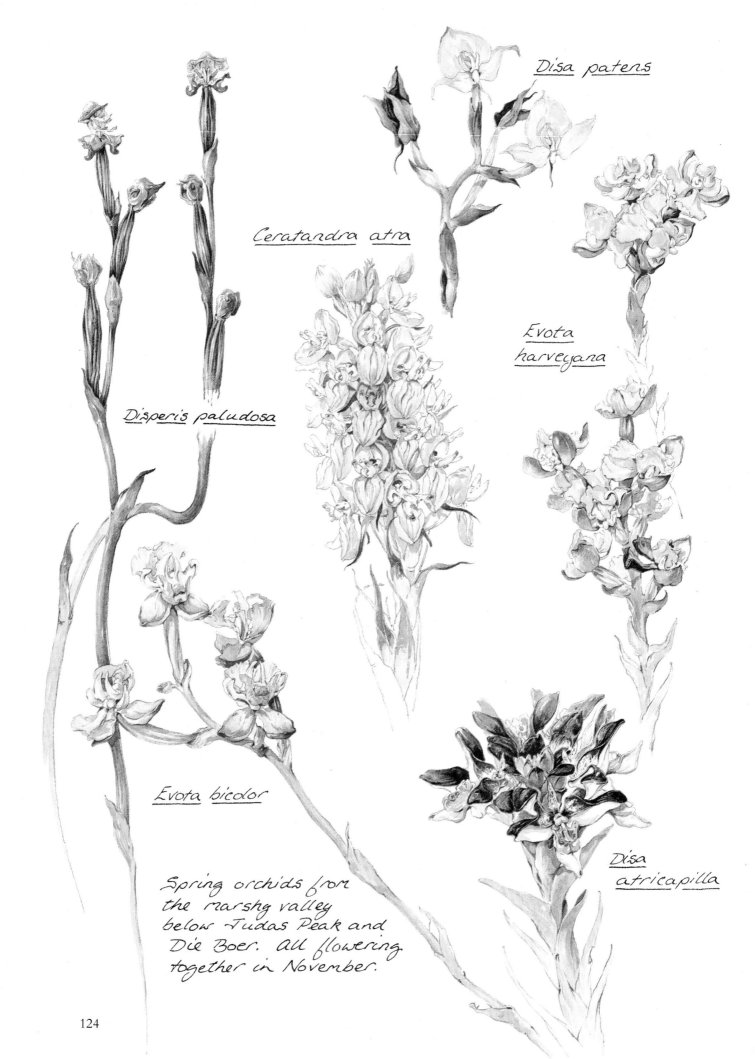

Disa patens

Ceratandra atra

Disperis paludosa

Evota harveyana

Evota bicolor

Disa atricapilla

Spring orchids from
the marshy valley
below Judas Peak and
Die Boer. All flowering
together in November.

In the swampy seep
near Skaife Centre
<u>Disa Racemosa</u> flowers
profusely after fire.

Blacksmith Plover Vanellus armatus
(Bontkiewiet)

The parent birds are ever alert
and at the first sign of danger
give their sharp "tink, tink"
alarm call. At which the
chicks crouch and remain
motionless.

discarded
egg shell

One of a brood of four chicks
from a nest near
Dias Monument.

Tell-tale signs of
Vlei Rats *Otomys
irroratus* are the
little heaps of chewed
plant stems which they
leave dotted around
their tussock marsh habitat.

Low tide at Bordjiesrif reveals a forest of kelp and a rocky-shore rich in marine life.

CHAPTER SIX

Periwinkles, Puffers and Prions

❀

Life Between and Beyond the Tides

We have so far described the wildlife of dryland and freshwater at the Cape of Good Hope Nature Reserve. Although the reserve boundary extends a meagre ten metres seaward of the low-tide line, between terra firma and this watery demarcation lives a variety of fascinating and beautiful organisms which it would be invidious to ignore. In describing life between and beyond the tides, we travel from the top of the beach down to the water's edge, along sandy shores and rocky cliffs, into rockpools and surf, and through the kelp forest to the open sea. With such a diversity of habitats, and with an abundance of animals and plants living in, on and under the water, the reserve's 40 kilometre coastline has at least an equal claim to your attention as the fynbos and vleis.

It is noteworthy, if not unexpected, that the first wildlife of any kind reported from southern Africa was seaweeds and sea creatures from the Cape of Good Hope. In April 1595 an expedition under the command of Cornelius de Houtman left Holland for the Dutch East Indies, rounding the Cape in July. An account of the voyage published in 1598 incorporated a rather crude map of southern Africa. Our interest lies in the drawings, equally crude, which embellish it. These depict 'birds drawn from life, such as are seen near the C. de Buena Esparansa, being a happy sign of the Cape' and 'Trombás, of which many are seen adrift, also signs of nearing the Cape'. Drawn from life they may be, but the identity of the birds paddling on placid waters is not immediately obvious. However, a process of elimination and a soupçon of imagination lead to Kelp Gulls, which, conveniently, are also harbingers of dry land, their furthest sorties to sea being roughly to the distance at which land would first be sighted by vessels approaching the Cape. Less problematic are the *trombás*. These are sea bamboos or sea trumpets, the long, hollow stems of the kelp *Ecklonia maxima*, which drift around on the surface when broken from the sea floor in nearshore waters. The *trombás* could be fashioned into wind instruments of powerful capacity, if limited musical range.

Another illustration from de Houtman's expedition report portrays a veritable swarm of marine life near his ships. These drawings are, again, more figurative than realistic, and it is all but impossible to identify species. However, the annotations allow the identification of Pintado Petrel ('birds like water-hens except that they are mottled or speckled all over'), although it is difficult to see any resemblance between this distinctive species and the illustration. Also featured are flying fish, seals and a whale which, if the double spout is anything to go by, is a Southern Right.

Despite the confusion which surrounds the precise historical position of the Cape of Good Hope, there is every reason to believe that these organisms were recorded at the very Cape, being the first land south of the African bulge encountered by de Houtman's little fleet once it had sailed east on the trade winds from the mid-Atlantic. With much less effort today you can still enjoy the *trombás*, Pintados, whales and seals at the Cape of Good Hope. We cannot guarantee a flying fish, but if ocean conditions are favourable, they do enter our waters in late summer.

Tideline treasures

A preprandial wander in the gathering gloom was a regular evening indulgence when we lived at Olifantsbos. With the baboons safely to bed (preferably theirs) and the *braai* fire burning cheerily, it was a pleasure to walk the kilometre or so to the wreck of the *Thomas T. Tucker* and back to see what the sea had washed in. Every tide would bring new treasures; nothing so romantic, perhaps, as a message in a bottle, or as valuable as glinting gold doubloons, but always something to inspect, admire or carry back.

Cephalopods and other odd bods

An array of Good Hope jetsam is illustrated on pages 148 and 149. All these and a multitude more may be found by even the most casual beachcomber. Only once, however, have we found the exquisite shell of the Paper Nautilus on our beach walks. An object of fragile and ethereal beauty, the shell is manufactured by the female *Argonauta argo*, named after the Golden-Fleece-seeking mariners of Jason's *Argo*. Although the living animal is rarely seen (any that are washed ashore quickly fall prey to gulls), one look at its

Goose barnacles
Lepas sp.

characteristic tentacular form would tell you that it is a cephalopod, a member of the class of octopods and squids. The delicately constructed shell is her buoyancy chamber and floating home, a nursery in which she lays her eggs, and board-and-lodging for the virtually parasitic male of the species (which is very much smaller than the female – about two centimetres compared with her 20 – and has no shell of its own).

Cuttlebones can be found washed up on any of the reserve's beaches, sometimes in large numbers. These are perhaps most familiar as the pale, bone-like, flattened-oval objects wedged between the bars of budgerigar cages. But how many budgies or, indeed, their owners appreciate that these are the internal shells of another squid-like animal, the cuttlefish? After death the soft, fleshy part of the cuttlefish is quickly eaten by scavengers, leaving the light-weight cuttlebone to drift, many subsequently to be cast up on the shore, some ultimately destined to keep the beaks of the budgies of the world in trim.

Seeds from far-off places found at Olifantsbos include those of the Broad-leaved Laurel and the Bonduc, trees which grow no closer than the Transkei. The hefty purplish seeds, the sea beans, come from the liane *Entada* which is found along riverbanks in tropical and subtropical Africa. The seeds are dispersed by water, but may take the tech-

nique a little far if they reach the ocean and are swept southwest along the south coast of the subcontinent.

Summertime blues

Every now and then during a good summer southeaster, the False Bay beaches can be strewn with a curious collection of stranded animals, many of which are coloured blue, while a few verge on transparency. Known, not inappropriately, as the Blue Community, this pelagic posse is rendered inconspicuous by its coloration as it drifts around the open sea.

The most infamous member of the Blue Community is the Portuguese Man-o'-War, known locally as the Blue-bottle. This may look like one but it is not, in fact, a single animal. Rather it is a colony of creatures, each with its own task and working for the benefit of the whole. The long tentacle, which inflicts a nasty sting, can stretch to 10 metres, but its contracted length is a more modest 30 centimetres or so. The whole entity drifts on the open sea, the bubble-float acting as a sail as well as providing buoyancy. Two variations of the float are recognised, a 'right-handed' and a 'left-handed' form. The latter is shaped in such a way as to reduce the chances of its being blown ashore by the southeaster and hence tends to drift the animal to the left. This form typically occurs in the southwest Cape.

The Blue Community also includes a number of jelly-fish species, a small crab called the Columbus Crab (that explorer is reputed to be the first to have recorded one), and the Bubble Raft Shell or Violet Snail, which eats Blue-bottles and secretes bubbles of mucus from which it suspends itself at the sea surface. These are all essentially warm-water creatures and most often come ashore in summer on the reserve's east coast, notably at Buffels Bay.

Also blue and happier afloat than washed up are the goose barnacles. These are not part of the Blue Community, but are found in the open seas where they attach themselves to floating objects. In the days before anti-fouling paints, the performance of sailing ships could be greatly handicapped by the drag caused by hitch-hiking goose barnacles, and the ships had to be periodically beached and careened.

A long spar cast ashore at Bordjiesrif was the source of our goose barnacles, densely packed in their thousands. Onto this overcrowded cruise-ship some small swimming crabs and sea slugs had also stowed away. Goose barnacles feed by extracting plankton and organic particles from the water with their cirri. These are long, hairy appendages extended from the shell in a curved fan shape. The cirri are attached to the legs, from which it can be deduced that the old barnacle essentially spends most of its life standing on its head waving its feet around. The goose barnacle is so called because of early attempts to explain the mysterious arrival in autumn of the Barnacle Goose. This is a black-and-white goose which nests in Greenland and two Arctic Ocean islands and spends its winter in western Europe. As their nests were never seen, it was concluded that the geese developed from these barnacles, and there is many a medieval manuscript illustrating the process.

Swimming stones

Like the goose barnacle, a potentially distant, but in this case inanimate, drifter is the pumice stone, which washes up, especially after strong northwesters. The nearest volcanic activity to the Cape is on the ocean floor along the mid-Atlantic and Walvis Ridges, although it is not known if our pumice originates there. In August 1993 we found small, black pumice which had the colour and relatively large pores typical of that from Tristan da Cunha, which the islanders there know as 'swimming stones' (p. 148). There seems no reason to doubt that, given time, these black stones can 'swim' all the way from Tristan. If you are still sceptical, support for our theory is provided by a 'float card' which we found in May 1984. These are small, plastic cards used by scientists to study ocean currents. Ours was one of a batch of 25 dropped off in the South Atlantic about halfway between Cape Town and Gough Island in May 1969. Its landfall near the Cape of Good Hope was made 15 years and 1,500 kilometres later.

Exciting as such finds are, the most important articles to be washed up on the beach are the glistening lengths of the Sea Bamboo. Like manna from heaven, the Sea Bamboo provides sustenance, directly and indirectly, for everything from bacteria to baboons. Without it, the reserve's beaches would be very different and certainly not as full of wildlife as they are. But where does this largesse come from, and what makes it so important?

The underwater forest

When not mimicking large and venomous snakes basking on the beach, the Sea Bamboo and other similar kelps may be experienced as gently writhing stems and waving fronds smothering the water's surface at many spots along the coast. Extensive beds occur on the coastal platforms at Buffels Bay north to Venus Pool and along most of the west coast. In a regional context, the kelp forests are very much a west coast speciality, and gradually peter out along the south coast until vanishing at Cape Agulhas as the water warms up and supply of dissolved nutrients diminishes.

The kelp comprises a holdfast, a root-like structure which anchors it to the rocky sea-bed; and a long, hollow stem (the 'bamboo') at the top of which are the 'leaves', fronds or blades, which are strap-like to reduce resistance to the water and which extend from a gas-filled float that serves to keep them on the surface. The weed can attain 12 metres in length and will grow where there is suitable substratum to which it can attach. It grows extremely quickly (up to 13 millimetres each day in summer), and each square centimetre of its blades can, when fertile, produce up to 10,000 spores per hour. (Spores are reproductive units, the alga's equivalent of a plant's seeds.)

The depth to which the seaweed occurs is determined by the penetration of the sunlight required for photosynthesis. In the clear waters off Olifantsbos, for example, kelp flourishes down to 30 metres. With a supply of upwelled nutrients and an abundance of sunlight, the kelp thrives. Indeed, the amount of kelp growing at any one time between Cape Point and Cape Columbine, a distance of 180 kilometres, is estimated to be over half-a-million tonnes, of which 60 per cent is Sea Bamboo and 40 per cent the Split-fan Kelp. Exploiting this productive habitat is a wealth of creatures, ranging from microscopic plankton, through small invertebrates such as sea urchins and crabs, to fish, seals and, in the form of the angler and diver, ourselves.

Few animals feed directly on the living kelp, which may seem surprising given its abundance. Explanations for this absence of exploitation centre on the turbulence of the water in which the kelp grows and the slipperiness of the kelp stem, which together make it difficult for animals to attach themselves.

Kelp fronds which droop to touch the sea-bed are, however, eaten by Perlemoen, which clamp the weed beneath the front of their shell, where uneaten seaweed may also be stored for future consumption. A member of the widely distributed abalone family, the Perlemoen has a large, flat shell with a characteristic row of holes along its left side. Through these, waste products and deoxygenated water are expelled. It is a slow animal in all its activities, the more so in the cold waters off the Cape of Good Hope where it can take a dozen years or more to attain 12 centimetres in size. Spawning takes place in spring and autumn; up to 15 million eggs may be produced at one time by the bigger individuals.

The Perlemoen takes its name from the Dutch word *paarlemoer*, meaning mother-of-pearl, but long before it was thus christened it was well known to the original inhabitants of the Cape. Indeed, Perlemoen probably has the longest history of exploitation of any seafood in southern Africa, having been eaten for more than 125,000 years by indigenous and immigrant peoples. Their shells have been found in prehistoric middens at the reserve, and many are fished out by divers today. Chronic over-exploitation has, however, necessitated the introduction of catch restrictions. Recreational fishermen are allowed four per day, with a minimum size of 114 millimetres. There is no upper limit, no doubt to the dismay of the Perlemoen recently caught off Cape Point which measured 190 millimetres across and weighed a hefty 2.5 kilograms. The fact that when cooked this shellfish often resembles a casserole of rubber bands seems never to have dampened enthusiasm for it. On being shown a real live Perlemoen (as opposed to the diced ingredient of *bouillabaisse*), however, with its exploratory tentacles and oozy grace, one person we met at the reserve swore he would never eat one again. We are happy to have struck a blow for gastropods against gastronomes.

Rock lobsters revealed

Although yet to be fully investigated, the denizen of the kelp beds, the West Coast Rock Lobster, is thought to be one of the few creatures which use ocean currents to transport their offspring away from parent populations, only for the young to return many months later to resettle on home ground. The female rock lobster carries her eggs (up to 240,000 of them) under her tail for 80–90 days before they hatch into tiny, leaf-like larvae. In the southern Benguela, hatching occurs in late winter and spring, and the larvae then enter the South Atlantic gyre, the huge circular current which flows anticlockwise round this ocean. Within this current our local lobster larvae are joined by those of other Atlantic species from the mid-ocean seamounts and islands and from South America. This great seafood soup drifts around, feeding on zooplankton, for many months. When the appropriate point is reached in their travels, the larvae of each species alight at their respective natal area, having whizzed around the Atlantic past the birthplaces of near-relatives. How each species recognises its home is not known, but presumably some nuance of water chemistry or angle of the sun provides the necessary cue. Thus the Cape larvae, in turn, drop anchor back at the Cape, notwithstanding the attractions of Tristan or Brazil or wherever else it has been on its travels. Be a lobster and see the world.

Like so many creatures previously found in abundance and generally available to all and sundry (oysters and salmon, not to mention Perlemoen, also spring to mind in this context), the rock lobster has become something of a gourmet's delight and presently realises the most outrageous prices in restaurants. It is difficult to understand why this humble invertebrate has been elevated to such dizzy heights and is held in such esteem. It's not as if it's *so* tasty (many of the culinary *cognoscenti* would reckon it grossly over-rated), nor does its capture require even a modicum of sporting or cerebral skill (ducking for apples at Hallowe'en is marginally more challenging). Be this as it may, the pursuit and capture of the rock lobster, crayfishing, has become a popular, nay obsessional, pursuit of South Africans. Strict quotas are set for commercial and recreational crayfishermen, and sanctuary areas have been established at the reserve to protect the species.

Sandy beaches

There is only one sandy shore, Buffels Bay, on the reserve's east coast. The west coast, in contrast, is more generously blessed and is bounded by long ribbons of the most glorious, dazzling beaches.

From the wildlife point of view, sandy beaches are not as rich, at least superficially, as the rocky shoreline. However, there is a wealth of animals here, although many of them do require a microscope and some biological skills to appreciate. It is recognised that the sandy beaches that border the Benguela Upwelling exhibit some of the highest biomass values (that is, the weight of all living material – plant and animal – combined) for this type of habitat anywhere in the world. This is the result of the organisms benefiting from a high input of nutrients (a consequence of upwelling) and of kelp.

Kelp consumers

Kelp is cast onto the beaches with every tide, but the amount is greatest in winter when storms wrench the kelp from the sea-bed and hurl the glistening fronds onto the shores in monstrous mounds. At some spots, notably Olifantsbos and Strandbank, just north of the *Thomas T. Tucker*, there is an almost continuous input of kelp and other weeds. Great slimy, oozy terraces are formed, but these are consumed at a rate almost as fast as they are deposited. Which is just as well, as the kelp found at any one time on a metre-wide strip of beach from low to high water may weigh as much as 80 kilograms. Over a thousand kilograms of kelp may be deposited over the same area every year. Multiply this by the length of coastline to see just how much there would be on the shore were it not devoured.

The most important kelp-consumers of the sandy shores are probably the little Beach Hoppers, also known as sand-fleas because of their shape and jumping ability, if not their taxonomic status (they are amphipod crustaceans, not insects). These air-breathing animals occur in countless millions and generally emerge at night during low water from their above-tide retreats to feed on any weed which has been dumped ashore by the previous high tide. Lift a frond of damp kelp and you will likely disturb a gathering of these beasts, who will hop hysterically like animated rice pudding until they can collect their wits and bury themselves safely in the sand. Beach Hoppers consume over 300 kilograms of kelp per square metre each year, producing as a result 151 kilograms of droppings. These form the finest fertiliser, which provides nourishment for other sandy-shore animals, enriching what would otherwise be a very impoverished environment.

Also great devourers of kelp are the kelp flies or, at least, their larvae. The fly lays its eggs on stranded kelp at the top of the beach after spring high tide. This level is not reached by the water for another month, the intervening tides being lower. The eggs hatch and the larvae feed furiously and then pupate. After a total of 22–28 days the flies hatch, just in time to escape the next spring high tide. The swarms of flies are eaten by a variety of birds, from gulls to swallows, and the maggoty larvae are much sought after by waders, particularly Sanderling. On warm days after a hatch the flies form a low, grey haze just above the beach, on which the gulls stand with their bills wide and eyes narrowed in epicurean rapture as the insects cooperatively, if inadvertently, gather in their gapes.

Kelp does not, of course, discriminate between the types

of beach upon which it is stranded. On sandy shores, however, productivity is severely limited by an absence of stable or solid surfaces to which seaweeds and animals can attach. Consequently, a sandy beach community relies on kelp for its nutrients much more than does a rocky shore.

Ploughs and wedges

Two relatively large molluscs inhabit the reserve's sandy beaches. Both are adapted to withstand the rigours of existence here (life on the shore demands more than a beach towel and a brolly), but display a marked contrast in feeding habits. The one is the Finger Plough Shell, a pale-shelled snail-like creature which remains for much of the time buried in the sand. It is a scavenger and will eat any animals which wash up. Come the arrival of largesse in the form of a dead fish or Bluebottles, the plough shells emerge from the sand and converge upon the victim. This speedy response is accomplished through an ability to detect minute quantities of a chemical which is released by decomposing flesh. This chemical is trimethylamine, and can be registered by the plough shell at concentrations of one drop in a million.

When the tide rises, the plough shell sends up a periscope-like siphon with which it samples the water. If it detects the appropriate chemical, it exhumes itself from its sandy tomb and, in another remarkable adaptation, 'hoists' its great pancake-like foot. This seemingly unwieldy appendage catches an incoming wave and the shell surfs up the beach with aplomb. After a few such surfs and a little crawling of its own, it arrives at its target. It then eats as much as one-third of its own body weight before allowing itself to be carried by the receding waves back down the beach to its original position. Here it buries itself again and waits for the next delivery of edibles. This can take quite a time, and a single meal may have to sustain the shell for a fortnight or more.

Somewhat less at risk from the vagaries of food supply than the plough shell is the White Mussel, the second mollusc which typifies sandy beaches. This is not a true mussel, but a wedge clam of the family Donacidae. The White Mussel burrows into the sand with its powerful spade-like foot. Ensconced a few centimetres below the surface, it extends one long and one short tube out into the overlying water when the tide advances up the beach. Water is sucked through the shorter of the tubes, a filtering system excluding sand and extracting nutritious particles. The waste water is then expelled through the long tube. This can be a risky business as a favourite food of Whitefronted Plovers is the tips of these siphons, which the birds nip off when they protrude through the sand.

Growing against the grains

In addition to the decomposing kelp, an important source of nutrients is that fraction of the receding waves which does not flow back down the beach, but percolates into the sand. Here the water is filtered and particles of weed and other goodies trapped. The receding waves also leave a filigree of foam on the damp sand. This is a frothy, surf-constituted soup of macerated weed and detritus which also boosts the nutrient content of sand and helps a whole community of animals to live within it.

With individual members which are smaller, almost infinitely so, even than the flies and sandhoppers, this community comprises animals which live in the spaces between the grains of sand. These animals can be categorised according to size, and a convenient rating of macro-, meio- and microfauna has been agreed upon by biologists. Macrofauna are veritable giants, being more than a millimetre long and comprising annelid (segmented) worms, crustaceans and molluscs. They live near or on the sand surface and are predators, scavengers or filter-feeders.

Next on the list are the meiofauna, animals which are between 0.045 and 0.5 millimetres in length, are extremely diverse, and feed upon detritus as well as grazing upon bacteria and diatoms (algae with silicon-rich cell walls). Nematodes (round worms), oligochaetes (segmented worms) and harpacticoid copepods (crustaceans) predominate in this group, and a million or more of them may inhabit a square metre of beach.

Finally, the microfauna. Members of this group are extremely small, as their name indicates, occur in huge numbers and comprise mainly bacteria and protozoans (single-celled animals). These are important decomposers of detritus, making nutrients available to other plants and animals, and are themselves preyed upon by the meiofauna further along the food chain.

Data obtained from sandy beaches receiving moderate to large amounts of kelp (which would happily describe the Cape of Good Hope's west coast) yield values for macro-, meio- and microfauna of 3.1, 4.2 and 24.4 kilograms, respectively, per metre strip of beach per year. Such figures are very low compared with the biomass of rocky shores, but more than respectable for an environment which to the unsympathetic eye is as bleak and barren as a minor planet. If the sandy beaches at first glance seem sterile and dull, therefore, remember that with every step you take you will shadow thousands of organisms going about their business unseen and unappreciated.

Rocky shores

The reserve's rugged and beautiful rocky shores include cliffs which drop straight into the sea, jumbly boulder beaches and broad, gently sloping shelves and wave-cut platforms. In sharp contrast to sandy beaches, these rocky shores provide dependable shelters and solid foundations in and on which animals and plants can anchor themselves. Organic matter also accumulates in pools and gulleys, providing food for sessile or slow-moving shellfish and other organisms, which are, in turn, preyed upon by fish and crabs.

The distribution of plants and animals on these rocky shores is determined by the time they can spend out of water at low tide. The tolerance of each species to different periods of exposure and submersion is such that bands or zones can be distinguished at different levels on the beach by the communities found in them. The width of these ecological zones depends upon the slope of the beach: the steeper the rock, the narrower the zones. Any rock-face near Venus Pool at low tide will illustrate these zones at a glance if you are finding difficulty in discriminating them on the more gently sloping shores.

Horned Isopods

The distribution and abundance of plants and animals in these zones have been studied on rocky shores at Buffels Bay and Olifantsbos, and at an unstable boulder beach at the former site, where the rocks and stones can be shifted by heavy waves.

At the very top of the shore, which is submerged only briefly on a few days each month by the spring tides, is the Littorina Zone. This is a very simple community, comprising almost entirely a diminutive marine snail, the African Periwinkle (formerly known scientifically as *Littorina*, hence the name of the zone). These feed on the sparse algae and lichens which grow there. The periwinkles avoid contact with the heat of the rocks (which can become uncomfortably hot in summer) by suspending themselves by mucous threads from the rock surface or even from each other.

Beach Hoppers

Below the Littorina is the Balanoid Zone. *Balanus* is the scientific name of a group of barnacles which is found in this zone elsewhere and from which it gets its name. This is the first of the intertidal levels, which is inundated at every high tide, and it may further be divided into Upper, Middle and Lower.

The reserve's Balanoid Zone as a whole is home to the Granular Limpet. This mollusc occurs low down the shore when it is young, higher up when it gets older. Elderly individuals are bigger, with more domed shells than the youngsters, allowing the size of the animal inside to increase without a proportional increase in the size of their shell-opening. This reduces water loss and prevents drying out in the relatively long time for which this high shore zone is exposed at low tide. Hence the upshore migration of older, more domed individuals.

The Upper Balanoid supports rather few marine algae (seaweeds). Those that do occur are abundant only in winter and spring, when they grow most rapidly. The dominant alga here is the grey-green, limp-lettuce-like Purple Laver (as in the Celtic 'laver bread' made from a near-

relative). The zone is characterised by filter-feeding barnacles, of which the grey Volcano Barnacle (p. 153) and Toothed Barnacle are the most numerous. Chitons, or coat-of-mail shells, occur here in large numbers. These distinctive shellfish move around almost painfully slowly, scraping diatoms and algae from the rocks. One of the smaller species, the Brooding Chiton, often congregates in little groups, youngsters and adults huddling together like select gatherings of armoured sheep.

The Middle Balanoid Zone is also dominated by barnacles, with Common Dogwhelks and limpets occurring amongst a scattering of algae. A much greater variety of algae is found in the Lower Balanoid Zone, where barnacles are actually rather scarce, but whelks and limpets are abundant. The sandy tubes of the Cape Reef-worm make their first appearance here. These are sedentary polychaetes (many-bristled marine worms that stay in one spot) which construct their own tubular homes from sand grains. These form substantial and solid reefs, although fragments broken by the waves are commonly found on the tideline (p. 149). The tube provides protection from many predators, but the Cape Reef-worm has yet to hit upon a defence against the Pustular Triton (p. 150). This predatory whelk simply inserts its tubular snout in the reef-worm's front door, injects a dose of sulphuric acid (manufactured in special glands), and then draws up the resultant chowder.

The Lower Balanoid Zone is also characterised by larger numbers of limpets, represented by five or more species. Nevertheless, it should not be confused with the zone beneath it, which is completely dominated by one species of limpet, the Pear Limpet, whose scientific name is *Patella cochlear*. The name of the band in which it is so abundant is, consequently, the Cochlear Zone.

Resting between the low-water neap and low-water spring tides, the Cochlear Zone is a limpet enclave shared by very few other animals – the odd sandhopper-type and little or nothing else. Although one of the least diverse communities on the shore, the Cochlear Zone is one of the most interesting. Limpets are highly territorial and defend areas of rock against other limpets. After grazing (or, more accurately, rasping with their serrated tongue-like radulae) their 'patch', they return to the same position as the tide drops. Long-term occupation of these spots gives rise to scars on the rocks, and the shell fits snuggly into the miniature contours which they create. Such site-fidelity and territoriality result in regular, if crowded (over 2,600 per square metre at their densest), distribution of the animals. Within their territories the occupants incessantly graze algal sporelings, such that virtually the only algae which grow to any size are found in almost the only place the limpets can't reach them – on top of their shells! The otherwise bare rock is dotted with little algal clumps; these, on inspection, reveal themselves as tiny, lush, mobile roof gardens, molluscan Birnam Woods (p. 150). Limpets determine the growth and abundance of algae in this zone; if they are removed, the algae very quickly establish and form dense mats or beds. There is thus a sharp contrast between the low numbers and density of seaweed species in the Cochlear Zone and the veritable algal jungle in the next, and last, intertidal zone.

This is the Sub- or Infratidal Zone, which is at the lower extreme of the beach and only exposed by the lowest of spring low tides. Here is a wealth of plants and animals, few of which can tolerate exposure to the air for very long. Myriad microhabitats amongst the weeds provide home for a rich and diverse assemblage of small molluscs, crustaceans and errant polychaetes (those bristly worms again, but ones which move around). Where the shores are exposed to heavy wave action, filter-feeding animals occur in dense communities, notably the Ribbed Mussel and the Eight-shell Barnacle on the west coast, Brown Mussels and Red Bait on the False Bay coast.

Seaweeds

Seaweeds are some of the most conspicuous components of the seashore and near-shore coastal waters. Like their terrestrial counterparts, they provide food and shelter for a multitude of animals. In addition, the shade and moisture they afford prevents many intertidal creatures from drying out at low tide. They also dampen the force of incoming waves, a task most effectively executed by the beds of kelp.

Seaweeds are simple plants which have no true stems, roots or leaves, at least as we understand them in more complex plants. They come in three colour forms – green, red, and brown. Each absorbs different wavelengths of sunlight and occurs at broadly different levels in the water: the intertidal zone is occupied mainly by green algae, the lower shore by browns, and reds are found from here to the deeper subtidal.

Marine algae also vary greatly in size and structure, from tiny unbranched filaments to the metres-long stipes of Sea Bamboo; from diminutive balloon-like bladders to long ribbons; from crusty fans to slimy sheets. Although 'seaweed' may not conjure up a picture of anything as pretty as a flower, many of these marine algae are very beautiful.

The richness of the reserve's terrestrial plants is paralleled, in a relative way, by a wealth of seaweeds. The abundance of species is a consequence of the reserve's wide variety of marine habitats. Even the type of rock can influence the species of seaweed which grows upon it – a small intrusion of dolerite (a coarse volcanic rock) at Smitswinkel Bay, for example, supports a very different seaweed population from those growing on sandstone and granite nearby. Superimposed on these factors are the degree of wave exposure and differences in water temperature and nutrient levels which characterise the two sides of the Peninsula. These peculiar environmental attributes also result in the Cape of Good Hope being a transitional zone between warm-water south coast and cold-water west coast forms. Many species thus find themselves at the geographical limit of their range on one or other coast of the reserve. False Bay as a whole supports some 217 species of seaweed, including 34 brown algae, 43 green and 143 red – a remarkable richness. On the cold west coast a distinct seaweed flora is to be found, and the Benguela region as a whole supports more than 300 species.

Rockpools

You will never have to walk far to find plenty of pools to explore on the reserve's coastline. Twenty paces from the Cape of Good Hope car park, between the sandy bank and the rocky reef where the cormorants roost, the runnels and ill-defined pools are a treasure trove of marine life. The shallow water and gentle slope make the hunt for animals easy and safer than the steep shores, and much pleasure can be obtained from simply being a spectator and observing just how different life can be a few paces from the familiar and reassuring plants and animals of dry land.

Another fine stretch for rockhopping is the False Bay coast between Black Rocks and Venus Pool. Here are more conventional, steep-sided, deep rock pools to be explored. Check your tide tables and make a visit at spring low water (which, conveniently, always falls between nine and ten o'clock in the morning in this part of the world) on a calm day. Peep into a puddle or part the forests of weed overhanging the deeper canyons and gulleys dissecting the rocks to discover the most exquisite marine gardens encrusted with coralline algae and sponges, bejewelled with anemones and starfish, adorned with urchins and seashells. Klipvis dart around, perching on their stiff front fins and eyeing the intruder with mischievous, if endearing, expressions. Crabs scuttle back and forward, prawns fidget hither and thither, sea slugs slither, and grazing gastropods glide over lawns of algae green as grass. All very idyllic, and on a warm day the gentle slop of the waves and the dreamy sway of seaweed fronds in limpid pools paint a picture of watery bliss.

This is about as far from the truth as one can get. Here is a veritable battlefield, where a creature eats or is eaten, faces fiercesome competition for food, shelter and mates, and where an array of defences and weapons and devious stratagems is employed to meet or counter these demands. Not only do the animals make life uncomfortable for one another, but the battering of the twice-daily incoming tides, often accompanied by rapid changes in temperature (if the pool has heated up in the sun) and salinity (if rain has diluted the seawater), does not make for a relaxing lifestyle.

False Plums, hedgehogs and hermits

Unmistakable in this marine war zone are the sea anemones. No, they are not plants, but hollow-bodied animals which cling to the rocks and wait, like gorgeous mute sirens, for something edible to fall fortuitously (dislodged mussels) or be attracted (curious klipvis) into their flower-like, tentacle-encircled mouths. The tentacles envelop the victim and stinging cells paralyse it before it is manoeuvred inexorably to the mouth. Anemones are speedier than they look – they respond in a flash to a touch, the tentacles embracing their prey or withdrawing into the sanctuary of the body depending upon the stimulation. An exception to this general rule is the False Plum Anemone, which can only retract its tentacles rather slowly. This species may be fire-engine red or, like our specimen (p. 161), pale orange with pink-tipped tentacles. They also are surprisingly mobile and can move slowly around their pool to find a more salubrious position or to maintain territorial advantage over enemy anemones.

Everyone is familiar with those celestial bodies of the intertidal, the starfish. The most numerous species at the reserve is probably the Dwarf Cushion Star. Their mosaic patterning is a perplexing mixture of chaos and conformity, pentagonal Florentine on pincushions into which one would be loth to stick a pin. Some sport shades of red, from brightest crimson to palest pink. The more dramatically disposed opt for a mystery of midnight blue with needle-points of white. Yet others are more rustic and choose the seasonal assembly – vernal greens or autumnal browns. Some stars go totally overboard and combine the lot. Whatever the combination, never does the result jar the eye; the embroiderer's art would be tested to achieve such well-composed and expertly stitched designs. We are told that their colouring is cryptic, but we see so many on sharply contrasting backgrounds that this is hard to credit. Indeed, a carpet of pink encrusting algae can be liberally decorated with an array of cushion stars of every colour *except* pink. If their upper surface indicates considerable artistic inclinations, their under tends more to the practical. Their feeding technique involves extruding the stomach out of the mouth and contouring it onto the rock surface upon which they digest tiny algal growths. This might not be an easy concept to grasp, but for the sake of good taste we shall not attempt to describe an analogous situation in humans, adding as it could a whole new dimension to the concept of 'eating out'.

More conventionally starfish-like than the cushion star is the Spiny Starfish (p. 159), characterised by a spiny body which is usually orange, occasionally grey. It can exceed 20 centimetres across and is found under rocks and overhangs in pools and gulleys. A predator of sedentary organisms, it specialises in feeding upon mussels which it prises apart by sustained pressure on the two valves. When the latter separate, the starfish slips its stomach through the gap and begins digestion of the mussel flesh.

Everyone is also familiar with sea urchins. Their scientific name, Echinodermata, means 'skin like a hedgehog'. Need we say more? Some of the low-shore pools at the reserve, particularly at Bordjiesrif, are jam-packed with Cape Urchins, mainly shades of purple, with the occasional red or green one dotted around. Some look like intertidal rag-and-bone men with a cloak of adhering shell fragments and scraps of weed.

Not 'true' crabs, but closely related to them, are the hermits. Little groups may be found gathered under boulders in rock pools on both sides of the Peninsula. These are celebrated for their occupation of the empty spiral shells of gastropods, such as whelks and winkles. They have a curved abdomen and a pair of short, horny back legs which are used to wedge the creature into the shell of its choosing. The hermit crabs are an estate agent's dream as they are forever moving house, even before they have outgrown the one they are in.

Whereas the hermits have adopted a shell, other rockpool creatures seem to be in the process of losing them. The keyhole limpet has reduced its shell to little more than a small hat, possibly because it has substituted armour plating with poison as a defence strategy. Through the 'keyhole' in the shell protrudes a funnel which voids waste products. The dark, slug-like animal beneath rumbles along at sometimes surprising speed, and executes fluid and graceful movements as it travels (p. xxx) in its search for seaweed to graze.

The Alikreukel, or Giant Periwinkle, illustrated on the same page is made the more interesting by the Slipper Limpets which it carries. These are filter-feeders which are invariably attached to other shells. A single Slipper Limpet on a shell is always a female; the next to settle is a male. If another settles on top of him, the newcomer will be a male and the one now below him, our original male, changes into a female, and so on. At the end of the day, the topmost limpet is a male. Oblivious of the licentious behaviour on its roof, the Alikreukel goes about its business of feeding on seaweed and growing slowly.

Klippies and their kin

Rockpool fish generally are small, cryptic and carnivorous. They tend to live on or near the bottom and will rapidly take cover as your threatening shadow passes over their pools. A not-too-long wait on your part will see them relax and emerge again, affording you the opportunity to watch them going about their business.

The fish which characterise the Peninsula pools belong to the goby, Rocksucker, blenny and klipvis (literally 'rock fish') families. Whereas the first three are represented by one or two species each, at least 16 of southern Africa's 39 klipvis species occur here, and the family as a whole is endemic to the subcontinent's coastal waters.

The major factor influencing the abundance, number of species and biomass of rockpool fish is the amount of rock cover in the pools. On this basis, a large pool does not hold more fish than a small one purely because it is bigger, but because, generally, it provides more cover. The significance of cover rests not only in its obvious importance as a sanctuary from turbulent waves or predators, such as kingfishers and egrets, but in the fact that other organisms also live in nooks and crannies and beneath overhangs and rocks. Many of these, such as shellfish and crabs, are favoured prey of the fish. It is not surprising, therefore, that the fish tend to loiter with intent where food is to be found.

The diets of most of the rockpool fish are varied and overlap to a greater or lesser extent. Many species show preferences for certain food types, however. The klipvis eat large numbers of isopods and amphipods. The Rocksucker displays size-related trends in its feeding habits. Small ones (less than 2.5 centimetres) eat only small crustaceans; ones over 15 centimetres ignore this food almost completely. The Banded Goby is a veritable vegetarian, feeding almost entirely on *Enteromorpha*, the sea lettuce. A few molluscs and worms are eaten, but one wonders if these are consumed accidentally while eating the algae, in much the same way that you might swallow a slug with your salad.

Fish and fishing

The fish fauna of the reserve's coastal waters has been most intensely studied by those who take the greatest interest in it – the anglers. An idea of the types and sizes of fish caught at the Cape of Good Hope is available from information collated by the Oceanographic Research Institute in Durban. As part of its investigation into marine sport fishing, the Institute requests anglers to record and submit on special cards details of their catches (the species, numbers and weight of fish caught at a particular location, together with the time spent catching them and the number of rods involved). Such statistics rely on the goodwill and help of fishermen who are willing to supply such details and will, in the long term, benefit fish and fishermen alike.

The Oceanographic Research Institute data indicate that almost 30 species of fish are caught from the reserve's coast. The most commonly caught fish are Hottentot, Galjoen and Yellowtail. The first two species are caught predominantly on the southwest coast, the last-named almost exclusively at Rooikrans, the locality which accounted for about 50 per cent of the cards.

The Rooikrans ledges

Among the angling fraternity, the Rooikrans ledges rank among the finest sites from which to fish, not just in South Africa, but in the world. Here on the False Bay coast a rough track at the foot of Vasco da Gama Peak leads along the cliff edge and down to the ledges a couple of metres above the sea. In very few places elsewhere in South Africa is deep water accessible from the shore, and the natural topography and currents at Rooikrans seem to encourage the nearshore coasting of fish more traditionally found farther out to sea. This brings them within striking distance of the land-based fisherman.

The 'discovery' of the Rooikrans riches has been attributed to a certain Mr Reynolds who, while camping on the east coast in 1905, took a walk towards Cape Point with his dog. Returning to his campsite, he informed his friends that he had found a 'wonderful place' for fishing. The next day they all went to investigate his claims and saw for themselves the fish swimming close to the surface below the perfectly positioned (for angling) ledges. It was not long before some of the fish joined them on dry land, although the biggest ones got off the hook (don't they always?).

Since then, Rooikrans has become something of a point of pilgrimage for anglers. It is also a superb site for sitting and watching fish, large and small, from sardines to sharks, swim past within a few metres of the cliff edge. The major spectacle, as well as a target of the anglers, is provided in summer by Yellowtail, Rooikrans's most celebrated fish. Yellowtail are found in temperate southern oceans, and in South African waters migrate rapidly (up to 50 kilometres per day) and extensively in enormous shoals along the south and east coasts. Spawning occurs off the coast of Natal in the summer and autumn until April or May. It is a fast-growing fish, reaching 40 centimetres in the first year. The biggest Yellowtails weigh up to 60 kilograms.

In the 1950s and 1960s 'flashes' of Yellowtail in the summer attracted many anglers to Rooikrans, and some memorable catches were made, both in the numbers (up to 400 Yellowtail a day) and in the size of fish landed. The bounty did not last, however, and by the 1980s the species had virtually disappeared from the bay. A ban on commercial netting in False Bay in 1982 had the almost immediate effect of improving recreational and commercial line catches, and life improved for the Rooikrans faithful. Shoals of Yellowtail may remain in False Bay for a few days at a time, but changes in currents or a drop in water temperature will see them moving on. Cold water discourages them from coming into the bay, as it did for much of the 1994 summer season when catches from the ledges were very meagre. No amount of legislation will warm up the water, so the anglers are still at the whims of the elements.

Snoek, line and sinker

The barracuda-like Snoek, that most famous of Cape fish, was formerly caught in quite large numbers from Rooikrans but has become scarce in recent years. It is still caught in varying numbers from boats not far out in the bay; the sight of a silver stream of fish being hauled in over the gunwales being somewhat

Pelagic crab eating Goose-barnacles

galling to the anglers ashore who cast their lures in vain. Weighing up to about nine kilograms (ours on pp. 162–163 is a small specimen), the fish demands care and respect because of its very sharp teeth, which will lacerate the unwary. The Snoek has become a feature of Cape Town's fishing folklore and, not least, its seafood cookery. There seem to be limitless ways in which it can be prepared, and it is the major ingredient of canned, pickled or curried fish (and familiar as such the world over; in World War Two it joined the ranks of horse flesh and whale meat in efforts to boost the ratings of rations). Snoek, incidentally, is Dutch for 'Pike', and reflects the habits and, to some extent, the looks of that well-known European freshwater pirate.

All the fish described so far are voracious piscivores (eaters of other fish). Their presence in False Bay can be attributed to the abundance and behaviour of the shoals of their main prey. The appearance of Snoek from more northerly waters between May and August certainly co-incides with the arrival of the shoals of juvenile Pilchard and Anchovy from the Agulhas Bank where they are spawned. On their migration, these small fish often take a dog-leg into False Bay, swimming close to the surface and, on calm days, manifesting themselves as large 'thumbprints', great discs of rippling water dotted across the bay. As well as predatory fish, these attract dolphins and seals below the surface, and seabirds above it.

When the gamefish are not running, the angler must modify his technique or move locality if he wants to try his luck with some of the other species found in the reserve's coastal waters. In addition to Rooikrans, rock angling is popularly practised on the west coast from Hoek van Bobbejaan south to the Cape of Good Hope. Here are rocky shelves indented with numerous gulleys and geos which provide foraging areas for the fish.

The fish sought at these sites are predominantly members of the sea bream family (Sparidae) and other species which are solitary, or occur in small numbers, and feed mainly on sedentary organisms. A conventional hook and sinker and a variety of baits (but particularly Red Bait) are used to catch these. Of course, it is not always possible to dictate exactly what species of fish will take your bait, and many of those hauled ashore are inedible and undesirable from the angling point of view. These include Spearnose Skate, Spotted Gulley Shark and Lesser Sandshark. A species which does make a particular nuisance of itself, as far as anglers are concerned, is the Evil-eye Puffer, which is a common inhabitant of sandy-bottomed areas and frequently takes bait intended for other fish.

But is our puffer (p. 152) in fact a Milkspotted Blaasop, which it so closely resembles that taxonomists are not sure if the two are not actually the same species? No matter, as one or both are members of the family Tetraodontidae, a group of fishes which displays many unusual features. One of the most remarkable of these is their ability to swallow water or air and essentially blow themselves up. In becom-ing more spherical, they look correspondingly more formidable, and would-be predators are less likely to have a go at them. Another aspect which makes them somewhat unappealing as a meal is the fact that their internal organs are lethally poisonous. Nevertheless, the blaasop's flesh is highly prized by the Japanese, who know it as *fugu*. Specially trained chefs expertly (one hopes) remove the nasty bits before serving it up to discerning gourmets. This fashion has, however, yet to catch on in South Africa where methods of doing away with oneself have not reached the levels of refinement practised in the Orient.

Other species of fish caught at the reserve make excel-lent eating without involving extreme personal risk, and are thus more sought after. One such is the Galjoen, which investigates frothy, turbulent gullies after the first winter storms have churned around the accumulated seaweed and other organic detritus of the summer. From April or May onwards, fishermen hunt this species along the reserve's rugged west coast, favouring spots such as Neptune's Dairy and Pappiesbank. It is succulent and, although an acquired taste, is reckoned to be second only to Snoek as a local favourite.

Outclassing both of these, in our opinion, is the Roman. Not only is this a splendid fish to eat, but is handsome to boot (p. 165). The origin of the name is a little obscure, but may derive from the cross-mark on its back (the side view shows one 'arm', a white smudge, of this cross). According to one source, the name was given to the fish as a label of derision by the Protestant emigrants to the Cape, the Huguenots, who fled their Roman Catholic per-secutors in France in the late seventeenth century. Alternatively, the name may be a simple corruption of the Dutch *rooi man* meaning 'red man'. The Roman is caught occasionally from Rooikrans, but is more often encoun-tered off the west coast. The largest attain four kilograms. This species shares with others in the sea bream family the curious phenomenon of sex reversal. When born, all the Romans are female and congregate in small shoals. As life progresses and the numbers of that particular age-class diminish as a result of predation and disease, an age is reached at which the survivors turn into males. They also become unsociable and solitary and ensconce themselves in small caves, which they defend against encroaching males. At breeding time they accumulate a harem of jeal-ously guarded females. The population of Romans at any one time, therefore, comprises lots of young, frisky females and a few old cantankerous males.

Turtles and terrors

We have hinted that Rooikrans can be a source of inter-est and excitement not just to the fisherman but to the wildlife enthusiast in general. Although much patience may be required, plus a dollop of good fortune and, not least, calm and clear water, it is possible to see some remarkable sea creatures from the ledges. The summer of 1992, for example, when the water was particularly warm, brought a Leatherbacked Turtle. An individual which swam past was reportedly not much smaller than a VW Beetle. A slight exaggeration, perhaps, but it is certainly not too dissimilar in shape, and the full-grown Leatherback can weigh up to 700 kilograms.

The migration routes of Leatherback and Loggerhead Turtles take them along South Africa's south coast and west to the Cape of Good Hope. Youngsters marked at the Zululand breeding beaches have been found in False Bay, and some may round the Cape in autumn in warm water.

The Leatherback which appeared at Rooikrans approached and investigated each of a group of divers in turn, which must have been a thrilling experience, if only for the people. Divers here have the chance to experience very close encounters with marine animals. Not the least exciting are the sharks which are common here and can also be seen from the relative comfort and safety of the ledges. Bronze Whalers are the most abundant; other species recorded include Smooth Hammerhead (whose curious head-shape may enhance binocular vision) and, every now and then, Great White.

There is one confirmed record of a shark attack at the reserve, which involved a swimmer bitten at Buffels Bay. The disappearance of at least one diver off Rooikrans has, however, been attributed to a Great White. Or, as some old salts would ruefully conclude, *the* Great White. Being the infamous 'Submarine', a massive and semi-mythical Great White rumoured to patrol False Bay and spice up its menu of fur seals at Seal Island with the occasional human being. This creature has entered the local folklore alongside the *Flying Dutchman* and, like the phantom ship, is rarely observed, but does not seem to be able to vanish from the scene.

False Bay is reported to contain the highest density of Great White Sharks in the world, which may or may not be the sort of statistic that should be bandied about when trying to attract tourists. The fact remains, however, that swimmers and divers are infinitely more likely to come to grief on their journey to the sea than to fall victim to a shark when they get there. Between 1925 and 1988 there were 123 documented Great White Shark attacks on humans *worldwide*, of which 25 were fatal.

There she blows

Seven species of whale have been recorded from the reserve, of which the commonest is the Southern Right Whale. This is something of a South African celebrity. It enjoys special protection, and it is source of delight to the many visitors who come to enjoy its heavyweight aquabatics. The right whales (there is a Northern one, too) were so called because they were the right whales to harpoon – they yielded high-quality oil and baleen and conveniently floated when killed, making them relatively easy to retrieve for

processing. The oil was a valuable illuminant and lubricant and the baleen was put to a variety of uses, ranging from umbrellas and hairbrush bristles to chair springs and corset stays. It is certainly ironic that a whale of enormous girth should be sacrificed to disguise the figure of similarly constructed ladies.

Buffels Bay was one of a number of shore-based whaling stations which operated in False Bay during the last century and early years of the present one. After an initial period of hunting in which the whales provided a seemingly limitless source of revenue, it was not surprising that their numbers not so much dwindled as plummeted. The last-recorded attempt to harpoon a whale from an open boat in False Bay seems to have been made in August 1929. In 1935, protection was extended to those few remaining whales which could benefit from such legislation. These conservation measures came just in time, and although it would be premature to declare the species safe and sound, the Southern Right at least has increased slowly and steadily to a relatively healthy level today.

Southern Right Whales grow up to 14 metres and 47 tonnes (males) and 18 metres and 67 tonnes (females). They are dark blue-grey on top with a variable amount of white on the underside, sometimes spreading to the upper surface. Occasionally, all-white animals are recorded. Distinguishing features of the species are the absence of a dorsal (back) fin and the callosities, pale growths of cornified skin infested with parasites, which decorate the head. When observed from the appropriate angle, the spout can be seen to be a double one, which forms a V-shape if not distorted by the wind.

They arrive in South African waters around May and spend the winter and early spring in sheltered coastal waters. Calves conceived the previous year are born, and courtship and mating between the adults take place. It is the nuptials of these great beasts which provide such a display, and they can be witnessed from almost anywhere along the reserve's False Bay coastline, less frequently on the west. When they are displaying, up to a dozen whales may gather in loose assemblages in False Bay where they can be easily watched by visitors. Courting couples prefer shallow water of about 12–15 metres deep, in which they spend a lot of time standing on their heads, their tail flukes projecting above the water and waving around in a most beguiling way. Males and females both leap from the water, launching almost their entire bodies out before executing a half-twist and crashing thunderously to the sea with the mother of all splashes. Individuals will make these leaps, known as breaches, ten or more times in fairly quick succession.

Having paired up, the couple face the daunting task of mating. Lining up the two enormous bulks into the appropriate position must be about as straightforward as docking two orbiting space capsules. But the whales manage to consummate their relationship through a combination of embraces (which would look affectionate if biologists were permitted to accord emotions to animals) and assistance from attendant supporters and helpers (which would be indecorous to a degree if psychologists were allowed to apply morals similarly). The resultant whale mêlées are accompanied by powerful thrashing of the water with the flippers and vigorous exhalation of air through the blow-holes. Both these activities are audible from some distance. Gestation takes almost a whole year and expectant mothers return to the calving grounds, give birth and may sometimes leave before the other adults arrive to mate.

In early spring the Southern Right Whales move south to Antarctic waters where they gorge themselves on krill (astronomically abundant shrimp-like crustaceans). The seasonal disappearance of the whales from local waters was interpreted in a quaint way by some of the early whalers. It was believed that friction between a whale's skin and its blubber was occasionally sufficient to set it on fire. Having thus ignited, the creature would set off southwards at full tilt, fumes billowing out behind, to cool itself in Antarctic seas!

Marooned mammals

In a decidedly bulkier category than the sea beans which we described earlier, whales do occasionally wash ashore at the reserve. The most recent strandings have involved an unseasonal subadult Southern Right Whale (a real baby at about five metres long) on the rocky coastline below the Meadows in March 1994 and, even more unusually, a Pygmy Right Whale from about the same spot in May the previous year. The latter is a Southern Ocean species which has a circumpolar distribution, but of which very little is known.

In a similar class of rarity, but delving a little further into the past, was a Layard's Beaked Whale which was found, probably at Buffels Bay, in about 1865. The specimen, or what little remained of it, was inspected in the summer of 1873 by Henry Moseley, the biologist aboard HMS *Challenger*, which was on a pioneering round-the-world scientific expedition. Moseley met up with Mr McKellar of Buffelsfontein and was informed about the whale. It had, said McKellar, washed ashore some eight years previously and had yielded a very superior oil, which fetched twice the price of ordinary (presumably Southern Right Whale) oil. To add insult to injury, only the top part of the skull now remained, and it was propped up in the sand to be used for target practice!

Dolphin delights

At least ten species of dolphin have been recorded from southwestern Cape waters, but only three of these – Common, Dusky and Atlantic Ocean Bottlenosed – have so far deigned to show themselves at the reserve, the last-named only rarely.

The Common Dolphin we associate with False Bay and its feeding frenzies. Often the dolphins seem to be leading the hunt and move through in a tight pack at considerable speed, with the seabirds trailing in the wake. It is difficult to determine the numbers involved, but we feel that a figure in excess of 4,000 would not be unreasonable for some of the bigger congregations. If this seems excessive, it is worth noting that schools of up to 300,000 have been recorded elsewhere in the world. The sight of a school of dolphins on the hunt is an impressive one. They scythe through the water not just with enviable ease and grace, but with unmistakable killer instinct which seems to sustain them just above the water for longer than they are in it. Every now and then one will leap clear of the surface and execute a succession of half-twists, smacking down on the water with some force. When not in pursuit of Pilchards, Common Dolphins mill around and cruise slowly and languorously through the water. Often on calm days they perform delightfully engaging and balletic routines. We have seen particularly flamboyant individuals carry out the most startling and accomplished gymnastics involving forward and reverse somersaults, twists and rushes. No doubt there is some deep-seated biological basis for this demonstrative behaviour, but only the most hardened scientist would deny that sheer unadulterated pleasure must be the prime motivation.

Dusky Dolphins are about 25 per cent bigger than Commons, attaining 2.1 metres, and have a much blunter snout. They have black upperparts, greyish sides and are white underneath. In our experience they are rare in False Bay, occurring almost exclusively in the cold Benguela on the western side. Very little is known about them despite the fact that they occur widely in the southern hemisphere south of 30°. Even their diet is obscure, although around New Zealand and the Falkland Islands they eat mainly squid.

Seals and sea elephants

A marine mammal which you may encounter on your beach walk, although it is often visible at sea, is the Cape Fur Seal. This pinniped (meaning 'fin-footed') does not breed at the reserve, but is found ashore now and then. Some of these animals may leave the sea voluntarily, and enjoy a snooze on the rocks in the warmth of the sun. They may stay for a few hours before slipping back into the water, of their own choice or if disturbed by visitors. Other fur seals on the beach are less fortunate, being sick or injured and come ashore to die.

Schools of many thousands of seals may sometimes be seen porpoising speedily in pursuit of shoaling fish. Such schools are most readily spotted from the False Bay coast of the reserve, and are often accompanied by seabirds in the way that foraging dolphins are also associated with feeding frenzies. If you don't find a seal on the beach or spot a school offshore, your best chance of admiring one of these graceful creatures is to peer down from the viewing sites at Cape Point. At the base of the cliffs here, the sleek seals can be watched wallowing indulgently in the swell or cruising underwater like refined torpedoes.

Three other species are rare visitors to the reserve – Leopard (one record), Subantarctic Fur (two), and Southern Elephant seals (five). The last-named have all hauled out in the months of November to April. The most recent was a young female which came ashore at Neptune's Dairy in February 1994 and spent most of the month there soaking up the sunshine and moulting merrily. It is postulated that elephant seals recorded in this country are not, as might be expected, from the closest colonies at Gough and Marion islands, but from the much more distant island of South Georgia.

Birds on the beaches

The birds of the Cape of Good Hope coastline are a motley crew. They come in all shapes and sizes, belong to diverse families, are resident or are seasonal visitors from far-flung corners of the world. The shore may be used for any or all of the activities of feeding, breeding and roosting. If the term 'shorebird' encompasses any bird which at some time or another visits the shore, then our scope is broad. Indeed, one of the most interesting facets of the reserve's coastline is just how many traditionally terrestrial birds find their way there. The majority of the shorebirds, or birds on the shore, are, however, more conventional coastal species, the cormorants, waders, gulls and terns.

'A sort of bird'

An immediate addition to this list is the Jackass Penguin. For many people the concept of a penguin on a sweltering African beach is an incongruous one. Surely these are birds of icebergs and snowy Antarctic wastes? If the illustrators of Christmas cards are to be believed, penguins share their floes with Polar Bears, which is about as accurate as positioning the Star of Bethlehem somewhere over Honolulu.

Despite staunch popular efforts to keep them on ice, the Jackass Penguin is a genuine African article and is a regular visitor to the reserve, coming ashore singly or in twos and threes (p. 156). An eighteenth-century editor, commenting on the writings of Abbé Nicolas de la Caille, a visitor to the Cape, says of the Jackass Penguin: 'The penguin is a sort of bird which stands erect on its feet, the wings have no feathers, and hang down like sleeves, striped and cross-striped with white. It does not fly, and lives apart from all other birds. There is in it something of man, of bird, and of fish.'

The 'bird' component we take to be the bill and feathers; the 'fish', the accomplished swimmer. The 'man' part we would delegate to the fact that the Jackass spends a good deal of its time on the beach lounging around doing nothing other than making large amounts of noise and smell for no readily apparent reason.

Sea ravens and sheldgeese

The cormorant, according to our dictionary, is a 'large lustrous-black voracious sea-bird'. Which I suppose is as good a definition as any, although a little variation on the theme is required to account for the almost thirty species of marine cormorant found worldwide. Four of these occur at the reserve and two, the Whitebreasted and Cape, breed here. They are more sea- than shorebirds really, but your best views will be had of them roosting on the rocks or beaches.

The largest, and easiest to identify, is the White-

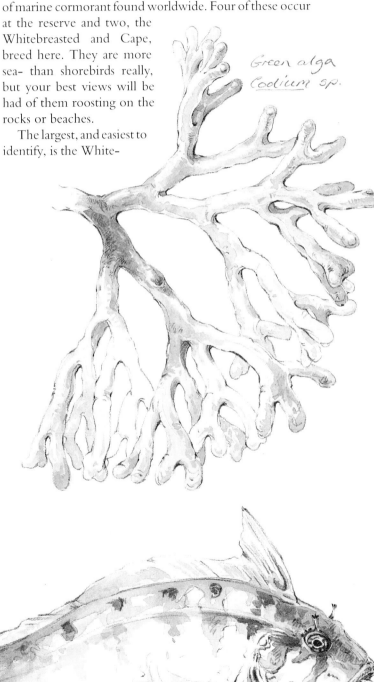

Green alga
Codium sp.

Super Klipvis
Clinus superciliosus

breasted, the local form of the wide-ranging Great Cormorant, whose scientific name, *Phalacrocorax carbo*, means 'charcoal-coloured sea raven'. In South Africa the species is found on fresh- and salt-water, and the hefty heap of sticks, foliage and sundry artefacts which it calls a nest is placed on the ground, up a tree or, as at Cape Point, on seacliffs. It is some time since a census was carried out, but at least a hundred pairs breed on the sandstone ledges of the Point and Cape Maclear and possibly elsewhere in the southeast and northeast of the reserve. Their large size and white breast make them unmistakable, although immatures are less boldly marked.

Far more numerous as both a breeder and visitor is the Cape Cormorant. Endemic to the southern African coast, it is exclusively marine and occurs in vast feeding flocks in False Bay in winter. The great dark strings of small goose-like birds which you may see pressing past the Point are almost certainly Cape Cormorants. Thousands often come ashore to roost on Dias Beach where, from a distance, they look like a huge black amoeboid organism, which intermittently engulfs or ejects black particles as birds join or leave the throng. The reserve's 2,300 or so pairs are but a fraction of the entire population of half-a-million birds, but is nevertheless significant as the largest mainland breeding colony. The Point holds the greatest numbers, but there are small colonies at Batsata Cove and, possibly, near Rooikrans.

The Cape Cormorant's nest is an untidy but solidly constructed heap of sticks lined with fresh plant material. At the Cape of Good Hope car park at nest-building time, the cormorants lollop along the ground, bickering and jostling in their efforts to tear up straggling stems of a grey, creeping *Helichrysum* with which to pad their nests. The plant is mildly aromatic and one is tempted to believe that the birds select it for its redolence or any insecticidal properties it may have (nests and their occupants are often infested with fleas, ticks and lice). Having selected or stolen from another bird their length of plant, like satanic thurifers looking for a light the cormorants disappear around the corner of the continent.

Two other cormorant species are non-breeding visitors to the reserve. The one is the small, long-tailed and jauntily crested Crowned Cormorant. Just how relatively diminutive they are is apparent when they sit next to a towering Whitebreasted. The other visitor is the Bank Cormorant, which is all-black, with a white rump in breeding plumage. The dark bottle-green eye is distinctive if you confront a bird at close quarters. It is restricted to the Benguela Upwelling System and found only where the Bladder Kelp grows in sheltered rocky lagoons and coves landward of the great forests of Sea Bamboo.

The Cape of Good Hope is a dependable spot at which to see all four species together. Those cormorants with their wings outspread are not spinning tales about the size of the fish they just lost, but are drying their feathers. Cormorants are unusual among water birds in having flight feathers which become waterlogged during their underwater foraging trips. They thus are obliged to hang them out to dry like the weekly wash every time they return from a fishing expedition. Feather maintenance and preening are also carried out at the roost, and oil from their uropygial (preen) gland at the base of the tail is rubbed over the plumage to keep it sleek and in good trim (p. 157).

For a bird associated with freshwater everywhere from the Okavango Delta to suburban swimming-pools, it might be surprising to find the Egyptian Goose in our seashore chapter. Nevertheless, this sheldgoose (it is not a true goose, or a duck for that matter, but somewhere between the two) is very much a mariner at the reserve. In the absence of much freshwater, they have adapted, quite happily it would seem, to a life on the ocean wave. The largest numbers are found on the west coast, with peak counts of over 70 at The Fishery.

It is remarkable that the flightless young can survive exclusively in saltwater for the fifty or more days before they fledge. In the summer months there is no rain to create puddles in the rocks, and the birds occur anything up to three kilometres from the nearest freshwater outfall.

We must conclude that the youngsters, if not their parents, drink seawater or obtain the moisture they require from their food (which, being marine algae, is unlikely to be very thirst-quenching). Genuine seabirds such as albatrosses and penguins have special glands which allow them to desalinate seawater and excrete the salt, but how the geese maintain a physiological balance and survive on the shore is something of a mystery. The excretion of salt by the salt-glands is controlled by hormones produced by the adrenal glands. Saltwater birds have larger adrenal glands than freshwater birds; where species live in both habitats, those which frequent the sea have larger adrenals. Since the Egyptian Goose is not recognised as having such dual citizenship, it would be interesting to see if the Cape of Good Hope birds are unique among 'gypos' in having large adrenal glands.

Resident waders

An almost universal feature of seashores is the presence of long-legged, long-billed birds which feed on the beach, at the water's edge or in the shallows – the waders. Plenty of birds wade, but this doesn't make them, in the ornithological sense, waders (so we will not be describing here the Ostrich which every now and then has a paddle at Olifantsbos). Strictly speaking, it is a term applied to the birds belonging to the family Charadriiformes. In our context it includes species which spend some part of the year at the shore, some which are long-distance migrants, and all of which, when at the reserve, obtain their food at, near or just beyond the water's edge. The waders also include some of the trickiest of species to identify, as well as some which are mercifully straightforward to recognise.

The latter category is topped by the African Black Oystercatcher, the most distinctive wader found on the reserve beaches (p. 185). The call, a loud *kleep kleep*, is also unmistakable. The reserve population of some fifty pairs is found mainly on the west coast.

The African Black Oystercatcher feeds on a variety of intertidal invertebrates, but its long and solidly constructed bill makes it an effective priser and chiseller of shellfish, its preferred food. Slight differences in bill morphology result in the females specialising in mussels, the males in limpets. The mussels are 'stalked' by the oystercatcher in shallow rock pools or at the water's edge where the bivalves are still open and feeding. The bird jabs its beak between the valves, severing the major mussel muscle, the posterior adductor, disabling the shellfish and preventing it from closing up. The flesh is then extracted on site or the shell wedged in a suitable crevice to facilitate removal of the tasty bits.

If you have ever tried to dislodge a limpet from the rocks you will appreciate how difficult a task it is. The oystercatcher is an accomplished limpet leverer, combining timing and technique to perform the operation. Limpets do not adhere tightly to the rock surface until the tide has dropped. When the water is shallow or the waves are still splashing over them, they continue to move around or fail to secure themselves. At this stage they are vulnerable, and a sharp blow to the bottom of the shell, followed by a hefty push, is often enough for an oystercatcher to dislodge large specimens. Failing that, the oystercatcher then pushes its bill under the limpet and levers it off. Smaller limpets are less of a challenge and normally require one sharp whack to detach from the wet rock.

The oystercatchers breed in high summer, the eggs being laid from December to February, and chicks appearing from January to May. Clutch size is one, two or, very occasionally, three eggs. Both parents take part in the incubation, and if all progresses smoothly the eggs hatch after about 32 days. Rarely is breeding a smooth operation, however. In the first instance the oystercatcher is a student of the school of architectural minimalism. The nest is but a shallow, saucer-shaped depression, often on a slightly raised hummock of sand, and often below the spring high-tide line. No effort is made to conceal the clutch or nest site, and the incubating bird generally is highly conspicuous, being black against the almost white sand. It does slip off the eggs quietly when approached. Although the eggs are mildly cryptic, the nest is almost invariably located next to an object, such as a bit of beach litter (a bottle will do) or a twist of dried weed, as if some direction finder is required to relocate it. None is needed by would-be predators, however, as a series of oystercatcher footprints converges on the nest site like roads at a multiple intersection, and it is a simple matter to follow the trail straight to the eggs. Few of the clutches that we have found over the years have successfully hatched, and even fewer of the chicks have survived to fledge. A survey carried out by Howard Langley illustrates the hazards which the oystercatchers face. One summer he found a total of 24 nests containing 40 eggs; of these, only a clutch of two hatched. Of the others, 22 disappeared down the throats of Water Mongooses, three eggs were washed away by the high tide, and primate disturbance (baboons and humans) accounted for two more. Nine other eggs disappeared without trace or the cause being identified. The birds laid up to three replacement clutches, but even this productivity was insufficient to guarantee success.

Pale plovers

The little white birds which run ahead of you along the top of the beach are Whitefronted Plovers. They are numerous on the west coast sandy and mixed beaches. A most attractive little bird, as are the plovers as a group, the Whitefronteds' warm sandy-grey upperparts and bright white underparts, often with a tinge of buff on the sides of the breast, distinguish them from any other small wader you will encounter here. In breeding plumage a narrow black bar above the white forehead is distinctive. They feed by day and night, scuttling along the shore in search of kelp fly and their larvae and various littoral crustaceans.

The plovers seems to have attended the same design school as the Black Oystercatcher, their nests also being a shallow scrape and, almost invariably, with a twist of kelp to set it off. Although we have not found a nest below the high-water mark, one in a human footprint at Platboom was possibly living a little dangerously.

The Whitefronted Plover lays two eggs, and we have found them nesting from October to March, although it is likely to breed all the year round. Many eggs doubtless fall to predators, although the Whitefronted Plover has gone a step further towards egg protection than the oystercatcher in that, when disturbed at the nest, it rapidly scuffs up sand with its feet, spraying it onto the eggs, often to the extent of burying them completely. There is some debate whether this is a deliberate ploy to conceal the eggs or to protect them from the sun, or is a nervous response, a displacement activity in response to the conflicting demands of personal safety and the welfare of its eggs. Only the bird can tell.

These are the resident waders which you are most likely to encounter at the reserve at any time of year. In spring, however, the relative tranquillity of the shore and the established daily routines of the locals are rudely interrupted by the arrival of flocks of tourists from the north. Although referred to as 'northern hemisphere' species, it is appropriate to note that these birds actually spend a greater part of their life south of the equator than north of it.

The Russians are coming

The northern waders begin arriving in August, the majority make an appearance in October, and they leave by April or May. While on our beaches, they undergo a moult and, towards the end of their stay, lay down deposits of fat to provide energy for their long return journey. Shortly before leaving, therefore, many are in summer plumage and noticeably plump.

Eight species of migrant wader are regularly found on the reserve's beaches; six others are scarce or occasional visitors. The most abundant overall, although its numbers can vary greatly within and between years, is the Sanderling, sparkling white below and pearly grey above. Their numbers vary tremendously, but flocks of up to 420 have been recorded on migration in April. Smaller numbers (up to 150, but generally tens and twenties) frequent the west coast between November and February.

Curlew Sandpipers are second in the league of abundance to Sanderlings, occurring in flocks of some hundreds on arrival and departure, with smaller and variable numbers between times. They also hail from the Sanderlings' Siberian breeding grounds on the Taimyr Peninsula. Brown above, white below, with a conspicuous white rump, these sandpipers are leggier and have a longer bill than Sanderlings. They are also found on rockier stretches of beach, as well as amongst the rotting kelp.

The third most common visiting wader here is the solidly built Turnstone, its plumage pied with autumnal tints and tortoiseshell (p. 158). There are few more attractive species on the shore than a Turnstone in full nuptial dress just prior to its departure for the tundra. With it are less brightly coloured immature birds, hatched the previous year, which will remain here for the winter and following summer before flying north to breed when almost two years old. At the reserve, Turnstones are birds of the kelp mounds and algal mats and mussel beds of the rocky coast.

A twist of lemming

The numbers of Sanderlings, Curlew Sandpipers and Turnstones visiting the reserve vary from summer to summer. Perhaps the reserve is a suboptimal habitat for them (particularly Curlew Sandpipers), and they only occur here when their preferred sites are disturbed or overcrowded (with birds, that is, leading to spillover to the reserve). On a broader scale, the numbers of these species found in the southwest Cape have been linked, not altogether surprisingly, with breeding success in Siberia. There are, however, fascinating twists to this tale. Research by ornithologists in Russia and South Africa, the latter spearheaded by the Western Cape Wader Study Group and Professor Les Underhill of the Avian Demography Unit at UCT, has determined that these waders are most abundant in the Cape in years when the numbers of lemmings at the waders' breeding grounds are at their highest. The lemmings, it has been discovered, exhibit a distinct cycle – a good year followed by a population crash, then two lean years during which they build up their numbers again. In the good years, when lemmings are abundant, Arctic Foxes prey almost exclusively on these rodents and the waders are, for the most part, left in peace. When the lemmings are scarce,

however, the foxes switch their attention to the waders and eat large numbers of their eggs and chicks. This results in low breeding success and few youngsters surviving to fly south. Who would have thought that Siberian lemmings could determine the number of waders you see on the beach at the Cape of Good Hope on a hot summer's day?

Gulls and terns

Three species of gull occur at the reserve, the Greyheaded infrequently, Hartlaub's and Kelp in large numbers. Hartlaub's is small, silvery-grey above and white below, with red bill and legs. It is another 'Benguela special', breeding between Swakopmund in the north and Dyer Island in the south and rarely straying more than 20 kilometres from the coast. The adult Kelp Gull is a brute of a bird, black on the back and white underneath. Immatures are speckly brown in their first year, gradually attaining the distinctive adult plumage over three or four years. Both species are abundant, although Hartlaub's occurs in larger flocks, the Kelp often in pairs or small groups. Neither species breeds here (although it would not surprise us if the odd pair of Kelp Gulls nested on the Cape Point cliffs).

At Olifantsbos the Hartlaub's feed on small invertebrates associated with stranded kelp, notably Horned Isopods and Sea Slaters and kelp-fly larvae and pupae picked from the heaps of rotting weed. Kelp Gulls at Olifantsbos feed on much the same creatures as Hartlaub's, but rather than pecking their prey off the surface, they rake amongst the weed, lifting pieces to expose the larvae underneath. This is such an attractive food source that over 90 per cent of the Kelp Gulls at Olifantsbos spend their time exclusively on the kelp heaps. Only a few of them potter amongst the boulders at the water's edge, where they capture Horned Isopods, Black and Mediterranean Mussels (a recently arrived alien species), and Cape Rock Crabs.

An intriguing feeding ploy adopted by Kelp Gulls is the dropping of shellfish, notably mussels, from a height onto a hard surface to break them open. A traditional rock shelf is often used, and the remains of hundreds of shattered molluscs litter these 'anvils'. Car parks, particularly the one at Bordjiesrif, are also popular anvils. If you, like us, have one of those cars which are dented by a rise in atmospheric pressure, you would be advised to inspect the surroundings for mussel-shell fragments and myopic gulls before parking.

Closely related to the gulls, and represented at the reserve by two local and four international visitors, are the terns. Three of the latter are welcome harbingers of summer, arriving on our shores from September. Terns are long-winged, short-legged and often fork-tailed birds; they catch fish in the coastal waters and use the shore for roosting, often gathering in large numbers at favourite sites.

The Swift Tern is an abundant non-breeding visitor, its loud, harsh cries being the most evocative sounds of the shore. The slightly drooping yellow bill is distinctive, and a shaggy black cap distinguishes the adults in summer. About

Mediterranean Mussel
Mytilus galloprovincialis

5,000 pairs breed in South Africa, the nearest nesting grounds to the reserve being the west coast islands; many ringed at Marcus Island at the entrance to the Langebaan Lagoon are recorded at the reserve.

Of the migrant terns which visit the reserve in summer the most common is, you guessed it, the Common. It is predominantly a summer visitor, but non-breeders frequently opt to stay for the winter as well, rather than head north. The numbers of summer birds vary greatly from year to year, pre-sumably in response to the availability and location of their food supply. Roosts regularly contain a few thousand birds, but none has since exceeded that at Die Mond which, on 30 December 1986, contained an estimated 45,000 birds. A further 42,000 were present that day at six other roosts in the reserve. In the evening we watched spellbound from the stoep at Skaife as, against a sickeningly beautiful and cinematic sunset, tens of thousands of terns dipped and dived just offshore. Their shrill *kik kik kik* and *kree-aarr* cries continued to carry across the water after dark, the twinkling of trawlers' lights indicating that the terns were not the only fishermen abroad that night.

The Common Tern at a distance can resemble the Arctic Tern, another visitor from northern climes. The birder who is not sure what he is looking at, but wishes to avoid embarrassment, calls them 'Comic' Terns, but we can confidently say that Arctics are scarce at the reserve. We attribute this not to oversight on our part, but to a lifestyle which keeps the Arctic feeding further out to sea and rarely coming ashore. We have seen the occasional one or two in roosts of other terns, their relatively very short legs making them stand out, if that is not a contradiction in terms. The Arctic Tern is notable in that it probably experiences more daylight than any other animal. Those at the most northerly breeding grounds in the high Arctic are bathed in virtually constant sunlight, albeit cool and often clouded, for the couple of months they are nesting. In July and August the birds migrate south, and by December (mid-summer in the southern hemisphere) some of them have reached the Antarctic pack-ice, where they also witness the midnight sun.

The austral counterpart of the Arctic Tern is the Antarctic. Solid, tubby little terns, in good plumage they have grey underparts with a contrasting white cheek stripe. Roosts at Platboom number up to 125 birds, mingling with Swift and dilatory Sandwich and Common Terns. May to August are their customary months in Cape waters, but late leavers have included individuals in full and splendid breeding plumage in October. Antarctic Terns breed at some of the most remote and isolated islands in the world – the

Sea Bamboo Ecklonia maxima *cast ashore at the Cape of Good Hope.*

Tristan da Cunha group and Gough in the south Atlantic, and Prince Edward and Marion, Kerguelen and Crozet in the southern Indian Ocean. The terns' ability to locate these specks of land in the watery vastness reflects impressively on their navigational prowess.

The Sandwich Tern, named after the town of that name in southeast England, is an abundant summer visitor from the northern hemisphere. One bird ringed as a nestling in Northern Ireland in June 1974, was found at Buffels Bay in February 1994, a few months short of 20 years and 10,145 kilometres later, a journey it presumably had carried out 19 times before. Twenty years might seem an impressive age, but Sandwich Terns are known to live for over 30 years.

Common and Antarctic Terns at the reserve have been observed shuffling along the ground and picking up Beach Hoppers, but this is a most unusual feeding technique. More customary is the capture of small fish by plunge-diving after a short hover. A tern will sometimes catch a fish and play with it in mid-flight – dropping it and swooping down to catch it before it hits the water. Occasionally one tern drops the fish and a second will catch it. They then alternately drop and catch the fish until both birds lose interest and the fish is dropped to the sea for the last time. We have seen Swift and Sandwich Terns playing with the same fish, so the residents seem quite happy to play water sports or beach games with the visitors.

They are also not averse to sharing their beaches, and mixed roosts of Swift, Common and Sandwich Terns may be found on any rocky shore in summer. Favourite spots are Buffels Bay, Olifantsbos Bay and The Fishery. Great flocks also gather on the rocky shore at Bordjiesrif at low tide, and every boulder seems to be topped by a bird. Indeed, no stone is left unterned.

Ocean wanderers

The Cape of Good Nature Reserve ranks as the best spot from which to observe one of the richest gatherings of seabirds in the world. Seabirds concentrate in areas of upwelling along continental lee shores, and the rich feeding grounds of the Benguela off the west coast consequently attract spectacular concentrations of pelagic (open ocean) species, including albatrosses, shearwaters and petrels.

Winter is undoubtedly the best time to gaze optimistically seawards. This is the season when birds which breed on the sub-Antarctic and Antarctic islands visit these coastal waters. To see these species at their nesting grounds would require major effort and expenditure, particularly for the albatrosses. So why not sit at the Cape of Good Hope and let the birds come to you instead?

Binoculars or, much preferably, a tripod-mounted telescope are essential for 'seawatching', as the mildly masochistic activity of looking at, or for, oceanic birds is termed. Generally speaking, a strong onshore wind is also necessary to blow the birds close to the coast and into view. 'Close' is a relative term, of course. Birds tend to drift past one or two kilometres or more offshore; but sometimes they come within a few hundred metres of the beach or even very occasionally venture over it.

Having positioned yourself on the top ledges at the Cape of Good Hope on a windy day and set up your telescope, look directly south towards the foaming maelstrom halfway to the horizon that is the sea breaking over the Bellows (having a point of reference in an otherwise featureless ocean is useful). If you strike lucky, you will witness one of the finest spectacles in the birding world. Birds fly past or mill around in their hundreds or thousands, and are most abundant just before or after the passing of a cold front. The fronts may sweep over the Cape at hourly intervals or so, and you can see them approaching ominously from the northwest, great banks of leaden clouds, the sea whipped white beneath them. They can hit you with some force, with torrential rain and shrieking winds, but after a little while the sky clears, the rainbows decorate the heavens and you can enjoy the spectacle of seabirds in the depression's wake. Albatrosses glide past with consummate ease – Shy and Blackbrowed by the dozen, a Yellownosed every now and then. These are the 'mollymawks', a family of small

Thousands of Common Terns, migrant visitors from the northern hemisphere, sometimes visit Die Mond to bathe and rest.

albatrosses, black on top and with distinctive underwing patterns. They really are sensational birds, even at a distance.

Moving down the scale, the Whitechinned Petrel is one of the most regular species here, a dark chocolate-coloured bird whose pale beak, if not white chin, is a distinguishing feature. It would seem that the smaller the birds are, the more abundant they become. The Sooty Shearwater has a wingspan of about a metre, about half that of the molly-mawks, but it occurs in astronomical numbers. They are particularly abundant at the beginning and end of the winter, when on passage to or from their sub-Antarctic breeding islands. Our peak counts of one thousand careening south every minute are not thought to be the product of slipped lenses. There really are zillions of them out there, and they flow past in never-ending streams, their silvery underwings twinkling in the sun.

Only slightly less numerous overall, although at times more abundant than all the other birds put together, are the prions. These tend to occur in tightish flocks, as opposed to the filamentous strings of the Sooties. The prions are small, dove-grey and white petrels whose most remarkable feature, not visible at any distance, is their wide, flattened bill. The inside of the top part of the bill, the upper mandible, is fringed with lamellae, which constitute a baleen-like 'sieve'. This is used to filter krill and plankton from the seawater in the way that whales do ('Whale-bird' is an old name for them). Although the identification of the prions as a group is easy, the individual species are more problematic. Nevertheless, the most abundant prion seen from the reserve is certainly the Broadbilled, which has a veritable Donald Duck of a beak. On good days, many thousands skip and dip offshore, often pausing to feed but, like many of the seabirds, just pressing through with an inexplicable urgency to reach who knows where.

The black-and-white Pintado, a smartly chequered petrel whom we have met before, is a less frenetic flyer than the prions. It occurs in small numbers throughout the winter. Softplumaged Petrels (our favourite pelagic species), with their switchback flight and distinctive black underwings and white body, may amount to a few score in the course of a morning. Add to these the occasional rarity (Antarctic Fulmar and white-phase Southern Giant Petrel spring to mind), a healthy sprinkling of Wilson's Storm Petrels and masses of our local gulls, gannets and cormorants, and you have a wonderful and memorable display, one which can outshine any other avian attributes the reserve may have to offer. The fact that many of the birds involved hail from such romantic and far-off places as Adélie Land, Nightingale, South Signy and Marion Island, reinforces their already considerable appeal as masterful flyers and navigators, scorners of Adamastor and the Cape of Storms.

Tubes of Cape Reef-
worms
Gunnarea capensis

Ossified skin of box fish
Family *Ostraciidae*

Softplumaged Petrel skull
Pterodroma mollis

Ram's horn
Spirula

Pumice stones

Cape Cormorant skull
Phalacracorax capensis

Cuttlefish bone
Sepia

Paper Nautilus
Argonauta argo

Whelk egg capsules.

Mermaid's purse.
Egg case of a shark
or ray.

Sea beans,
seeds of Entada (Seeboontjie)

Jaws of White Musselcracker
Sparadon durbanensis
(Witbiskop)

Terebellid worm
tubes

149

Pear Limpets
Patella cochlear
with their roof
gardens of algae

Ridged Burnupena

Burnupena cincta

Pustular Triton
*Argobuccinum
pustulosum*

Keyhole Limpet
Dendrofissurella
scutellum

a limpet lunging!

Alikreukel or
giant periwinkle
turbo sarmaticus
bedecked with
Slipper Limpets

fleshy foot
from underneath

Evileye Puffer (Boosoog-blaasop)
Amblyrhynchotes honckenii

Found in rock pools and
in the open sea to depths
of 400m. Not eaten by
other fish or seabirds
as it is highly poisonous.

Grey Volcano Barnacles
Tetraclita serrata

Spider Limpets
Patella longicosta

Limpets Patella and
False Limpets
Siphonaria

Barnacles,
Cirripedia

153

Swift Terns *Sterna bergii*, with
their yellow beaks and shaggy caps,
and Antarctic Terns *Sterna vittata*
roosting at Platboompunt.

Dozing Jackass Penguins
Spheniscus demersus
at Potbank.

Whitebreasted Cormorants *Phalacrocorax carbo*
roosting at the Cape of Good Hope.

Turnstones *Arenaria interpres*
nest in the arctic tundra
but spend their winters south
to the Cape. (Steenloper)

Menskoppunt, April.

158

Sping starfish
Marthasterias glacialis

Dwarf Cushion Star
Patiriella exigua

Reticulated Star-
fish Henricia
ornata

Red Starfish
Patiria granifera

159

Once a real reserve rarity,
this unmistakable species
began to appear in some
numbers in late 1990 and
is now a common sight on
sandy beaches. Here they
probe for invertebrates
in the rotting seaweed.

Sacred Ibis
Threskiornis aethiopicus
(skoorsteenveër)

False Plum Anemone

Pseudactinia
flagellifera

Impossible animals to
paint as they
constantly change
their shape!

Knobbly Anemone
Bunodosoma capensis

A shoaling species,
the Panga _Pterogymnus_ _laniarius_
undergoes sex reversal
at about five years old.

Steentjie _Spondyliosoma emarginatum_
The common name is Afrikaans for
"little stone", and perhaps refers to its
size and choice of rocky habitat.
   Snoek _Thyrsites atun_ can grow up
to two metres in length and weigh
as much as 8kg. This is a small one.

An assortment of lures
for catching Yellowtail.

Oval lead sinker
for fishing in
the kelp.

164

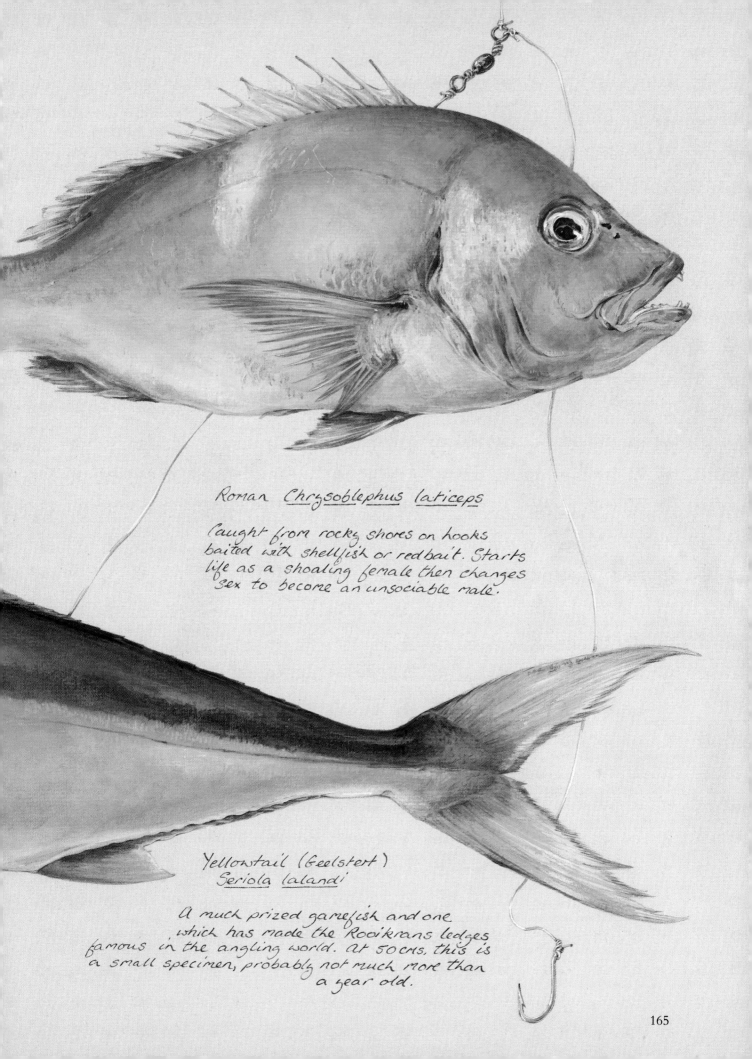

Roman *Chrysoblephus laticeps*

Caught from rocky shores on hooks
baited with shellfish or redbait. Starts
life as a shoaling female then changes
sex to become an unsociable male.

Yellowtail (Geelstert)
Seriola lalandi

A much prized gamefish and one
which has made the Rooikrans ledges
famous in the angling world. At 50 cms, this is
a small specimen, probably not much more than
a year old.

CHAPTER SEVEN

Wattles and Wilderness

Conservation, Research and Management for Wildlife and People

The establishment of the reserve in 1939 was the culmination of a hard-fought and often acrimonious battle. Having emerged on the victorious side, the Divisional Council of the Cape suddenly found themselves responsible for a great tract of land and a multitude of plants and animals. What were they to do with it and them?

Any decisions regarding active management of the new reserve were postponed by the outbreak of the war, during which the reserve was under the control of the military. But come 1945, Council was faced with the choice – should the Cape of Good Hope Nature Reserve be primarily a recreational area for Capetonians, a wilderness area, a game park, a wildflower preserve, a zoo, a garden, or any combination of these?

The bucks stop here

Since its establishment, the reserve had been viewed in different lights by its Advisory Board and the public. Despite persistent and impassioned pleas for the flora to be given priority, a selection of animals was introduced to the area in response to perceived public demand, the 'game ranger' syndrome and the perception, in some quarters, of the reserve as a glorified zoo. Over the years the 'zoo' was the recipient of, amongst other creatures, Peacocks, Blue Cranes and over a thousand tortoises. Into the 'game park' came Blue and Black Wildebeest, Burchell's and Hartmann's Zebra, Eland, Bontebok, Springbok, Red Hartebeest and Fallow Deer. The immigrants extended even to fish – the vleis were stocked with Small-mouthed Bass and Banded Tilapia donated by the Department of Nature Conservation. With the exception of Eland, none of these animals occurred here naturally.

To accommodate the alien antelopes and perhaps to placate the botanical contingent, a fence was erected across the width of the reserve about one quarter of the way down, confining the animals to the southern sector while the northern was set aside as a 'floral reserve'. Initially, some of the buck seemed to fare quite well and their populations increased. This was a short-lived phenomenon, however, and they soon displayed general ill-health, malnutrition and

symptoms of copper deficiency. At the root of the problem, as the farmers had recognised years ago, was the fact that all the introduced animals, apart from the Eland, were grazing species. That is, they feed almost exclusively on grass, which is a scarce commodity in fynbos, and what vegetation does grow here is very low in essential nutrients.

Why were such animals introduced in the first place? Unfortunately, wildlife management has wallowed for much of this century in the stereotypic image of 'African' conservation – savannas with big game and big wardens, all muscled and hairy. As a consequence of this popular conception, as well as the absence of appropriate training, the reserve staff often included people who were, essentially, frustrated game rangers. Arriving from up-country they were, understandably, somewhat disillusioned to discover that the most important animal on the whole reserve was a toad. None daunted, they pressed on in the attempt to bring Kruger Park to the Cape Peninsula, as one ranger expressed it in his monthly report of May 1967: 'I certainly look forward, with no little impatience and anticipation, to the not far distant day when – the trees having been planted, the grasses having been sown, the dams having been built and sedged around, and the wild herds at maximum strength gloriously on view – I can turn with humble pride to my principals and assure them that this reserve is now what a Game Ranger expects a reserve to be.'

With sentiments such as these being aired, it is perhaps not surprising that the Advisory Board took such a long time to put its house in order. That the early management of the reserve foundered on the rocks of suspect ecological advice and the demands of an ill-informed public was not necessarily or entirely the staff's or the Board's fault. Nevertheless, the failure to appoint an ecologist to run the reserve, and the absence of a qualified ecologist or botanist from the Board, were inexcusable. It was not until the 1980s that an ecologist was appointed to its ranks. It is gratifying to record that today, 55 years after the reserve's establishment, the Board at last comprises experts in the fields of ecology, botany, ornithology, wildlife management, environmental sciences, and tourism.

The policy of indiscriminate introductions and efforts to create a game park at the Peninsula's tip have come to an end. The remaining antelope populations are now continuously monitored, and if the carrying capacity is judged to be exceeded or the veld shows signs of overgrazing, surplus animals are captured and translocated to other nature reserves. If the animals are undernourished or show signs of distress, they are removed. There remains, however, an urgent need for a scientific assessment of the impact the remaining introduced animals, the Bontebok, Red Hartebeest and Eland, are having on the indigenous flora.

The aliens have landed

'Aliens', also known as 'exotics', are plants or animals which have been introduced by Man into areas in which they do not naturally occur. This is the opposite of 'indigenous'. Where such an organism establishes itself and succeeds in spreading beyond its original point of introduction, it is termed 'invasive'. A White Milkwood is, therefore, 'indigenous', an oak tree an 'alien', and Rooikrans (an acacia or wattle from Australia) an 'invasive alien'.

There are over 80 species of alien plant at the reserve, ranging from the tallest trees to the tiniest herbs. Many alien grasses and other small herbaceous plants are established around old homesteads. Road verges provide suitable corridors to outlying parts of the reserve for European weeds such as clover, fleabane and sowthistle. What effect these have on the indigenous fauna and flora, and what danger exists of their spreading further into the veld, is unknown. Beyond all doubt, however, is the fact that the woody invasive aliens, notably the Australian gums and wattles, are an ecological disaster.

Although the more subtle, but still pernicious, effects of aliens are only now being recognised, it has long been appreciated that their sheer volume was enough to simply swamp the indigenous plants. This was certainly happening at the reserve. Seeds which were washed down the Krom River had germinated in the relatively fertile soils of the floodplain, and a great alien forest stretched down the valley almost to the sea. The ruined homestead at Theefontein was at the centre of a grove of giant eucalypts and many thousands of tall, slender saplings, densely packed and all straining heavenward for a glimmer of light. Underneath them, nothing grew. Here was a sight to gladden the heart of any Koala Bear. Up the slopes of Teeberg the Cluster Pines had raced, to be met on the other side of the hill in the Schusters River valley by a great barrage of

Zoology students from the University of Cape Town fishing for frogs in Suurdam. The reserve is a valuable outdoor laboratory for scientific research.

Port Jackson. The thickets of Rooikrans at, amongst other places, Buffels Bay and Vasco da Gama Peak were utterly impenetrable, the ground beneath completely shaded and lifeless and deep with their seeds, leaf-litter and dead wood. At Olifantsbos, the river running across the coastal plain was imprisoned by a jungle of Grey Poplar, Port Jackson, Black Wattle, Spider Gum and scrambling Canary Creeper. Below the towering pines and eucalypts at Klaasjagersberg, the forest floor was deep with needles and leaves, and supported barely an indigenous sprig. At the simplest level, therefore, one or two species of alien were occupying the land, to the complete exclusion of the fynbos vegetation.

Perhaps the scale of the task was all too overwhelming, or resources were still lavished on the introduced buck, but it was not until the early 1980s that there was an injection of motivation and funding into the task of eradicating alien plants at the reserve. This is now the most important management undertaking and the most expensive item on the reserve's budget sheet, accounting for almost half of the total annual expenditure. The reserve's strategy of dealing with aliens is, in fact, now the envy of other reserve managers, as the problem is not, of course, confined to the Cape of Good Hope, or to South Africa. Indeed, a distinguished ecologist is of the opinion that the reserve's alien-clearance programme is the best of its kind *in the world*, something about which the authorities would be justified in blowing their trumpet a bit more loudly.

Research for conservation

The reserve is the perfect outdoor laboratory, providing as it does a combination of near-natural environment and accessibility – there are three universities and a variety of academic and research institutes within two hours of the Point. The area has witnessed studies as varied as the habitat requirements of long-tongued flies, and the concentrations of chlorofluoromethanes (CFCs) in the air. The latter forms part of an important programme of long-term atmospheric and physical research carried out from a laboratory on Cape Point Peak run by the Council for Scientific and Industrial Research.

There are at present almost forty research projects under way at the reserve. Some of these are part of more wide-ranging studies and include investigations of everything from waterfleas to Peregrine Falcons, from blood parasites to Bonteboks. The results of much of the research are then used to determine how best to manage the plants and animals which make the reserve so special. If rarity is the most important factor determining management policy in the reserve, then eleven species of plant demand particular attention. These are the species presently considered to be endemic, occurring only in the reserve and nowhere else in the world. Five of these are heaths (*Erica blancheana, Erica capensis, Erica clavisepala, Erica eburnea* and *Erica fontana*); the others are single members of the cabbage (*Heliophila cinerea*), protea (*Leucadendron macowanii*), restio (*Restio dodii*), vygie

(*Ruschia promontorii*), brunia (*Staavia dodii*) and orchid (*Pterygodium connivens*) families. An overall 'community' management approach has been adopted, however, within whose framework all those animals and plants, including these particularly rare ones, indigenous to the area live under a regime that resembles as closely as possible that which occurs under natural conditions. This is achieved through the removal of all alien plants and animals, veld-burning every 15 or 20 years, and the sensitive development of facilities for visitors.

Appealing to visitors

Over 400,000 visitors a year come to Cape Point, the great majority of them over the summer holiday season. This is a far cry from the 2,889 vehicles which passed through the gate in 1939. Numbers of visitors peaked at 440,000 in 1970. A moderate decline thereafter is attributable to a shift in policy away from promoting the reserve as picnic site and to a rise in the cost of petrol. The entrance fees have, in contrast, remained very reasonable. In March 1939, G. A. Leyds declared that 'the expense of visiting Cape Point for a day per family would be no more than visiting a bioscope'. A family of four going to the cinema nowadays find themselves more than R50 the poorer when they come out. Entrance to the reserve for the same family may be had today (1994) for R17 (R5 per car and R3 per person).

How does the reserve cope with the hundreds of thousands of people who pour through its gates every year and who all need to be fed and watered. Can, or should, the reserve provide these facilities, and at what levels should it attempt to do so? In the past, Bordjiesrif and Buffels Bay were inundated with busloads of people whose main concern was to 'eat, drink and be merry'. A feature of the picnic sites over the summer holidays, they were, unfortunately, notorious for their high spirits. The time and effort spent by reserve staff breaking up fights, treating the wounded, and clearing up the mess afterwards, far outweighed any benefit which the reserve might have gained from the additional visitors. Buses are now not allowed to these sites, and further control is placed on the numbers visiting them in summer to prevent overcrowding.

Today's emphasis, therefore, focuses on downgrading the reserve's function as a picnic site, and promoting its unique wilderness qualities. Such a step can only be taken if the very aspects which attract people are not destroyed by so doing. It must also be borne in mind that 400,000 visitors do not, mercifully, all want to hike across the veld. They are, however, the people who, on their short visits, spend far more money in the reserve than the locals who walk the trails or come to fish or birdwatch. They must be made to feel welcome and should, within reason, be provided with all the facilities they have come to expect at a major tourist destination, without compromising the natural environment of the reserve.

The last word

When we started writing *Between Two Shores*, we found ourselves at something of a loss for an opening sentence, as there seemed to be nothing of great substance or artistic merit concerning the Cape of Good Hope that could be called upon to serve as our curtain raiser. This was not such a handicap; rather, it emphasised the fact that the Cape of Good Hope speaks most eloquently for itself. For those of you who have been there, memories may centre on the discovery of such remarkable wildness less than an hour's drive from a swarming metropolis. Perhaps the grandeur of the Cape Point promontory impressed, or you were moved by the historical ambience of the Cape of Good Hope itself. You may have deliberately avoided the very tip of the Peninsula and were happy instead to pause for thought on an east coast craggy perch with distant views of Cape Hangklip and the widening sea, or inhale deep, satisfying lungfuls of essence of vintage kelp at Olifantsbos, or scuffle unselfconsciously through the sand on a startlingly deserted beach at Platboom.

Certainly it would be difficult to overstate the reserve's importance as a sanctuary for fynbos and seashore plants and animals. Once you have come to an appreciation and acceptance of the fact that this is no place for the 'big and hairies', you can enjoy the reserve for what it is and be delighted by what you do find instead of disappointed by unrealistic and, consequently, unfulfilled expectations.

To us, the Cape of Good Hope is many things. It is a place of great frustration, not least when the wind howls for days or even weeks on end, and staying upright is cause for the celebration of a job well done. It is a place of undoubted beauty, from the grandest scale of sea- and landscapes, down to the most diminutive of fynbos flowers and insects and the undemonstrative inhabitants of tidal pools and coastal shallows. It is a timeless place; the past is fascinating, the present captivating and the future tantalising. Most of all, a place of anticipation. Although the landscape is solidly permanent, many of its occupants, past and present, are transient, rare and enigmatic – the flowers that bloom for a day or two, then wither, to become dormant for many years; the wind-blown birds from the New World which make fleeting and grateful landfall, then vanish as mysteriously as they appeared. Anticipation in an inspirational setting.

Having proposed that the Cape of Good Hope Nature Reserve can speak most eloquently for itself, what justification had we, therefore, for producing this book? Speak for itself it may, indeed, but softly and to those who care to listen. It does not speak loudly enough for those who choose to ignore it, those who are deaf to the sounds of nature. The Peninsula is a very special place. The reserve at its very tip may be secure, but the few remaining undeveloped areas nearby are no less deserving of conservation efforts, and many are under threat.

Cape Town has, for the moment, the all but unparalleled opportunity to be the world's wildest city. How many others can boast such a superb setting, magnificent landscapes and wealth of ridiculously rare flora and fauna all within a hop and a skip of the city centre? Despite these singular assets, 'The Tavern of the Seas' presently follows with disconcerting enthusiasm the rest of the world, in which intrinsic character (by which we mean natural landscapes and indigenous plants and animals) is swept aside and replaced by urban blight and convenient cosmopolitan weeds. The few as yet untouched areas are eyed greedily by developers and politicians, and the formerly rural areas follow the city and suburbs along a path of unrelenting tattiness. Instead of wearing a crown, in which the Cape of Good Hope is one of many jewels, Cape Town and the Peninsula have donned the mask of the mediocre at very best and the unprintable at worst.

Between Two Shores is our appeal for the continued and appropriate conservation and management of the Cape of Good Hope Nature Reserve, for the enjoyment of its visitors and the benefit of its natural inhabitants. We hope it will also contribute to a greater appreciation of the remaining unspoilt areas of the Cape Peninsula, and earn them the protection which they urgently require.

Viooltjie
Lachenalia sp.

The veld is aglow with
spring flowers after
last autumn's fire.

Olifantsbos,
October

Hesperantha
falcata

Nemesia versicolor
Weeskindertjies

Wahlenbergia
capensis

Gladiolus
debilis

Homeria
ochroleuca
Apricot Tulp.

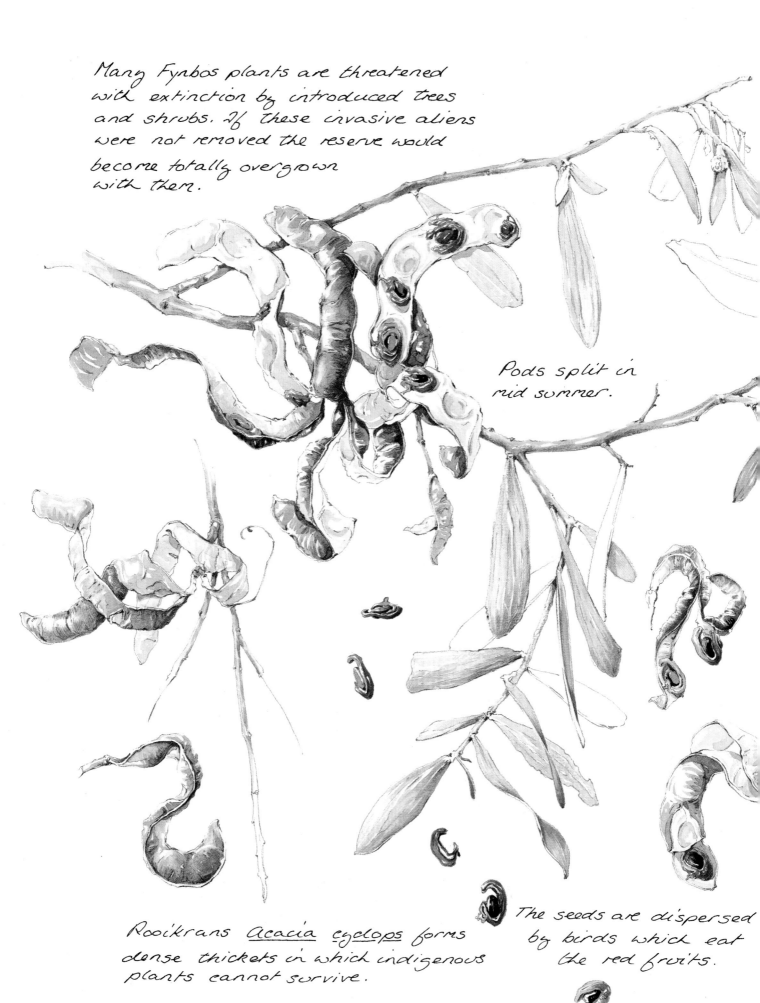

Many Fynbos plants are threatened
with extinction by introduced trees
and shrubs. If these invasive aliens
were not removed the reserve would
become totally overgrown
with them.

Pods split in
mid summer.

Rooikrans *Acacia cyclops* forms
dense thickets in which indigenous
plants cannot survive.

The seeds are dispersed
by birds which eat
the red fruits.

Port Jackson
acacia saligna
Introduced to the
Cape in about 1833.

Long leaved Wattle
acacia longifolia
with wasp-induced
galls.

White Milkwood
Sideroxylon inerme

Flowers and fruits.
Olifantsbos,
18th March.

A brood of Redwinged Starlings
Onychognathus morio from under
the eaves at Klaasjagersberg.
January.

After ten days or
so the chicks are more
presentable. They are well feathered
and their orange-patched primaries
are beginning to show.

The Common Platanna
Xenopus laevis has all
the grace and poise of
a Sumo wrestler in
battle dress.

The reserve is the world
stronghold of the diminutive
Cape Platanna _Xenopus gilli_,
an endangered species.

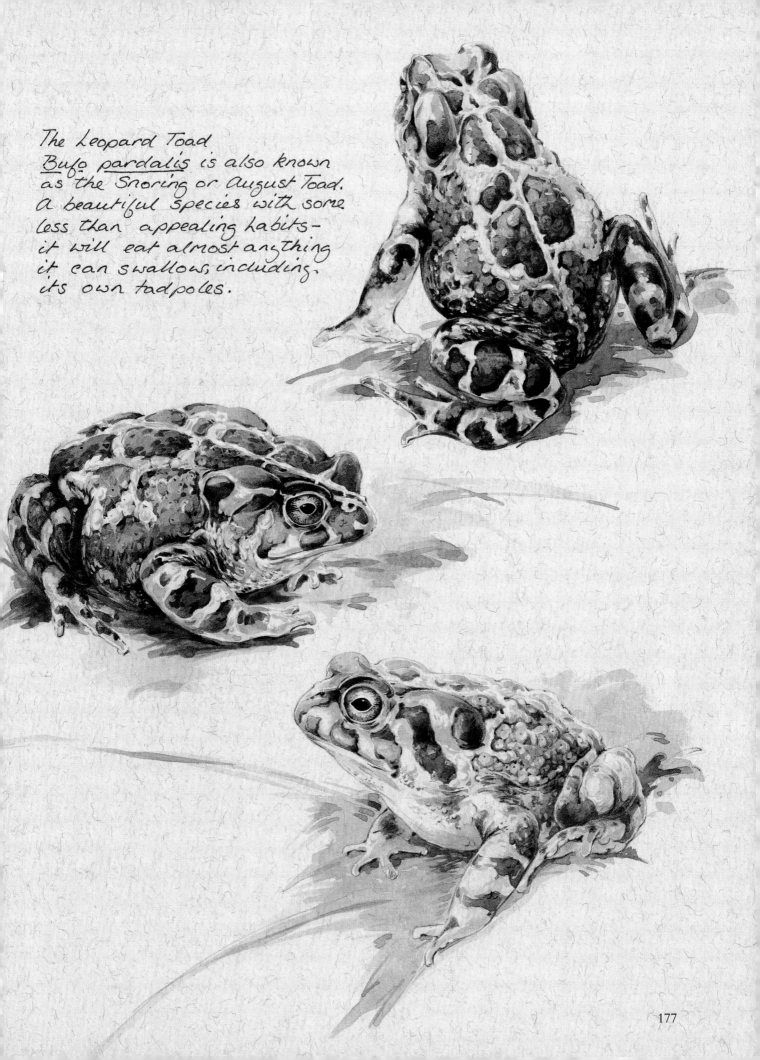

The Leopard Toad
Bufo pardalis is also known
as the Snoring or August Toad.
A beautiful species with some
less than appealing habits—
it will eat almost anything
it can swallow, including
its own tadpoles.

Studies of Bontebok
Damaliscus dorcas dorcas
in young veld near
Smith's Farm.

178

179

Adult males have black feathering
and white plumes. The front of
their legs turn red in the breeding
season. Females and youngsters
are brown.

Ostrich *Struthio camelus* (Volstruis)

The reserve birds probably are
descended from farming stock
introduced to Buffelsfontein by
John McKellar in the mid-nineteenth
century.

Buffels River, 1st March.

A few buds were emerging
from amongst last year's
withered leaves.

Candelabra *Brunsvigia orientalis*
(Koningskandelaar, Perdespookbossie)

The baboons had snapped off almost
a hundred plants, chewing the bottom
inch or two of the stalk before tossing
them aside. If the discarded blooms
land upside down, like this one, the
individual flowers reorient to face
upwards again. Perhaps they can still
be pollinated and set seed.

Tread carefully along the
beach in midsummer –
amongst the dried kelp
and other tideline debris
the oystercatcher chicks
crouch motionless and
unseen.

African Black Oystercatcher
Haematopus moquini (Swarttobie)

Rare and endangered plants.

Bokmakierie's Tail
Witsenia maura

Disa salteri
(above)

Leucadendron
floridum

Staavia dodii
Diamond
Eyes

(endemic)

186

Bobartia gladiata
subsp. _major_
(endemic)

False Heath
Audouinia capitata.

Resprouts after
fire.

Leucadendron
macowanii
(endemic)

Index of Scientific Names

✿

(Text references in roman type, illustrations in italics.)

List of Subscribers

Sponsors' edition
Steve Bales
Allen Miller

Collectors' edition
Africana Book Collectors
Alex A. Barrell
The Brenthurst Library
Mr & Mrs J.M.R. Dower
J.P. du Plessis
Eugéne & Lalie Fourie
Mrs H.L. Hurwitz
Keith E. Kirsten
O.J. Mackenzie
Peter Martens
University of Stellenbosch
Maureen Viljoen

Standard edition
Clement W. Abbott
D.J.J. & J.J. Ackermann
Joan Ackroyd
M.P. Adams
Africana Book Collectors
M. Alberts
Liz & Jumbo Anderson
E.M. Ardington
Michael & Elisabeth Arndt
Geoffrey & Heidi Ashmead
Jill Attwell
Graham Avery
Dick & Monetta Badnall
Colleen & Brian Bain
Ian Balfour Paul
Marijke & Ken Ball
Gerald & Peggy Baromen
Peter Bayly
Hope M. Beaumont
Mark A. Beeston
Alan Crawford Begg
Graeme Bell
Bergvliet Primary School

Prof. Gerhard & Isolde Beukes
John E. Bishop
David & Sheena Blyth
S.M.R. Boehmke
Avril Booth
Mrs G.M. Borcherds
Philke Borgelt
Z.D. Botma
Gillian & Razi Bovrov
Helen & David Bradley
Kenneth Bradshaw
Dieter & Susan Brandt
Keith & Morag Brockie
Jean-Jacques Brossy
Athol Brown
Kate Brown
Paul & Kathie Buley
Cape of Good Hope Nature Reserve
    Library
Cape Nature Conservation
Graham & Lesley Charnock
Elaine Rosemary Clark
Nicholas Cole
Pam Cole
Tony Colling & Nancy Gordon
Donald Cook
Lilla D. Copenhagen
Dr Graham Coupland
Richard & Shirley Cowling
R.B.E. Croft
Patrick Cullinan
Harry & Lorna Dalzell
Dr David Davies
Frances C. Davies
Richard & Maureen de Beer
Sandra Fay de Coning
Brigitte de Kock
Tom de Roo
Noel & Margie Descroizilles
J.M.P. Desmidt
Danie & May de Villiers
Don Africana Library
Margot & Ewen Duncan and family

François du Randt
François & Wilhelmina During
Cedric Edwards
Erinvale Hotel
Roy Ernstzen
Rodney Charles Esau
E.E. Esterhuysen
F. Evans
G.P. & U. Evans
Elaine Eyre
R.F. Fasham
S.G. Ferguson
Nathan & Hillary Finkelstein
Dalray Fox
Elizabeth Fraser
Joan Fraser
John, Alison, Ian & Andrew Fraser
Kenneth & Kathlyn Fraser
Norman & Muriel Fraser
Ian Garland
Kathleen Garrity
Mrs M.S. Gibbons
Barrie & Pam Gibson
Leon Glaser
Renée & Peter Gleeson
Belinda Gordon
G.L. Goulding
John Graham
T.A.L. Greaves
Nelson, Winnie, Jack, Cynthia & Shane
    Green
Elizabeth Jane Greenwood
M.J. Grier
Sheelagh Groenewald
Barbara Hall
Pentti Hallapera
Jim & Sue Hallinan
Madeleine & David Halstead
M.B. Hardy
W.L. Hare
Mike Harris & Sarah Wanless
Colin Hayne
Glynn & Anne Herbert

Birdie Heron
S.S. Herselman
Win Hewitt
David Hicks
Raymond Hoog
Craig & Claerwen Howie
Peter Humphrey
Joyce Hunter-Blair
Ian B. Huntley
Erika Huntly
Jacana Education
Antoinette Jacobson
Kate & Bryan Jagoe-Davies
Elodie Janovsky
Ralf Johannsen
Neil & Jean Jones
Dr A.C.C. Joosting
Cliffie & Peter Joubert
Vicki Käsner
J. & E. Kent
Marianne Kien
Marie & Doug King
M.W. King
Chris & Mary-Lou Kinross
Brian Kirsch
Kirstenbosch Garden Shop
Nicholas Klapwijk
Jean & Tony Knight
L.E. Kreutzer
J.D. Krige
Franci & Mariaan Krone
V. Krone
Noelline Kroon
Chris & Val Kuhn
Kathy La Grange
Howard Langley
K.A.S. Latham
Joan Laubscher
Belle Leon & Gabriel Epstein
Reinhard Le Roux
Jean Marie & Astri Leroy
Letaba Arts & Crafts
The Lishman family
Liz Livesey
Betty Louw
David A. Louw
Nicole Ludeke
Richard Ludeke
Don & Penny MCArthur
Heather K. McBurnie
Ian McCall
Goldie Macdonald
Wendy McKeag
Anna McMahon
Jenny McMahon
John & Marjorie McMahon
Joseph McMahon
Pat & Nancy McMahon

Rose McMahon
Mike Main
William & Jean Malley
Gavin W. Maneveldt
Michael & Diedie Marais
Joan Martin
Adam & Dorothy Mecinski
Adv. Abri Meiring
Pauline Michaelis
Hans & Jessie Middelman
H.F. & J.E. Möller
Mike & Ann Munnik
Bruce & Cilla Nel
Geoff, Lynne & Douglas Nichols
R.M. Nicholson
Carl Nortier
Dr Barbara Norton
Pat Oettlé
Miss Penelope Palmer
Susan Ruth Parker
Tom & Jane Pellatt
Patricia S. Pickstone
P. & A. Pohl
Brendan & Charmaine Pollard
Stanley & Moira Pollard
Miss Fiona Powrie
A.M. Preston
Mike & Tessa Rakow
Suzette M. Raymond
Everard Read
Dave & Corlia Richardson
Mrs Mary H.S. Ritchie
Mary Roberts
Barry Robinson
F. Ulrich Ruch
J.A. Rupert
Peter & Coleen Ryan
Helen Schipper
Rudolf Schneebeli
Donty Schrire
Sylvia Schrire
Dawn Lois Schröck
Robert & Kate Semple
James Sheard
R. Sieboldt
I.R. Simms
R.G. Simms
J. Simpson
Ansie & Dennis Slotow
Jennifer Slotow
Keith & Dorothy Smith
The Smuts family, Franschhoek
Peter Smuts
Somerset House Preparatory School
Stephanie S. Sperber
Sally Starke
Basil & Ines Stathoulis
Jan & Ann Stekhoven

R.S. Stobie
J.C. & M.F. Stormonth Darling
B. & C. Street
Ken & Shona Sturgeon
Eric & Fiona Sutton
May Sweeney
Professor & Mrs M.B.E. Sweet
Mrs J. Taylor
Vincent & Pam Taylor
Colin & Ann Tedder
Annette Theron
Dr Walther Thiede
Peter & Noreen Tonkin
John & Jill Tresfon
Elizabeth Triegaardt
Di & Bill Turner
Mr & Mrs J.J. Turner
James W.D. Turner
Muriel van Breda
Dick & Liz van der Jagt
François van der Merwe
Marié van der Merwe
S.W. van der Merwe
Arnold van der Riet
Antony van Hoogstraten
H. van Kerken
M. & M.A. van Rijswijck
Marius & Lenette van Wyk
Rhoda M. van Zijl
Kirsten, Dirk & Carl Venter
Audrey Joy Viljoen
Jannie & Anne Lise Vlok
Julian & Doreen Vollmer
O.M. von Kaschke
Derek John Wade
C.J. Ward
C.E. Weaver
David C. & Cynthia Weaver
Marion Went
Ilse & Stephan Wentzel
Gill Wheeler
V.E.M. Whitmill
Yvonne Whyte
Alen H. Wilkinson
William Poulton Library
Geraldine & Alistair Williams
E.M. Witham
Arne & Harald Witt
Hilda & Jürgen Witt
Bob & Myfanwy Wood
Barry & Diana Woode
Dawn Louise Woods
John Woolley
David & Joan Wootton
John & Catherine Wootton
Gerald & Helen Wright